Memorial Book of Bolekhov (Bolechów), Ukraine

Translation of *Sefer ha-zikaron le-kedoshei Bolechow*

Original Yizkor Book Edited by: Y. Eshel

Published by the Association of Former Residents of Bolechow in Israel, 1957

Published by JewishGen

**An Affiliate of the Museum of Jewish Heritage - A Living Memorial to the Holocaust
New York**

Memorial Book of Bolekhov (Bolechów), Ukraine
Translation of *Sefer ha-Zikaron le-Kedoshei Bolechow*

Copyright © 2015 by JewishGen, Inc.
All rights reserved.
First Printing: Septmeber 2015, Elul 5775
Second Printing: March 2019, Adar II 5779

Editor of the Original Yizkor Book: Y. Eshel
Translation Project Coordinator: Alex Sharon
Layout: Alan Roth
Image Editor: Larry Gaum
Cover Design: Nina Schwartz
Indexing: Moshe Kutten

Published by JewishGen, Inc.
An Affiliate of the Museum of Jewish Heritage
A Living Memorial to the Holocaust
36 Battery Place, New York, NY 10280

Printed in the United States of America by Lightning Source, Inc.

Library of Congress Control Number (LCCN): 2015949061
ISBN: 978-1-939561-34-3 (hard cover: 254 pages, alk. paper)

Cover photographs: Courtesy Charles Burns (www.galiciantraces.com)

Acknowledgements

Special thanks to the National Yiddish Book Center in Amherst, Massachusetts and the New York Public Library for supplying the high resolution images used in this book.

Special thanks to Ala and Larry Gamulk for providing missing translations, so that the fully translated book could be published.

Notes to the Reader:

Note: There were a great many redundancies in the original English language version of this book to incorporate minor inconsistencies between the Hebrew version and the Yiddish version of the book. The redundancies resulted in some stories being told as many as four different times throughout the book. To prevent this duplicity, we have slightly restructured the Bolekhov story to reflect one complete version of the history of the Town and its people, from the beginning of the Town's formulation to the final destruction of the Town and its people during the Holocaust.

Also please note that the Table of Contents is organized to provide two different page references. The first page reference is the actual page number in this translated book. The second page number is the location of the content in the original Hebrew document (page number noted with an "(H)" and/or the location of the content in the original Yiddish document (page number noted with a "(Y)".

Within the text the reader will note "{34}" standing ahead of a paragraph. This indicates that the material translated below was on page 34 of the original book. However, when a paragraph was split between two pages in the original book, the marker is placed in this book after the end of the paragraph for ease of reading.

Also please note that all references within the text of the book to page numbers, refer to the page numbers of the original Yizkor Book.

The original book can be seen online at the NY Public Library site:
http://yizkor.nypl.org/index.php?id=1006

A list of this book and all books available in the Yizkor-Book-In-Print Project along with prices is available at:
http://www.jewishgen.org/Yizkor/ybip.html

JewishGen and the Yizkor-Books-in-Print Project

This book has been published by the **Yizkor-Books-in-Print Project,** as part of the **Yizkor Book Project** of **JewishGen, Inc**.

JewishGen, Inc. is a non-profit organization founded in 1987 as a resource for Jewish genealogy. Its website [www.jewishgen.org] serves as an international clearinghouse and resource center to assist individuals who are researching the history of their Jewish families and the places where they lived. JewishGen provides databases, facilitates discussion groups, and coordinates projects relating to Jewish genealogy and the history of the Jewish people. In 2003, JewishGen became an affiliate of the **Museum of Jewish Heritage - A Living Memorial to the Holocaust** in New York.

The **JewishGen Yizkor Book Project** was organized to make more widely known the existence of Yizkor (Memorial) Books written by survivors and former residents of various Jewish communities throughout the world. Later, volunteers connected to the different destroyed communities began cooperating to have these books translated from the original language—usually Hebrew or Yiddish—into English, thus enabling a wider audience to have access to the valuable information contained within them. As each chapter of these books was translated, it was posted on the JewishGen website and made available to the general public.

The **Yizkor-Books-in-Print Project** began in 2011 as an initiative to print and publish Yizkor Books that had been fully translated, so that hard copies would be available for purchase by the descendants of these communities and also by scholars, universities, synagogues, libraries, and museums.

These Yizkor books have been produced almost entirely through the volunteer effort of researchers from around the world, assisted by donations from private individuals. The books are printed and sold at near cost, so as to make them as affordable as possible. Our goal is to make this important genre of Jewish literature and history available in English in book form, so that people can have the personal histories of their ancestral towns on their bookshelves for themselves and for their children and grandchildren.

A list of all published translated Yizkor Books in the project with prices and ordering information can be found at:
                    http://www.jewishgen.org/Yizkor/ybip.html

Lance Ackerfeld, Yizkor Book Project Manager

Joel Alpert, Yizkor-Book-in-Print Project Coordinator

JewishGen
Yizkor Book Project

This book is presented by the
Yizkor Books in Print Project
Project Coordinator: Joel Alpert

Part of the
Yizkor Books Project of JewishGen, Inc.
Project Manager: Lance Ackerfeld

These books have been produced solely through volunteer effort
of individuals from around the world. The books are printed and
sold at near cost, so as to make them as affordable as possible.

Our goal is to make this history and important genre of Jewish
literature available in English in book form so that people can have
the near-personal histories of their ancestral towns on their bookshelves for themselves and for their children and grandchildren.

Any donations to the Yizkor Books Project are appreciated.

Please send donations to:
Yizkor Book Project
JewishGen
36 Battery Place
New York, NY 10280

JewishGen, Inc. is an affiliate of the
Museum of Jewish Heritage
A Living Memorial to the Holocaust

Title Page of Original Yizkor Book

ספר הזכרון
לקדושי בוליחוב

בעריכת
יונה ומשה־חנינא אשל

לא למכירה

בהוצאת ארגון יוצאי בוליחוב בישראל
תשי״ז—1957

Translation of the Title Page of Original Yiddish Book

Memorial book
of the Martyrs of Bolechow

Edited

Yona and Moshe-Chanina Eshel

Not for resale

Published by the Association of Former Residents of Bolechow in Israel
5717 - 1957

MAP OF UKRAINE IN 2015

Map of Bolekhov in the Ukraine

Geopolitical Information:

Bolekhov (Bolechów), Ukraine is located at 49°04' North Latitude/ 23°52' East Longitude

Alternate names for the town are: Bolekhov [Russian], Bolechów [Polish], Bolekhiv [Ukrainian], Bolechov [Yiddish], Bolechiw [German], Bolechiv, Boleḥov

	Town	District	Province	Country
Before WWI (c. 1900):	Bolechów	Dolina	Galicia	Austrian Empire
Between the wars (c. 1930):	Bolechów	Dolina	Stanisławów	Poland
After WWII (c. 1950):	Bolekhov			Soviet Union
Today (c. 2000):	Bolekhiv			Ukraine

Nearby Jewish Communities:
Wołoska Wieś 1 miles W
Mezhdurechye 5 miles NE
Vygoda 9 miles SSE
Dolyna 10 miles SE
Staryy Mizun 10 miles S
Sokołów 11 miles NE
Stryy 13 miles N
Verkhneye Sinevidnoye 13 miles W
Broshniv-Osada 15 miles ESE
Svarychiv 16 miles ESE
Skole 16 miles W
Rozhnyativ 16 miles SE
Orov 18 miles WNW
Golyn 18 miles E
Lysyatychi 19 miles NNE
Sukhodol 20 miles SSE
Stebnik 21 miles NW
Truskavets 22 miles NW

Perehinske 22 miles SE
Hnizdychiv 23 miles NNE
Zhuravno 23 miles NE
Kalush 23 miles E
Dovhe 24 miles WNW
Zhidachov 25 miles NNE
Boryslav 25 miles NW
Drohobych 26 miles NW
Medenychi 26 miles NNW
Skhidnitsya 26 miles WNW
Yalynkovate 28 miles SW
Lavochnoye 28 miles SW
Dolzhka 29 miles ENE
Lukvitsa 29 miles SE
Voynilov 29 miles E
Rozdil 29 miles NNE
Berezdivtsi 29 miles NNE
Pryslip 29 miles SSW
Cherniv 30 miles ENE

2009-2010 Photographs of Bolekhov by Charles Burns
Not in original Yizkor Book

Table of Contents

Table of Contents
Hebrew contents translated by Mary Jane Shubow
Yiddish contents translated by Susannah R. Juni

[Hebrew page 5 & Yiddish page 157]

A Word from the Committee

In the annual memorial meeting in Tel Aviv in 1954, it was decided to establish a memorial for our relatives who perished in sanctification of the Divine name during the Holocaust.

It was impossible to actualize this by erecting a memorial monument in our town, the place of the murder. Therefore, we established the idea in two particularly fitting and appropriate forms:

a. We planted 1,000 trees in the Martyr's Forest on the land of the Keren Kayemet LeYisrael, at the approach to Jerusalem. 900 trees were named for the victims whose names were given to us by their relatives. 100 trees were in memory of the anonymous victims who left no relatives to perpetuate their memory.

A monument was erected in that grove upon which is inscribed "To the martyrs of the community of Bolechow".

b. The memorial book. Its publication was delayed for four reasons.

1. As long as the pledges for the grove were not collected, we could not become involved with the publication of the book.

2. Because of the lack of replies from our brethren, natives of our town, from the Diaspora.

3. Because of the difficulties that piled up in the collection of material, pictures and photographs.

4. Our paltry budget did not allow us to hire external people for editing and translations. (We received material in Yiddish, German and Polish.)

It is conceivable that this book is lacking in breadth, content, and number of photographs. However, in contrast to the few resources that we had at our disposal for this purpose, this was also a benefit!

Our esteemed friend, a native of our town, the well-known historian and pedagogue Michael Hendel, edited the historical section. He did this without expectation of recompense. He invested the best of his talents, spirit, power and love to his native town. He invested the best of his time and energy to this task. We express our sincere thanks to him!

Other parts of the book – the Holocaust and day to day life – were handled by Yonah Elendman-Eshel and Moshe Chanina Hausman-Eshel. They edited, translated and corrected these sections in a voluntary fashion, with dedication and tireless diligence. They never despaired despite the many trials and tribulations. They continued their work without flinching.

Moshe Chanina Eshel must be singled out for special recognition. He toiled tirelessly. Thanks to his dedication, seriousness and great persistence, we overcame all the obstacles in our path. He directed the publication of the book. He actualized it. Blessings of grace upon he and his wife!

With satisfaction and joy we announce that we succeeded in actualizing our plans solely though out own efforts. We succeeded at the difficult endeavor.

We offer our thanks to Yosef Adler and the brothers Benno and Max Reisman – all three of them eye witnesses to the Holocaust – for their participation in the section about the destruction of our city. May blessings come upon them!

Thanks to the efforts of the scholarly Dr. A. Y. Brauer, we were prepared to publish the "Memoirs of Reb Dov of Bolechow" in the historical section. However, we were forced to forego this on account of the paucity of our financial resources. Through the intermediary of Professor B. Tz. Dinur, we turned to the Mossad Bialik (Bialik Institute). The institute promised us that at the soonest appropriate time, a proper volume of the writings of Reb Ber Bolichower would be published, edited by Dr. A. Y. Dinur.

To Professor B. Tz. Dinur, Dr. A. Y. Brauer, Mossad Bialik, we express heartfelt appreciation for your willingness and good intentions.

We hereby thank all institutions and individuals who assisted us at the time of the publication of the book.

We express special thanks and appreciation to our friend Shlomo Altbauer-Katz, a native of Stryj, for his kind agreement to translate Dr. Hendel's historical chapters into Yiddish.

We must make note of and thank the "Ot" publishing company which attempted to impart a beautiful form to the book. We would especially like to thank Aryeh Shen-Tal for his great efforts.

We were only able to carry out our difficult double task of planting a grove and publishing a book through the toil, sincere dedication discipline and seriousness of all members of the committee, who did not recoil from any obstacle, and did not spare any effort. Each person fulfilled what was asked of him. Congratulations!

To the Righteous Gentiles from among the population of our city who provided refuge to our Jewish brethren during the Holocaust, who took their lives into their hands are were slaughtered along with those they hid – honor and appreciation! With holy awe and deep appreciation we will bind their memory along with the rest of our martyrs!

This Yizkor Book is dedicated to the memories of the dear victims who were cut off, murdered and strangled with satanic cruelty; as well as to those who endangered their lives with humanitarian gestures as they saved Jewish souls.

May this Yizkor Book be a reliable testimony for generations to come about a tragic chapter in the annals of the era of the most frightful atrocities in human history.

In the name of the committee,

Michael Schneeweiss

Members of the committee:

(In Hebrew alphabetical order)
Eshel, Yonah
Eshel, Moshe Chanina
Hendel, Dr. Lipa
Weber, Avraham
Turkel, Dvora
Lustig, Pnina
Messinger, Yehuda of blessed memory
Reinhartz, Shmuel
Schneeweiss, Michael

[Hebrew page 7 & Yiddish page 159]

A Word from the Editorial Board

We have approached the task of editing the book with trembling, with holy awe, and with a sincere feeling of responsibility.

Layer by layer, we laid the foundations.

Honorable reader!

We ask your forgiveness for the material that is lacking in the historical section after the year 1900. To our great dismay, we were missing oral and written sources.

The chapters on experiences and folklore are not the fruits of the pen of professional, experienced writers. Rather, these are solely collections of memories and experiences, a slice of life in our city, of its people, happenings, struggles, desires and aspirations.

For reasons beyond our control, we are missing from the second part of the book aside from youth groups, such organizations as: various charitable organizations, the elder aliya (during the period of the partition), synagogues, kloizes, and prayer groups, bands, workers' organizations, and specific professions that characterized Bolechow and its environs.

You will find duplication in the chapters about the destruction of our community. Mr. Adler wrote his words in a general fashion, whereas the Reisman brothers described the events as personal experiences.

With regard to the spelling of "Bolechow" (Beit Vav Lamed Yud Chet Vav Veit), we relied on sources – the memoirs of Reb Dov of Bolechow.

To our dismay, not all of these chapters were translated from Yiddish to Hebrew.

The Yiddish translation in the book is not uniform for two reasons: 1) the translation was not done by one person; 2) we wished to speak to the reader in simple "Bolechow" language. [1]

We take responsibility for all lacunas and extraneous facts.

Despite its many lacunas, may this book serve as a modest comfort for the natives of our city and our friends! Would it be that every person can find in it an echo of what was, what was lost and is no more!

May it be that this book will not remain in the bookshelves as a stone that is not turned over!

May it be that our descendents take interest in it. As they study it they will realize that their predecessors were a living limb in a vibrant body, and that the most difficult conditions of the exile forged their essence of life. They will realize what was lost to the national pantheon in the tragic destruction!

Please, accept the book as it is!

Our intentions were sincere.

Translator's Footnotes
1. This paragraph only appears in the Yiddish version

[Hebrew page 9 & Yiddish page 161]

Yizkor
Bolechow

To you, our tiny town, negligible in the map of the world,
Your splendid, glorious tapestry was wide for us,
A tree with much splendor,

To you,
To mothers and fathers,
Grandfathers and grandmothers,
Brothers and sisters,
Friends and acquaintances,
Your scholars and erudite ones,
Workers and simple folk
Elders and children,
To the vibrant youth who dreamt of actualizing (aliya} and did not
merit –
We will erect a modest monument!
Your pure images will forever blossom in our memories!
That which was perpetrated against you and all of Israel
By the impure evil ones

We will remember and not forget!

We give our oath!

[Hebrew page 11 & Yiddish page 163]

Chapter I. Early History of Bolekhov - 18th and 19th Centuries

1. The History of the Jews in Bolekhov at the end of the 18th Century
Based on the book
"The Memoirs of Reb Ber Bolekhover" and other sources
by Dr. M. Hendel
Translated from Yiddish by Eszter Andor

A. Foreword

In times past, there were few towns inhabited by Jews that contemporaries found worth describing. Thus, we have few descriptions which can help us form a notion of the spirit of the town and its Jewish community, of the personalities and public figures of the community and the atmosphere surrounding it. The farther we go back in time, to earlier epochs, the fewer descriptions we find. A Jew would take a pen in his hand only to write about the Torah and the fear of God, and whatever was not related to the Torah and the fear of God was like "mud" in his eyes. So, the person, the author writing about himself, never comes to the fore; and even as we learn from his book important details about his life and business, his family and circle of acquaintances, his interests and aspirations, this is not because he wanted to arouse the interest of his readers in these details – but simply as the author describes God's greatness and kindness, who redeemed him when he was in distress or relates how God led him on the path to good fortune, we learn other details as well. This is why the memoirs of Reb Ber Bolekhover are doubly important for us – thanks to them, we can gain an insight into the life of a Jewish community in Galicia, South Poland, in the 18th century.

B. The founding of the town and the privileges granted to the inhabitants

Bolekhov is not an old town. It was founded some 350 years ago by the landowner Nikolay Gedzinsky. He transformed one of his villages into a town, hoping that it will increase his revenue. His aim was to reinforce the colonization of the Jews and to increase his holdings through their economic activity. He promised various privileges to the inhabitants of the town. These privileges, which were submitted to the king and approved in 1603, were very important. Most importantly, the Jews were granted equal rights with the Gentile inhabitants. Gedzinsky also delivered all the inhabitants from the various obligations with which they, especially the village population, were burdened.

[Yiddish page 164

These included the obligation to furnish means of transportation, provide men for the building of roads and highways and the repairing of bridges on the estate, pay the tithe of shearing the sheep and the tithe of beehives and so on. The only duty that Gedzinsky did impose was the guarding of the sluice to make sure that the water does not inundate, God forbid!, the surrounding fields. And as all merchants were interested in running their shops in the middle of the town, he granted them right to build houses and shops on the main square. Moreover, he granted a piece of land, for very little money, to each householder in which they could form a garden. Furthermore, he granted the Jews a favor and gave them a place to build a shul and a cemetery. He also promised explicitly that if the Jews built a house for the hazzan and the shames beside the shul, it would be free of tax forever.

Beside economic concessions, the Jews were given two very important political privileges. On the one hand, they were entitled, just like the Christians, to elect a mayor and a *"rada mieyska"* (town council). And on the other, if a Gentile sued a Jew, he was tried directly by the landowner or his substitute, and a representative – a respected Jewish man – was to participate in the trial and the verdict. As opposed to this, there was no such thing in a trial that involved Jews only because in such a case the trial obviously took place in the community and the mentioned respected man (a community elder) represented the Jewish community to the outside. In conflicts between Gentiles there was also no such thing because such trials evidently took place in the town or government court. However, in a subsequent law of 1660, we find a paragraph, which stated that only in the presence of a respected Jewish man could the town court issue a verdict in a trial between a Jew and a Gentile. Various documents indicate that the representative of the community always participated in trials taking place in the town court.

There is evidence that the privileges did not remain a dead letter but were enforced in everyday life. When taking the oath after the local elections in 1660, the mayor said the following: "I swear to live in peace with all the citizens, be they Roman, Greek Catholic or Jewish, poor or rich. I will respect and protect the privileges of all nations."

Gedzinksy's intentions were indeed good but the circumstances were not favorable. The Tartars often ambushed the town and in 1678 the community was compelled to get a loan from the landowner, who served as the bishop of Lemberg. It is worth noting that relations between the Jews and the Gentiles were friendly and decent and the Gentiles approached the Jews with respect and esteem.

[Yiddish page 165]

In Zhidotshuv, for example, when the archives burnt down and the document, which granted the privileges and ensured the reciprocal relations between the Jews and the Gentiles perished, the inhabitants of the town chose two Jews to file the documents with the government.

C. The town and its "Owners" in the 18th century

The shtetl lies at the foot of the Carpathian mountains. The Jewish population, which formed the majority of the townspeople in the 18th century, was rather small. The community, made up of the Jewish inhabitants of Bolekhov and those of the thirteen neighboring villages, numbered only 1,000 souls. Apparently, it was a very small community – but one should not forget that in those times even big towns were sparsely populated. The town of Brody, which was an *"ir ve-am be-israel"*, had at that time a population of 7,000 souls, and even Lemberg, the capital city of Galicia, where close to 80,000 Jews were concentrated after World War I, had no more than 7,000 Jews at the end of the 18th century.

As we have already mentioned, Bolekhov was, just like many other Polish towns, a "private" town, that is, the property of a landowner, which passed on as inheritance after his death. The "town owner" could sell the town, just like his other properties, to another landlord, exchange it or lease it to an arendator (tenant) who pleased him and ensured him a nice revenue from the taxes of the townspeople, their businesses, the cultivation of the surrounding land, etc. Most of the arendators were Jewish. Sometimes the arendator made a fortune from such leases, at other times, for example, if the town owner demanded too high a price or determined the lease contract as he saw it fit, he was impoverished. In some cases the town owner decided to manage his business alone through his own administrators and the Jewish arendator came "clean" out of the whole business. In the memoirs of Reb Ber we shall hear a great deal about arenda leases. There is the story of a very wealthy man from a neighboring shtetl who leased properties from the town owners. "He was very skilful in working in the fields and in cattle farming", but when the town owner changed, "he did not want to lease his properties but supervised them himself". His properties were managed by his administrators and the Jewish arendator was left without an income.

In the time of Reb Ber the town was ruled by a Catholic priest who had business ties with the Jews. Reb Ber used these connections for the benefit of the community. Once when the town owner changed, the Jews of Bolekhov faced a great danger. The story goes like this: the earlier town owner lost a lot of money in playing cards and in his tight financial situation he sold the town to his brother-in-law who paid a very high price for it.

[Yiddish page 166]

To get rid of such an expensive acquisition, he sold the town to another man. The new buyer sought various ways to increase his revenue and decided to move part of the inhabitants of Bolekhov to one of his villages in order to turn it into a town. "When the townspeople learnt about his plans, nobody wanted to leave the town where they were born and raised." The administrators of the town owner promised the would-be-colonizers "great luck" but when they saw that nobody listened to them, they resorted to force and compelled a part of the inhabitants to build houses in the new town. The rebellious were imprisoned and Reb Ber's house was designated to be the prison, where they were to be locked up in the rooms which were used as the synagogue and the community suffered *"yagunot, daagot and tsaar"* [grief, worry and regret]. Reb Ber's brother intervened and the harsh decree was annulled and the community could sigh with relief. However, when the landowner saw that he could not succeed in founding the new settlement, he wanted to get even with his Jewish subjects and forced them to lease the town revenues, especially the taverns and the mills, which meant losing money. The lot fell on Reb Ber. He did not like this idea. "But who can resist an influential person, if even the rabbi of the community advises him to take the arenda, reasoning that if the Jews of Bolekhov have good relations with the town owner, he will protect them vis-a-vis the lords who borrowed money from them and could not repay their debts by the set deadline. After much hesitation, Reb Ber accepted to take the arenda with some associates. The business did not succeed and after a certain time, he was compelled to ask for a concession from the lease money, justifying his request with the argument that he took over the business not to make money "but to take care of the lord's revenue".

The town owner was obliged to protect the Jewish community. But he could not always fulfil this duty even under normal circumstances, let alone in turbulent times, in times of war with outside enemies, in times of internal wars or when gangs of robbers were rampant in the country. On the other hand, the town owner was interested in protecting his Jews for his own sake because Jews made business and also increased the revenues of the landowner, so if he did not protect them, his revenues declined.

Beside the special taxes that the town owner imposed on the community, the community also had to secure the annual payment of the "rabbinate's salary". This was paid from the shekhita [ritual slaughter] income and the belt tax, which was in the hands of the petty merchants.

[Yiddish page 167]

It happened several times that the community was in a strained financial situation and it could not pay the taxes. To protect the community in such times, Reb Ber wrote requests asking for concessions and the alleviation of the taxes.

So much about the relations between the Jewish population and the town owner. The community also maintained relations with the king, the sovereign of the country; these relations consisted chiefly of paying taxes. The main taxes for the benefit of the country were as follows: tax on alcoholic beverages and poll tax. The first was paid directly to the Royal Treasury, while the second, and this was the main tax, the per capita amount of which was determined by the Jewish self-government, the Council of Four Lands, was collected by the central treasury from each community separately. Supervising the taxation was one of the main tasks of the Council of Four Lands as an organized administrative body in relation to the Jewish population and between the Jews and the central state authorities.

D. The Kahal and the Council of Four Lands

The internal Jewish authorities consisted of the kahal of each town and the Council of Four Lands of Poland. [1] The Polish Jews were subordinated to three authorities: the city hall and the lord of the town (if the town was a private property), the central state authorities and their own self-government, which they respected very much as it was their own [2]. When recalling a Jew who had a position in the self-government, Reb Ber always calls him by his due title: "intercessor of the Four Lands", "head of state", "major generals heads of state", "chiefs and leaders" – these expressions are repeated over and over in his book.

The kahal as the local Jewish authority dealt with the spiritual and material well-being of the Jewish populace and acted as the representative body of the local Jewry in its dealings with outside agents, such as the king, the clergy, the landowners and so on. In order to manage the affairs of the local Jewish population, the kahal was compelled to impose internal direct taxes – which were collected directly from each Jewish inhabitant – and taxes on commodities of first use. These included taxes such as midwife tax and fees for the services that the community set up for the benefit of the residents, such as ritual slaughter or public weights and measures. Reb Ber relates how he bought new weights for the community and how much money the community made from giving out permissions to use them for weighing honey. One of the most important tasks of the kahal was the collection of the poll tax. This tax, which put a heavy burden on the Jewish population of Poland, was ten thousand zloty in the middle of the 16th century.

[Yiddish page 168]

In the course of time, the amount of the tax increased and it reached 220,000 zloty at the beginning of the 18th century. The Council of Four Lands was responsible for dividing the tax among the communities and the kahals carried on negotiations about the distribution of the tax with the Council, since it often happened that certain communities were unable to pay the tax imposed on them. That happened to the Bolekhov community as well in the middle of the 18th century when the town was burnt down and looted and many inhabitants left it. This caused a loss of 300,000 zloty to the community. The kahal turned at once to the Council with a detailed memorandum and asked for a concession from the poll tax, and it also presented a memorandum to the town owner to ask him to defend them before the minister of finance. However, high society did not pay much attention to their efforts. The leaders of the Council gave a response which was not binding on them and the finance minister put the blame on the Council: "What can I do? Since the assessors have already determined the amount of the tax and the assignments [3] have already been distributed by the leaders of the Council in all the counties, the burnt-out Bolekhov community should ask the neighboring communities to help it so that it can pay the poll tax." [4] "The community was confused and frightened because of the repression it suffered from the cavalry troop which came to collect the poll tax." But Reb Ber consoles himself saying "God is our father and he will not abandon his Jewish children". Together with some other inhabitants of the town they intervened with the prince who ordered the payment. They described to him the great calamity that befell the town: "people lie around on the streets because they do not have a dwelling place and we have great pity for them; so how could we ask them to pay?" [5] This intercession, which cost money of course, yielded fruits: the payment was provisionally postponed until the next convention of the Council of Four Lands. The convention took place in Brody. The delegation sent from the Bolekhov community included Reb Ber's brother. They reached a compromise with the Council according to which the poll tax would not be paid all at once but in several installments in the course of three years (adding, of course, the interest). It seems that the Bolekhov community benefited from the postponement of the payment of the poll tax. Although Reb Ber promises to tell the reader about it, there is no more information about the matter in his memoirs.

Eventually the Polish government became convinced that collecting the poll tax through the Council, the official body of Polish Jewry was inconvenient. The economic hardships weighed heavily on the Jewish population in the 18th century when the foundations of livelihood and security crumbled and huge sums had to be invested to protect life and livelihood. The Council of Four Lands sank into massive debts and was not able to pay them back to the Royal Treasury.

[Yiddish page 169]

The government asked itself whether it would not be more sensible to impose the tax on each Jew individually without the mediation of the Council, in which case the Council would not be needed any more. There were also internal factors that undermined the competence of the Council: quarrels and intrigues, the putting of personal interests into the forefront at the expense of the community, the reign of a small number of rich members over the masses, the exploitation of the poor, etc. In consequence of this situation, the Poles disbanded the central Jewish authorities in 1764 and imposed, from that time on, a direct tax of 2 zloty a year on each Jew. The tax, however, continued to be collected by the kahals. The introduction of the new tax called for a census. So the government nominated a committee in each town, which consisted of community representatives and was chaired by a Polish landowner, and these committees were responsible for carrying out the census. From the materials preserved in the archives we can learn a great deal about the number of Jews, their family arrangements and, to a certain extent, their livelihoods. The census was carried out among the Jews of Bolekhov as well and 883 souls were counted in the town. However, because of the harsh decree concerning the payment of the tax many of the poor did not participate in the census; in fact there were another 400 Jews among the poor.

The debts of the Council reached the sum of two and a half million zloty and in order to repay it, the Council imposed a tax on each community that was to be paid in three installments. In connection with the arrangements for paying the tax, Reb Ber's brother achieved great distinction and he was nominated "head of state", that is, most probably chairman of the county council of Belorussia (Galicia), which, like other county councils, was still in existence for some time. The payment of the tax in three installments was imposed on the Bolekhov community as well. However, with various combinations, Reb Ber succeeded in saving the community from these expenses. Later when he went to Lemberg on behalf of the community, he managed to return the full amount of the money to the community. The government simply saw a source of revenue in the Jewish subjects and the Jews of Bolekhov, like the Jews of other towns, found a good excuse to undo the government decrees.

Reb Ber praises the moral value of the Council: "it was something of a deliverance that God, may he be blessed, was merciful and did not leave us, as it says in the Mosaic law: 'But despite all this while they will be in the land of their enemies, I will not have been revolted by them [a]'" and as he relates the dissolution of the Council, he forestalls others: "and I will now tell you about the great changes that took place in Poland, about the ignoble situation of our Jewish children and about the humiliations they have experienced ever since they settled.

[Yiddish page 170]

" Reb Ber also describes the relations of the Polish Sejm and the Jews, its intentions to limit the movement of the Jews and the heavenly intervention that always arrived in times of emergency: "and the Jewish children believed that when the Sejm harassed the Jews, the prophet Elijahu would appear in the guise of a member of the delegation and say, 'I do not agree with this decree and it will be annulled.'" [6]

E. The town and its livelihoods

The majority of the inhabitants of Bolekhov were merchants. There is no mention of craftsmen in Reb Ber's memoirs but there must have been various artisans in Bolekhov, just as in any other community, who produced commodities for the local Jewish population and for the peasants of the surrounding villages. Reb Ber who was a retailer was not interested in craftsmen, this is why he does not mention them in his memoirs. In Bolekhov, like in other towns, various branches of trade could be found: trading with food, beverages, garments for the Jews and for the peasants, trading with the landowner and his officials satisfying his needs on the one hand and selling his agricultural products (cereals, pelt, wool, flax, etc.) on the other. There was also a special trade which grew out of the local conditions: [7]in Bolekhov and its environs there were many salt mines [8] and this was one of the sources of trading activity. The other source was trading with Hungarian wines, since the shtetl was not far from the Hungarian border. The salt business brought profits to the town's rich people, who used to lease the salt mines, as well as to the petty traders, who used to buy salt and sell it for cash (or exchange it for cereals) to the local consumers and at fairs in other towns, for example in Brody or Lemberg. The peasants from the surrounding countryside often bought salt on credit and paid their debts after the harvest. We have no information on Jewish workers in the salt mines.

Wine trade had a very important place in Bolekhov. Polish landowners liked alcohol. Since Southern Galicia was very close to Hungary which was abundant in vineyards an extensive wine trade developed. The import of Hungarian wines was in the hands of the Jews of the border area, including the Jews of Bolekhov. Through the wine import, the merchants came into contact with a wide circle of customers and salesmen not only in Poland but beyond its frontiers as well because trading extended beyond the framework of local business into international commerce. It is not hard to imagine that this resulted in the widening of horizons, life styles and education of those who were involved in trade.

[Yiddish page 171]

Through their trade relations with the surrounding countryside, the Jews of Bolekhov came into closer contact with their Gentile neighbors, and as Reb Ber's memoirs show, the Christians turned to their Jewish neighbors with trust. One especially hard year, the Jews and the Christians agreed to present a request to the landowner to appeal to him "to take pity on the poor, Jews and, 'lehavdil', Christians [b] who were forced to borrow wheat and corn from the mills in order to appease their hunger and who, because of the hard times, cannot pay their debts before the new grain harvest". It was Reb Ber who wrote down the request because he was fluent in Polish.

The foreign currency businesses constitute a special chapter. The monetary system was very complicated in eighteenth-century Poland, where various types of coins from various countries circulated. Due to the economic decline and the wars, the value of the coins changed constantly, especially because a lot of false coins circulated on the money market. On the other hand, a new branch of commerce developed through money exchange, in which the Jews of Bolekhov also played an important role. Money business was also widespread in another form. The Jews used to lend money to the Christian inhabitants of the town and they themselves used to borrow bigger sums from the landowners and the clergy. The fact that they were not the money-lenders but they took loans themselves is a clear sign of the economic decline of the Jewry in the 18th century.

The tradesmen conducted their businesses alone or in partnership with their relatives or friends and there were also joint businesses with Christians. Many conflicts and quarrels arose because of the joint businesses and the women often intervened to straighten things out and find a compromise.

The merchants of Bolekhov had their own association, the 'Khevra Kadusha of the Merchants' [a merchants union], which used to gather once a year in the period between the first and last days of Succoth in order to elect the gabbaim [the trustees of the association] and other dignitaries. At Simkhat Torah, the association used to organize a banquet for its members, where they celebrated the end of the old year and the new activities of the coming year.

F. Events of the time

The 18th century was a turbulent period for Poland and her Jews. The repercussions of the events surrounding the changing of the kings and the internal and external wars which accompanied this had adverse effects on the lives of the Jews in every town and shtetl. Murder and looting were usual phenomena.

[Yiddish page 172]

During one war, Russian troops arrived in Bolekhov and the local rabbi, who was considered a wealthy man, had to flee (on horseback!) on the eve of Yom Kippur. The most important event in the lives of Galician Jews was the first partition of Poland (1772), when Galicia came under Austrian rule. Reb Ber does not describe how the local authorities were transferred from Polish into Austrian hands but he makes a remark which tells us that many Jews saw the partition of Poland as a divine punishment for having dissolved their self-government, the Council of Four Lands, eight years earlier. "What they did to the Jews, will be done to them (the Poles), they were deprived of their glorious country." Reb Ber seems to be content with the Austrian ruler, Joseph II. When he mentions him after his death, he adds *"zikhroyne-livrokhe"* [may his memory be blessed], which is a sign that he considered Joseph a true and noteworthy ruler.

During the reign of Joseph II, an important event took place in the history of the Jews of Bolekhov. In his striving to improve the economic and constitutional situation of the Jews, especially for the benefit of the Austrian Empire, the emperor decided to settle the Jews on the land. He did not understand the Jewish psyche and the needs of the Jewish public. His reforms contained a lot of edicts of prohibition but the idea of agricultural colonization was taken up enthusiastically by various Jewish circles. However, the endeavor was not successful because the government did not proceed whole-heartedly to create the conditions necessary for success. At the same time, the government also settled Germans on the land and if it had been willing to ensure the same conditions for Jewish settlers as for the Germans, the colonization would have been a blessing to the country and to the Jews. A Jewish agricultural settlement was set up near Bolekhov as well but the local officials displayed a very negative attitude to the whole undertaking.

Let us describe the conditions under which the new colony, Neu-Babylon, was founded. The name refers to the Babylonian exile of the people of Israel. The land of the colony was bad and, according to the explicit opinion of the colony's supporters in Lemberg, "it was established that the reason why it was not given to German settlers was because it was of such bad quality." It was decided that ten families would be settled there and each received 12 acres of land for which they had to pay a yearly lease money. The government gave the settlers building materials and agricultural hands. These expenses of the government and the yearly lease money of 14 and a half florin per person was added onto their account and they had to pay these back in four years.

[Yiddish page 173]

The settlers were obliged to start repaying the debt already in the second year after they settled, when their economic situation was still quite bad.

As opposed to this, the German settlers received cattle, tools and seeds for sowing immediately upon arriving. The Jewish settlers received this from the government only after the first harvest. This shows that the government budget for the settling of a German family amounted to 600-1,000 gulden. At the same time in the case of a Jewish family settling in the environs of Bolekhov the government gave no more than 100 gulden and the settlers usually had to repay the debt in four years. The same situation prevailed in all the Jewish colonies that Emperor Joseph II founded. The colony in Bolekhov was set up around 1788. The Jews started to cultivate land at around that time. Unfortunately we have no precise information neither on the origins of the settlers in general nor on those who settled around Bolekhov in particular. Because of the hard conditions, which affected especially the townspeople who had to become farmers in a short time, the colony soon sank into great debts. The government was thus compelled to reduce the taxes to 8 florins (instead of the 14 and a half florins paid earlier). But even this did not help because the settlers owed the government 2,660 florin in 1797. They appealed to the government to remit part of the debt, reckoning that they would pay the rest in a few years under more relaxed payment conditions. With this request, however, the settlers only precipitated their end because the officials that were asked to express their opinion on the appeal ruled that the Jews were lazy and did not work on their land themselves but leased half or a third of it to Christians. Therefore, they said, the debts should be called in from them and they should be expelled not only from Bolekhov but from all Galicia. The government approved of this opinion. However, the emperor granted a favor to the unfortunate settlers: they had to leave the colony but could remain in Galicia.

In the second part of the 18th century, two movements put their stamp on Jewish life in Poland: one led to conversion, while the other brought along a Jewish renewal.

The first was a continuation of Sabbetai Zvi's movement [c], still widespread even after the demise of the original, especially in Southern Galicia. This continuation found its clearest expression in the person of Jacob Frank, who started his activities as a kabbalist and ended up converting – both he and his sect – and spreading false accusations that the Talmud allowed the use of Christian blood.

[Yiddish page 174]

It is certain that people were interested in these matters in Bolekhov especially since one of its inhabitants, Reb Ber personally knew a leader of the sect and played an important role in the open debates (1759) that the Catholic priests organized between the Jews and Frank's sect. From the Carpathian region arose another movement which was destined to be the builder of the Jewish spirit and culture. This was the Hasidic movement of Reb Israel Baal Shem Tov. [d]

In his book on the history of the Hasidic movement, Dubnow writes the following: "In the last ten years of the Besht's [an acronym for Baal Shem tov] life (he died in 5520, that is, in 1760, one year before the above-mentioned debate), there were Hasidim in the towns from Podolia, Volhynia and Galicia. Someone from his generation concluded that in the year of his death the number of Hasidim reached 40,000." We have no sources on the basis of which we can establish precisely how many Jews from Bolekhov followed Baal Shem Tov's teaching. There is no doubt, however, that there were debates on the Hasidim and on Hasidism in the shuls. And there were both adherents and opponents in Bolekhov, just like in many other communities. Reb Ber himself, who was predisposed to Kabbala in his youth, seems to have disapproved of the new movement because he feared that it involved nullifying Torah study and he may have seen in it the dangerous signs of a new Frankism.

In the course of time, the Hasidic movement developed in Bolekhov, as in other towns of Galicia, and established its own rabbi as well.

G. Everyday life

So far we have described the situation of the Jews in Bolekhov on the basis of life in Galicia in general. Let us now depict the everyday life of the town itself. The inviting of a new rabbi when the earlier rabbi died or was offered a position in another community constituted a very important event in the life of the community. In his memoirs, Reb Ber describes it in the following way: "The local rabbi was elevated to the crown of rabbinate in the holy community *(kehile kadushe)* of Brody." [9] And when time came for his departure, the whole shtetl, young and old, came to accompany him. The *kheders* [religious elementary school] were closed and the boys with their *melamdim* [teachers] were all out on the streets. The rabbi took leave of the community with the words of the Torah and when the *kheder* boys went back to the *kheder*, the *melamed* made them memorize the rabbi's words. "And since then the words were engraved in the memory of the students." This was Reb Jacob Yoykel HaLevi Horowitz (1679-1754) who became the rabbi of Bolekhov in 1711, when his father Reb Meir, the earlier rabbi of the town, was offered the position of the rabbi in Zlatshev. Later when Reb Jacob Yoykel left Bolekhov to become the rabbi of the well-known community of Brody, his son Reb Mordke took over his post in Bolekhov.

[Yiddish page 175]

When Reb Jonathan Eybeshitz was suspected of Sabbetai Zvi-ist views and summoned to apologize before three rabbis,[10] one of them was Reb Jacob Yoykel. This shows that he was a very important and distinguished rabbi. Bolekhov had the honor of having well-known and great rabbis [11]. Reb Ber tells us that "rich Jews used to invite learned men to their homes and offer them jam and liquor as a sign of respect".

The events that brought a little liveliness into the life of the shtetl were the community elections and the feasts that the various societies organized, such as inaugurations or *mitsve* [good deed] feasts – a *bris mile* (circumcision) ceremony or a wedding. On the completion of a house, a tin flag was hung on the roof with the date engraved in Hebrew letters on it. When there was a wedding, people inquired carefully about the *yikhes* [distinguished descent], knowledge of Torah and financial situation of the parties. The age of the bride and groom was not taken into consideration. Reb Ber writes that he was married at the age of 16 and his son's wife was 11 at the time if their wedding. The young couple usually lived with the parents for a few years. Reb Ber writes that after the wedding he studied in the *bes medresh* [synagogue] under the guidance of the rabbi. When the young couple got married, they received presents from friends and acquaintances (wedding presents) and it was a great honor for Reb Ber when his son-in-law received the title of *"Morenu"* [our teacher] from the rabbi of Lemberg, which was a sign that he was a learned man.

The most important wedding gifts were dishes and jewelry because in those times it was important for people, especially among the rich, that their house looked nice. Reb Ber praises highly the silver and copper dishes in his father-in-law's house. He also gives a detailed description of the clothes and jewelry that his brother bought for his wife in Brody: they were "made of fine silk, embroidered with real gold; there is nothing like this in our country". The most valuable treasure of the family was, of course, the wife who helped her husband not only in the household but also in his business activities. She gave him good advice and dealt with landowners if her husband did not speak Polish and she did. There were also cases, however, when the jealousy of the wives caused problems in the business. This is how, for example, the partnership of Reb Ber and his brother ended because of his sister-in-law who was envious of Reb Ber's great success. It is also worth noting that there were also learned women in Bolekhov. The rabbi's sister, for instance, knew "by heart a *'Blat Gemore'* with Rashi" [a page of the Gemarah with the commentaries of Rashi].

The community experienced hardships as well. The houses were built of wood and they were frequently devastated by fire. The town often fell victim to plundering committed by soldiers passing through it or by robber bands. Reb Ber writes extensively about murders committed on the road. He also describes, however, the heroism the neighboring community displayed when it was attacked by bandits.

[Yiddish page 176]

"And there were armed watchmen and the rest of the inhabitants also kept watch the whole night", and this is how the town was saved. Bolekhov was not so fortunate and when the same bandits attacked it, it was pillaged. The Bolekhov community also made attempts to protect the inhabitants but to no avail. The story went like this: "When the day was breaking and the men who had been on guard during the night went home to sleep, a horde of *'goyim'* [non-Jews] arrived and they found a camp-fire that the guards had lit for the night. The community servant was asleep by the fire with his drum by his head. When the servant woke up, the bandits took the drum from him and threw it into the fire. Then they told him to call out loud his name so that the town's rich man would open the door for him." They thus penetrated his house with cunning. But when they first confronted the inhabitants, one of the robbers was immediately shot and after two further shots, two more were injured, among them the leader of the gang. This defeat enrage the bandits and they set fire to the rich man's house and to other houses in the town. They looted shops and broke into houses stealing money and jewelry. Apparently, the local Christians pointed out the rich houses to them.

Reb Ber was away on business in Lemberg when the looting took place in Bolekhov. His wife survived only because she gave all her jewels to the bandits. Reb Ber's house was set on fire and it was only thanks to their loyal Christian maid that a few household articles and, most importantly, the *sforim* [religious books] were saved. Some of the inhabitants ran to ring the church bell to arouse the population but people saw that they could not defend themselves. Desperate, they abandoned their houses and fled the town. The bandits reigned in the town undisturbed for half a day. They devastated Bolekhov, killed nine Jews and left the town in whoops of triumph. Reb Ber got back from Lemberg when the bandits had already left and he proceeded at once, together with the leaders of the community of whom he was also one, to draw up a list of the damages. The landowners of the neighboring estates, the town officials and the Christian town representatives helped him in this work. The case that Reb Ber describes in detail reveals the appalling conditions of security in which shtetl Jews lived, as well as their heroism, not uncommon even in those times.

H. Reb Ber's life and activities

The man from whose memoirs we draw most of our information deserves special attention. He was raised in Bolekhov and spent most of his life there. He was influenced by the spirit of the town just as he influenced it himself.

[Yiddish page 177]

As a man active on general Jewish territory, he doubtless brought honor to his home town. Through his person, which is of course unique to a certain degree, we learn a great deal about the norm, the same way as the history of the Bolekhov community teaches us much about the history of hundreds of other Jewish communities.

Reb Ber's grandfather was born in Mezrits, near Brisk and he fled to Bolekhov with his family at the age of eight because of Chmelnitsky's evil decrees. Reb Ber's father was a wealthy wine merchant, well-versed in Talmud. He also had an inn in Bolekhov. From Reb Ber's memoirs we learn that his father was no idle man. He spoke Hungarian and knew well the ways of the land, and he was also fluent in Polish. Thanks to these skills, he could protect the interests of the local Jews. Reb Ber was born in 1723. His father did all in his power to ensure a good education for his son. Reb Ber studied Talmud extensively and what he learnt in his youth was of great help to him later in his life, in his activities and in writing his sforim [religious books]. Reb Ber pursued not only Jewish religious studies but his father made sure that he received a general education as well, so he engaged a teacher to teach his son Polish. Reb Ber also learnt Latin with this teacher. As he writes, "I also understood Latin with its grammar". The Jews in Bolekhov frowned on secular studies and people did not stop talking about it. "They said that I was studying, God forbid!, not for the sake of Heaven." Perforce, he discontinued his Polish and Latin lessons. "And I devoted myself whole-heartedly to the study of our holy Torah." He later continued with his Torah studies but took up secular subjects as well. He perfected his knowledge of Polish. He learnt Hungarian during his business trips and when he established a partnership with a German merchant, he learnt German with his help. When he had the occasion, he apparently learnt French, too. From his memoirs, we can see that Reb Ber was a book-lover all his life and he took great care of his library. He writes with joy that most of his religious books were rescued from the great fire and "also the majority of the ancient authors". He praises his father-in-law's library: "He had a house full of rare splendid books." From Reb Ber's description of his library we learn that it contained not only Hebrew books but many foreign ones as well. He was especially interested in history books in which he found his belief concerning the special character of the Jewish nation and the special place of the Hasidim in the eyes of God confirmed. He took particular interest in the book of an English scholar, which he read in German and a part of which he translated into Hebrew, hoping that his translation "will enlighten the learned men of Israel".

We will learn more about Reb Ber's attitude to foreign literature and about why he read foreign books from the following passages of his memoirs that we will cite in full.

[Yiddish page 178]

"And I will make sure that one of my children would make an effort and read the book of the English author, either the original German version or my translation of it into the Sacred Tongue (i.e. Hebrew). He will discover many things, not only the kind of knowledge that we find in the holy books but he will also learn much about world events that are not well known among the sons of Israel, although we, Jewish children have to know everything so that the Biblical verse 'for this is your wisdom and your understanding in the eyes of the nations [e]' can be fulfilled through us. And although our sages offer a commentary to the verse in accordance with the sacred Torah, they say: it is good to study the Torah, but also to know the ways of the world *(es iz gut toyre mit derekh erets)* and it is very important for a learned man who understands a matter to know what is going on among the Gentile nations because it can come one day – as it happened to me when I had a discussion with the leaders and the priests of the Gentile nations – that he has to reply properly to their questions concerning the Jewish faith." We have before us the figure of a Jewish maskil [an adherent of the Haskalah] at a time when the Haskalah [f] movement was gaining strength and becoming an influential factor in Jewish life in Eastern Europe [g] in general and in Galicia in particular. Reb Ber's attitude to Hebrew is also typical. He sees Hebrew not as a language to be used to express holy things but as one in which a literature in the widest sense of the word can be created. He himself writes in a fluent Hebrew and from his youth he preserves in his memory the atmosphere of the shtetl Tismenits where he had spent some time. "And there are fine authors who write in the Holy Tongue there and there is one young man in particular who writes a splendid Hebrew. I greatly envied him and I have gained much to remember from his writings." Reb Ber's wife was born in the shtetl Tismenits. Her father was also a book-lover and we can well imagine the spirit of the Torah and wisdom that must have reigned in Reb Ber's house and the atmosphere in which his children were raised. It is worth noting that the shtetl Tismenits was well known for its merchants. A delegation from the shtetl took part in the district council of Belorussia, a right that not all shtetls were honored with. Bolekhov and Tismenits were small centers in the middle of the 18th century, when the Haskalah movement began. There is an important fact regarding the Jews of Tismenits. Reb Barukh Shklaver, one of the precursors of the Haskalah in Lithuania published, in 1771, an astronomy book from the Middle Ages, fourteen people subscribed to the book in Poland, among them one from Tismenits [12]. Reb Ber's general education did not affect his character, he remained a traditional religious Jew. When he spent some time in his youth in Tismenits, he started studying the Kabbala and became absorbed in the Zohar [the holiest mystical book of the Kabbala].

[Yiddish page 179]

He used to fast and torment his body but he quickly sobered up and left the Kabbala-Torah. He took up a position of intellectual balance by combining Torah with secular knowledge, the Jewish Law with secular scholarship. However, honoring the Torah and observing her *mitsves* [commandments] were more important for him than anything else and he could not tolerate the German maskilim who followed the ways of the *goyim* in their clothing and life style, and reviled the commandments of the Torah. In the quarrels between the Hasidim and the Mitnagdim [opponents of Hasidism] on the one hand, and the pious conservative Jews and the maskilim on the other, Reb Ber adopted a neutral position. "He is not a Mitnaged, nor is he a Hasid or a maskil. He was a special type." (A. I. Braver)

By profession he was a wine merchant who often traveled on business to Hungary. In his youth he tried other businesses as well: he was considering to work in money lending, although his parents had never done that kind of work. His family held him back from this plan and he opened a shop instead. For some years he traded with alcohol, herring and "various spices and was engaged in other businesses as well" and he used to ride his horse through towns and villages and sell his wares; he took leather and flax to Hungary. Once he invested his money in leasing and horse trade. In the end he worked only in the wine trade. He brought wine from Hungary and sold it in his depot in Lemberg. This commerce brought him in contact with various Polish landowners, as well as with various Jewish and Christian merchants: Hungarian, Greek, Armenian, German and French tradesmen. This is what Reb Ber tells us about these relationships: "We arrived safely with the wine in Lemberg and we sold it to the Jewish merchants from Danzig to Leipzig." He had a German guest staying with him "who is coming from Turkey and is going to Russia". "I commanded a well-known French personality to supply the types of wine that would be used in the *kire's* [kaiser of Austria] [13] court. He sold wine "to a merchant who travels to Petersburg in Russia". These businesses left their mark on Reb Ber's personality and it is not surprising that he was not at all narrow-minded but had a broad-minded and comprehensive conception of the world.

The debates with the Frankists that took place in Lemberg in 1759 played an important role in his social activity. In this debate, which the Frankists imposed on the Jews, they had to clear the Jews of the harsh accusations of using Christian blood. Reb Ber was one of the intimates of the famous rabbi of Lemberg, Reb Chaim HaKohen Rapaport, and served him also with his fluency in Polish. Reb Ber had to compose an answer to the false accusations of the Frankists because the rabbi, who did not really master the vernacular, laid the preparatory work on him.

[Yiddish page 180]

Reb Ber turned to Christian book traders "and I have taken books for this work and I called a Christian who was fluent in Polish and Latin and we wrote the whole night". In the morning, he showed his piece to the rabbi Reb Chaim. The memorandum demonstrates Reb Ber's great proficiency in the Torah, in Talmud and the Zohar, as well as in Christian literature from the Church Fathers to the polemical literature of his time. He provided smashing evidence against the blood libel and showed the libelers that they were ignorant and all their claims were repulsive lies. Reb Chaim Rapaport invited Reb Ber to participate in the debate. Reb Ber describes it in the following words: "When they (the Frankists) brought evidence from the Gemarah or the Shulkhan Arukh, the Rambam or other holy books, we told them that their translation was wrong and it was not written that way in the holy books." In the course of the debate Reb Ber was the "speaker" of the Jewish side vis-a-vis the Christian public. Let us quote what Reb Ber said: "German Christians and the town representatives of Lemberg were waiting for me and they asked me what these heretics wanted and what was their goal. They wanted to obtain a report which they could send to faraway countries." The debate ended. "The blood libel, which dates back to ancient times, was not substantiated but its falsehood was not duly demonstrated either", sums up Professor Baraban in his book entitled *A Contribution to the History of the Frankist Movement*. At all events, Polish Jews could sigh with relief even though they were still worried about the times to come. Reb Ber ends his description of the debate with the following words: "and I recognized the great miracle that God in his mercy did with the remainder of Israel and I praised and thanked God for it." Reb Ber transferred his business, he lived in Lemberg for some time, married out his sons – his daughter was married to a well-known physician – and occupied himself in literary activity in his old age. He died at the advanced age of 82 and was buried in Bolekhov.

We generally know Reb Ber as a maskil, a public person and a merchant. There were many positive traits in his personality: he loved his people, suffered their pain and rejoiced at their success; he was a very pedantic man and conducted all his affairs with great care. But he also had some negative characteristics: he was full of reproach viv-a-vis the people around him, he saw them as hard-hearted, jealous and so on. This may suggest a feeling of worthlessness compared to his brother, who seems to have surpassed Reb Ber in his communal activities and whom the community trusted and cherished. His brother was also active in the community of the capital, Warsaw.

[Yiddish page 181]

It is also displeasing to the eye that Reb Ber describes tricks and sly deeds without noticing what a shameful habit this is. However, we must not forget that the cruel life, the need to protect oneself against the evil decrees and the hard living conditions tempted many of our brothers in those times.

I. Reb Ber's literary activities

In the first place we must mention his memoirs, which he wrote in his advanced years. They are not complete, certain periods of his life are completely missing. From Reb Ber the manuscript made its way to England, but we do not know how, and it was discovered in 1912 among the manuscripts in the library of the Rabbinical Seminary of London. The memoirs as we know them are not arranged according to the date and there are incomplete chapters with the beginning and end missing. The manuscript was published by the historian, Vishnitzer, in the 1920s in the Hebrew original, as well as in Yiddish and English translation.

The book was not published, it remained a religious book of "words of wisdom," that contains chapters on the history of false messiahs, especially on the Sabbetai Zvi movement, as well as some autobiographical details, among them the debate with the Frankists in Lemberg. By writing this book, Reb Ber wanted to strengthen the faith of his folk and find satisfaction for himself, as well as compensation for his contempt of Torah study because of his business activities, and he pleads with God: "Remember me, God, for the good deeds that I have done when I sanctified your name in front of many priests, the Polish aristocracy and the common people among Jews and Christians alike." He intended to publish the book but influential people dissuaded him because they feared that it could bring harm to the Jews because of the numerous passages in which the Christian religion was mentioned with contempt. In the Shocken Library in Jerusalem there is a letter to Reb Ber from Reb Chaim Kurmash, who was the *shtadlan* [intercessor] of the Lemberg community in the debates with the Frankists. We learn from this letter that Reb Ber asked him to read the manuscript and comment on it. Reb Chaim's letter is written in a flowery language: "wise man and writer of science and wisdom, the famous rich man in the gate of *bat rabim* ". He confirms the correctness of Reb Ber's depiction of the debate with the Frankists. There is an important detail about Reb Ber's family in the letter. Sending his regards to Reb Ber's son, Reb Chaim addresses him as our wonderful master, wise man and writer". What he meant by "writer" we do not know [14].The book was not printed and the manuscript was discovered by the historian and geographer Dr. A. J. Braver in the library of the well-know maskil from Tarnopol, Joseph Perl.

[Yiddish page 182]

A part of the book was published by Dr. Braver in "Ha-Shiloach" [a periodical] (volume 35, page 38). Reb Ber also intended to translate historical works, polemical literature and pamphlets concerning Jews. Apparently he did not succeed in finishing this work. But he did translate some chapters from a historical book written by an Italian scholar in the 17th century and from the book of the above-mentioned English scholar, *On the Old and the New Testament.*

We must especially draw attention to Reb Ber's beautiful Hebrew style: it is not a flowery language with unnecessary flourishes. There are many grammatical and stylistic mistakes in his writing but we should not be too critical of the writer because Hebrew was not a living language in his time and Reb Ber's language was in a certain sense an individual creation.

J. Conclusion

Let us have a look: a small Jewish community with nothing special or important about it. Still its members conduct far-reaching business, know how to defend themselves in times of trouble. There are scholars learned in the holy books as well as experts of secular sciences. There is one that has contacts with Frenchmen and Germans, reads books written by French and English authors and protects courageously the Jewish honor.

As you can see, our forefathers in those times were no "idle, impractical people", who knew nothing beyond their own small spheres. On the contrary: they were practical, had many contacts with the surrounding world and lived their self-perpetuating lives to the fullest extent possible under the conditions of those times.

Translator's Notes:

[a]   Leviticus 26:44

[b]   The expression 'lehavdil' is used in Yiddish to make a distinction between the sacred and the profane. Its use to indicate an essential difference between the Jews and the Gentiles shows the enormous gap separating these two groups in the perception of the Jews as well.

[c]   He claimed to be the Messiah and said that he had the right to abrogate the accepted norms. After his conversion to Islam, the movement collapsed.

[d]   Hasidism was a Jewish religious movement, founded by Baal Shem Tov in the 18th century in Eastern Europe. It emphasized pious devotion and ecstasy more than learning and this is why it was very popular among the poor and uneducated Jews of this region. In the course of time, a

number of rebbes formed their own courts in which they received their followers from near and far.

[e]   Deuteronomy 4:6

[f]   Haskalah: Jewish Enlightenment movement which started in Germany in the 18th century and from there spread into other European countries. It aimed at breaking the isolation of the Jews by modernizing Jewish life and religion.

[g]   The text says Western Europe but it must be a mistake, otherwise the sentence with in general and in particular does not make sense.

Footnotes from Book Chapter:

[1]   The Jewish self-government in Poland consisted of three parts: the highest authority – the Council of Four Lands, the mid-level authorities – the county councils and the local authority – the kahal. In the coming pages, we will not distinguish between the central council and the county councils but will talk about councils in general.

[2]   The Bolekhov community, like other communities in Poland, also had financial obligations with regard to the Catholic Church. In his memoirs Reb Ber describes that once the cardinal of Lemberg ordered the closing of the shul because the community did not pay its dues to the church. The shul was closed from Pesakh to Shavuot and only after paying the due sum could the Jews pray in the shul again.

[3]   Assignment – a receipt for payment.

[4]   This is what the tax was called.

[5]   This was not a just claim because in the meantime new houses were being built.

[6]   According to Polish law, the Sejm could not pass a law if a delegate stood up and said, 'I do not agree (veto)'.

[7]   In the 19th century the salt mines in the vicinity of the town were closed down and only those within the town continued to be used.

[8]   On the agricultural colonization in Galicia see Dr. A. I. Braver's article, 'Yosef der tsveyter un di yidn in Galitsie' [Joseph the second and the Jews in Galicia], Ha-saloakh, vol. 23, pp. 336-343.

[9]   Brody was one of the most important Jewish centers at that time.

[10]   Dr. N. Gelber: Di geshikhte fun di yidn in Brod [The history of the Jews in Brody], pp. 54, 55, 57.

[11]   From Reb Ber's time, we know of two Talmud scholars from Bolekhov. One is Reb Zvi Hirsh, according to the well-known Reb Chaim Joseph Azulay, who negotiated with him when on a visit in Amsterdam in 1878 about organizing support for the yishuv in Palestine (Erets Isroel). "He is a disciple of the rabbi Jonathan (Yehonatan?) (he seems to sympathize with the Sabbetai Zvi movement). He served as a rabbi in Bolekhov but another rabbi came and took the rabbinate from him with the power of

the lord." The second is Reb Shniur Feybush Menakhen, and he is renowned among the Palestinian messengers. He went to Palestine (Erets Isroel) in 1749 and on the way published his book in Constantinople. He lived in Jerusalem for some years and won the trust of the Ashkenazi community there and they sent him on a mission to the Diaspora (1754). He accomplished his task wonderfully: "He was successful not only in the Ashkenazi communities of Amsterdam and London but he also succeeded in inspiring sympathy in some communities in Northern Italy, and they handed him over all the "Palestine money" for the Ashkenazi community in Jerusalem." (A. Yaari, Shalokhi Erets Israel?) The following appeal is addressed to the prospective donors. And the designation of the holy community (Maats?) as the center of the support for the yishuv in Jerusalem shows that he was an efficient man, worthy of the trust of those who sent him. Residing in Livorno (on his way to the North), he wrote a book entitled, which deals with the mystery of the leap year in the manner of the Kabbala. He published part of the book in Livorno and part in Amsterdam.

[12] Dr. R. Mahler: Yiddishe geshikhte, di letste doyres [Jewish history, the last generations], vol. 1, book 4, p. 35.

[13] The Kaiser, may his glory be enhanced.

[14] Dr. N. Gelber: Dray dokumentn vegn der geshikhte fun der frankistisher bavegung in Poyln [Three documents on the history of the Frankist movement in Poland], Zion, Bet (?), pp. 326-331.

[Hebrew page 27 & Yiddish page 184]

2. Maskilim and Haskalah (Enlightenment) Movement in Bolekhov in the 19ᵗʰ Century
by Dr. M. Hendel
Translated from Yiddish by Eszter Andor

A. The Haskalah in Galicia

When we talked about Reb Ber Birkenthal (Ber Bolekhover) we mentioned two movements which emerged in the second half of the 18ᵗʰ century, and we also gave a short summary of the relationship of Ber Bolekhover to these two movements. One of them is the Hassidic movement, which conquered masses in Galicia, and the other is the Haskalah movement, which was still in its infancy in Reb Ber's time and the first signs of which had only just emerged. The Haskalah movement arose from the economic changes that took place in the 18ᵗʰ century. A stratum of rich Jewish merchants and industrialists emerged in Prussia and in other German states, whose contact with the outside world inevitably led them to change their way of life. The outside world was experiencing an age of *"Sturm und Drang"* [Storm and Stress]. People behaved as if they had just opened their eyes and started looking at their surrounding in a totally different way, analyzing everything with the help of reason and intellect. This led to the weakening of the hitherto sanctified values in various areas of life: religion, society, economy, education, etc. This fermentation contained the seed from which the French revolution and the great transformations of the 19ᵗʰ century would develop. As a result of looking at the four ells [narrow confines] of the sanctified Jewish religious forms of life there is a change in the mind of the Jew as well. His naive faith is replaced by the critical stance, instead of shutting himself up behind the walls of an inner Jewish life, the Jew aspires to get to know the world with the help of science; instead of promoting the spirit and depriving the body comes the call for harmonious development, which includes special care for one's bodily health, and for finding aesthetic pleasure in the beauty of nature. In the case of some *maskilim*, these new elements which became part of their thinking strengthened their Jewish roots – because the *maskilic* awakening was generally closely connected to the love of the *Tanach* [Bible] and Hebrew, even though they transformed more or less the essence of the religious Jew. To sum up, a new type of Jew crystallized which in due course gave birth to Jewish nationalism.

In the mind of other *maskilim*, the new elements conquered the old ones and as a result of the struggle between "old" and "new", their soul was torn and they became estranged little by little from their Jewish roots, to the extent that some of them even converted.

[Yiddish page 185]

As we recall, the Haskalah movement emerged in the German lands but it spread beyond their borders. We can see its influence in the town of Shklov, Belorussia, the Jewish merchants of which came into contact with the Haskalah centers in Germany through their business activities. This is how the Haskalah movement emerged in some Galician towns, in particular in Brody, Lemberg and Tarnopol which were important commercial centers at the time.

One of the first *maskilim,* Reb Israel of Zamosc (1710-1770) comes from Galicia. Born in Boyberik [Bobrka], he spent the last twenty years of his life in Brody. He wrote an article on mathematics and astronomy. He published a book entitled *Netzach Israel* [Eternal Israel] in 1741. (He wrote a commentary in rationalist spirit on a passage of the *Shas* [the Talmud].) This Galician precursor of the Haskalah movement who was a *melamed* [teacher] in the yeshiva of Zamosc (hence his name), was in contact with the pillars of German literature (among them Lessing), and even Moses Mendelssohn, the leader of the German *maskilim,* was influenced by him.[1] A similar figure was Reb Shlomo Chelmer, rabbi of Chelm and Zamosc. He settled in Lemberg and died in Saloniki in 1871 on his way back from Palestine. In the preface of his book *"Marchevat ha-Mishna" – Chidushei Halachot le – "Yad ha-Chazaka shel ha-Rambam"* ["Chariots of the Mishna – Halachic Novellae to the book entitled "Strong Hand" by Rambam], he highly praises the sciences and complains that people neglect them, even though they are the seven pillars referred to in the Proverbs, chapter 9, verse 1.[2]

Another personality who belonged to this circle is Reb Shlomo of Dubno (1738-1813) who drew on the Torah knowledge of Reb Shlomo Chelmer of Lemberg. During some time, he participated in the translation of the Torah into German initiated by Mendelssohn. For a while he worked as a teacher in Mendelssohn's house. In the last years of his life he published a *Biur* [Hebrew commentary on the Bible by Mendelssohn and his disciples] to the Torah, without a German translation, and collected subscribers for this work. He died in Amsterdam.[3] Reb Zeev Wolf Büchner (1750-1820), born in Brody, also belonged to this circle. He traveled a great deal in Poland, Bohemia, Hungary and Germany because of his businesses, as well as for the publication of his books. For a while he was the secretary of the Jewish community of Brody. He displayed a passionate love for Hebrew and he saw the *maskil* as a Jewish ideal, who, among others things, studied the *Tanach* [Bible] with the commentators, as well as scholarly works, among them the Rambam.[4] An interesting figure among the precursors of the Haskalah movement in Galicia was Reb Pinchas Eliahu Hurvitz, who was born in Lemberg in 1765 and deceased in Cracow in 1821. His travels took him as far as Holland and England. In 1794, he published a work entitled *Book of the Covenant,* the first part of which is an encyclopedia of natural sciences.

[Yiddish page 186]

"The *Book of Covenant* played an immense role in diffusing basic knowledge about the universe", states the historian Mahler.[5] The pioneer of the Galician Haskalah movement was Reb Mendel Lapin of Satanov (1749-1826), who spent the last eighteen years of his life in Brody and Tarnopol. We are indebted to him for many practical plans in the spirit of the Haskalah and for practical activity for a particular goal.[6] This activity is connected to the negotiations concerning the Constitution of May 3 of independent Poland in 1791. In his pamphlet, written in French, he proposed, among other things, improvement of Jewish education, the spreading of scientific works, as for example, the *More ha-Nevuchim* [Guide to the Perplexed] of Rambam in easy Hebrew and he publication of popular scientific books.

From his literary activity we can trace his practical-daring plan, which was to translate the *Tanach* [Bible] into Yiddish, the only language that the common people speak. This went against the ideas of other *maskilim* who wanted to educate the people in German. It is especially noteworthy that Reb Mendel was one of the renewers of Hebrew language.[7] One of the main opponents of the translation of the *Tanach* [Bible] into Yiddish was the Galician *maskil* Tevye Feder (born near Cracow, died in Tarnopol in 1817). The activity of Mendel Lapin leads us already into the 19th century, where we find his friends and allies among the leaders of the Haskalah in Russia and Galicia. There are three personalities in the Galician Haskalah movement of the 19th century that are especially interesting to us. The first is the writer Josef Perl (1774-1839) who fought against the Hassidic movement and promoted a new type of education in Tarnopol. The second is Reb Shlomo Yehuda Rapaport (1790-1867) who, having served for a short time as rabbi in Tarnopol, was nominated rabbi in Prague, where he served for 27 years. He was one of the founding fathers of the *Wissenschaft des Judentums* [Science of Judaism] of the traditional spirit and of the founders of the historical critical research. And the third is Reb Nachman Krochmal (born in Brody in 1783, deceased in Tarnopol in 1840), the author of a profound work, the *More Nevuche ha-Zman* [Guide to the Perplexed of our Time] in which he put the Galician movement at the head of the forces which had an effect on the ideological strengthening of the Jewry.

Three characteristic features distinguish the pioneers of a new way of thinking in the Jewry:

a. from a religious point of view almost all of them remained within the framework of tradition, observing the *mitzvot* [good deeds] and fearing God;

b. they had a negative stance vis-a-vis the Hassidic movement because, as the leaders of the Haskalah movement argued, its strengthening led to the growth of ignorance.

[Yiddish page 187]

Photograph: the two lines under the picture read: Sincere thanks to Ch. David Zeman who found this document in the attack of his house in Bolekhov, brought it here from America and put it at my disposal.

[Yiddish page 188]

Mendel Lapin, for example, demanded that the publication of Hassidic and Cabalistic books be forbidden because "if the Hassidic movement strengthens, all hope of spreading scientific knowledge among the common people will be lost".[8] The *maskilim* were considering the idea of reforming the education hoping that it would lead to the emergence of the new man.

The Austrian government, which got Galicia at the partition of Poland in 1772, supported the *maskilim*. In the previous chapters on Ber Bolekhover, we described in detail the efforts of the government to transfer the Jews into agriculture. Now we will recall Emperor Joseph II who decreed that public schools must be opened for Jewish children and made it the responsibility of the Jewish community to ensure that children did attend school. When he realized that his orders were not successful, he decided to open German schools especially for Jews and introduced the following principles. A child was not allowed to attend *cheder* [religious elementary school] and study Talmud unless he had a certificate that he attended a German school. A Jew could not marry or be hired as a journeyman to learn a trade unless he had a certificate that he had gone to a German school or learnt German at home. In order to prepare teachers for these schools a seminary was founded in Lemberg, which was to be maintained from Jewish taxes. A Czech *maskil* Herz Homberg was nominated as chief-inspector and it was his task to establish and supervise the schools. The Jewish inspector set about his task with great zeal. In 1877, a year after accepting the nomination, he established 48 schools, among them a school in Stryj and in Dolina; four years later another 51 schools are added, among them a school in Kalusz, Skale, Zurawno [Zhuravne] and Bolekhov. Almost all the schools were designated for boys and the course lasted for one year; schools for girls were opened in two towns only, Lemberg and Brody. Beside the one-year course, a three-year institution was set up in these two towns as well, and a teacher training seminary was opened in Lemberg.

Until the graduation of the teachers from the Lemberg seminary, Homberg provided the schools with candidates from Germany, Bohemia and Moravia. However, Homberg did not live up to the expectations of the Austrian authorities.

Homberg approached with contempt all that was sacred and dear to the Jews and his only aspiration was to please the authorities and secure his career. His behavior and the behavior of his   teachers   was   foreign to the spirit of Galician Jewry and provoked an uncompromising hatred. When the Jews learned that he was among those who recommended the introduction of a tax on Sabbath candles, his authority and the authority of his teachers collapsed completely.[9]

The Jewish school in Bolekhov

The Jewish school in Bolekhov

(Sharper image of people in above picture)

[Yiddish page 189]

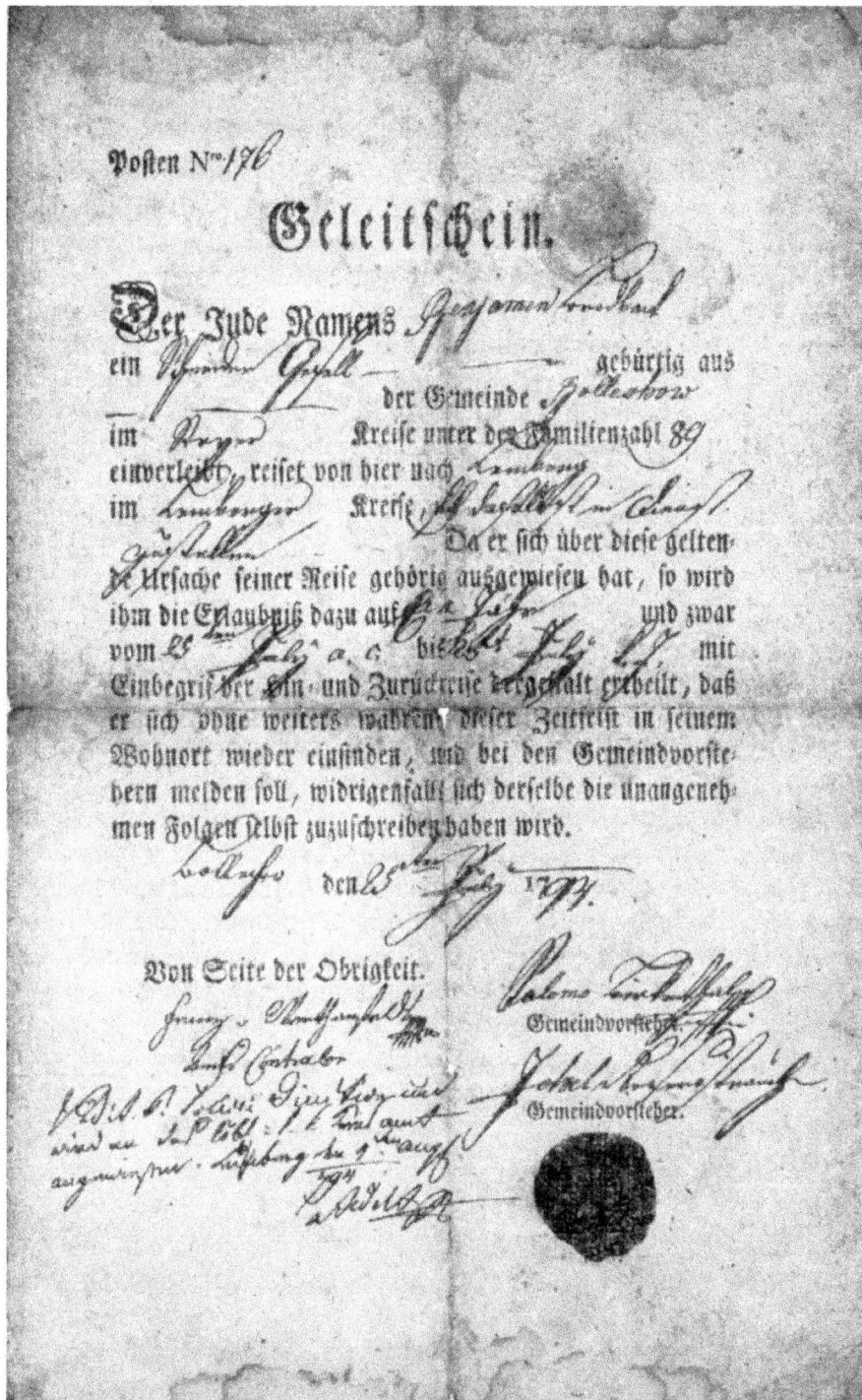

Hearty congratulations to David Zeman who found this document in the attic of his house in Bolekhov. He brought it from America and presented it us.

[Yiddish page 190]

As regards the school in Bolekhov, we know that there was a teacher called Jacob Blumenthal there; In the list of teachers in Galicia in 1790, assembled by the historian Gelber, he appears under the name Jacob Blum, which seems a mistake. We have an official document dated from 1794 which shows that the authorities took the issue of the school quite seriously. In that year a young man named Benjamin Bradbart received a permit signed by two community leaders (Shlomo Birkenthal and Yoel Rosenstruch) and validated by the administrative authorities, which allowed him to go to Lemberg and spend a year there (from July 29, 1794 to July 25, 1795) to improve his skills in the tailoring trade. Our young man traveled to Lemberg but it seems that the police made a mistake because on the pass which had been given to him on August 6, 1791, the police wrote the following remark: "the person in question will be sent back to his home town Bolekhov where he is obliged, in compliance with the laws passed by the authorities, to attend school and only after finishing school can he learn the tailoring trade." It can be assumed that the Jews of Bolekhov related the same way to the school as the Jews of other towns in that they did not want to rent a flat for the school, they made up various pretexts not to send their children to school and they tried to harass the teacher. Most importantly, the Jews took various measures not to send the children to school although, by order of the authorities, it was announced every year in the shuln [synagogues or schools] that young men could not get married or learn a trade unless they could read and write German, the number of students did not grow and the schools vegetated. The hostile attitude of the Jewish public opened both Homberg's eyes and the eyes of the government. Homberg left Galicia disgraced in 1801. In 1806 the government in Vienna discredited the plan for establishing schools for Jews in Galicia. Homberg summed up his activities in an anonymous article that appeared in the periodical Bikure ha-Ittim in 1820. In the article he claimed that "his educational activity bore nice fruit and it is undeniable that Galicia can be grateful to the schools for the many intelligent and useful persons educated in them.[10] The fact that in the discussions concerning the establishment of a school in Bolekhov in the 1840s neither the initiators nor the opponents mention Homberg's school shows that the school did not make much of an impression on the contemporaries. It should be pointed out that Bolekhov was one of the few towns in which the school teacher struck roots in the local community. Blumenthal married and settled in Bolekhov,[11] and it is more than likely that Berish Blumenthal whom we will talk about when we describe the new school was a descendant of the teacher who Homberg had brought into the town in 1790.

[Yiddish page 191]

To conclude our foreword which helped us familiarize ourselves with conditions in Bolekhov, we must recall that after the abolishment of Homberg's schools, new schools sprang up in Galicia which strove to combine "Torah" with "Derech Eretz" ["Torah with the ways of the world", phrase coined by S. R. Hirsch who wanted to combine traditional Torah observance with secular studies] and give their students both a Jewish and a general education. The two schools of Josef Perl, founded in Tarnopol in 1813 and in Brody in 1818, were typical of these endeavors.

In these two schools, the students learned general subjects, German, like in all other schools, and other foreign languages (French in Tarnopol, and French and Italian in Brody).

In the school in Brody practical subjects, such as bookkeeping and commerce, were also taught. In Tarnopol considerable attention was given to Jewish subjects: to the study of the *Tanach* [Bible] in Mendelssohn's translation, the Talmud, Jewish philosophy, as well as to writing in Yiddish and Hebrew. It appears that in the 1820s a mere 300 Jewish children attended these schools, of which 120 attended Perl's school in Tarnopol. The movement to establish schools in Galicia was renewed in the 1840s. Lemberg was the first with to open a four-year educational institute in 1844 and Bolekhov followed next. The founding and maintenance of the educational institute was part of the of the bitter fight between the *maskilim* and the Hasidim. Neither side refrained from denouncing and defaming the other before the authorities and it went so far that the forces opposed to Haskalah removed the rabbi, Abraham Kohn, who was the representative of the *maskilim* of Lemberg and a central figure in the founding of the local school, by poisoning him.

B. The Representatives of Three Generations of M*askilim* in Bolekhov

(1) Introduction

When we described the social and cultural centers of Galicia, we referred to three towns, Brody, Tarnopol and Lemberg. Contrary to these three centers, Bolekhov was a small shtetl but fortune favored it and it appeared on the stage of the battle of ideas together with the large towns, and moreover, very interesting maskilic characters emerged from this town who played an important role in the general Haskalah movement in Galicia.[12] We have seen that the first sprouts of the Haskalah movement in Bolekhov appeared with Reb Ber Birkenthal at the end of the 18th century. The evolution of the movement in the 19th century was a natural continuation of what Reb Ber had unintentionally laid down the basis of. In Bolekhov, as in other towns, the battle between the *maskilim* and the Hasidim was centered around the school. A few facts can show us that the shtetl was a maskilic center in the 19th century. In 1812, Samson Bloch, the well-known *maskil*, published the first volume of his geography book entitled *Shvilei ha-Olam* [Paths of the World] and among the 340 subscribers to the book there were six people from Bolekhov, 171 from Brody, 78 from Lemberg, 41 from Tarnopol, 13 from Zhulkover [?] and 13 from Jaroslaw. The following towns had fewer subscribers than Bolekhov:

[Yiddish page 192]

Risha [probably Rzeszow] – 5, Muscisk – 5, Tysmienica [Tysmenitsa] – 5, Tarnow – 3.[13] When the school in Lemberg opened in 1849, Bolekhov was the first to welcome it.[14] When the school in Stanislaw opened in 1849, the Bolekhov *maskil* Zelig Hirsch Mandschein was invited to give the opening speech.[15] Bolekhov gained the reputation of an active town and in the 1850s larger Jewish communities, such as those of Przemysl, Zlotshev [Zloczew] and Risha [?], consult Bolekhov in the matter of establishing schools.[16] In an appraisal published in 1858 in the monthly *Ben Chananja* [17], the author, who was in fact from Bolekhov, states the following: "The Jewish communities of Brody, Tarnopol and Lemberg, where progress and culture had struck root long ago were recently joined by the small community of the shtetl Bolekhov." This certainly enhanced the good reputation of the shtetl and encouraged the local *maskilim*.

Before we start describing the activities of the *maskilim* insofar as we can find their echo in the periodicals of the period, we will describe some maskilic personalities in Bolekhov. In the material at our disposal we can discern three generations of *maskilim,* whose representatives are the prototypes of their comrades ideological brothers-in-arms. Unfortunately, they were much smaller in numbers and weaker than the Hasidim and the conservative powers but, as well shall see, they made considerable achievements.

(2) The First Generation of *Maskilim* in Bolekhov

We will now introduce Reb Hirsch Goldenberg who represents the first generation. We do not know much about him. It can be presumed that he was a wholesaler and he made regular business trips to Greece. We have two reliable witnesses – pillars of the Haskalah in Austria with whom he maintained a regular correspondence on science and scholarship – who described Goldenberg. One of them is Shlomo Yehuda Rapaport, the other Shmuel David Luzzatto, professor of the rabbinical seminary of Padua, who impressed all *maskilic* circles in Europe. In 1831, Hirsch expressed his appreciation of S. Y. Rapaport's historical biographies and he made a parenthetic remark that Rapaport was wrong concerning a Greek word, "according to my knowledge of Greek and what I have heard in their country". But Reb Hirsch apologized for his remark saying that "I am still far from the threshold of wisdom and scholarship, and how could a fly speak among lions!".[18] Nevertheless, he displayed such a profound and thorough knowledge of Jewish cultural history that Rapaport reminded him in his answer to him that "You are one of the few who get to the core, to the heart of everything," and expressed his astonishment: "To tell the truth, I have not expected to encounter such a man in such a small shtetl as Bolekhov."

[19] These were unusual words. Rapaport was delighted at the deep knowledge of the scholars in Bolekhov. He expressed his delight in one of his letters to Reb Shmuel Reggio,[20] stating that Reb Hirsch "is a *maskil* who knows a great deal about Jewish *sforim* [religious books], he wrote me, too, very clever and dear remarks about my pamphlet".[21]

Let us now turn to our second witness S. D. Luzzatto. On December 15, 1835 Luzzatto replied to Reb Hirsch's letter in which the latter complained about the situation in the Jewish world, how the middle course is abandoned and everybody leaned towards the extremes – some towards uncompromising conservatism, others towards uncompromising progress. Luzzatto agreed with his judgement and said that he also believed that the right course was reciprocal communication, compromise and compliance, "but only the chosen ones follow such paths and you, Sir, are one of them".[22] A sentence from a letter that his son wrote to Reb Hirsch completes his characterization: "from your letter it appears that you are full of ardent aspirations that Jewish scholars should engage in translating useful scholarly works into our holy tongue in order to enrich and embellish it and to make it the lady of languages as it had been in the past." [23]

Reb Hirsch was a *maskil* who was deeply concerned for the survival of the Jewry and worried lest the sudden offensive of secular culture might harm it. However, he was not one to close his eyes and ignore the well of wisdom which could enrich the life of the Jewry and embellish our national culture as we progress.

As we shall see, a new generation of fighters emerged in Bolekhov in the 1830s who fought for modern Jewish culture and were not satisfied with aspirations only but prepared to take daring steps, as well.

(3) Representatives of the Second Generation of *Maskilim* in Bolekhov

The second generation is represented by Reb Hirsch's two sons, Shmuel Leib and Jacob, and Zelig Zvi Mandschein and his circle, whose members are each a chapter in themselves. Here we will only treat Reb Shmuel Leib Goldenberg and Zelig Zvi Mandschein. Goldenberg was born in Bolekhov in 1807. He got married at the age of 16, left Bolekhov at the end of the 20s and settled in Tarnopol. He died in 1846, leaving five children behind. Two of his children were abroad studying: one studied philosophy and the other was preparing for a teaching position. Shmuel Leib studied a great deal and from his youth on he was in contact with the prominent figures of his generation discussing with them the sciences and Haskalah. In the 1830s he planned to publish a periodical treating sciences in general and the science of Judaism in particular, in the form of a correspondence between learned men. This is how the periodical *Kerem Chemed* [Vineyard of Delight], which was the continuation, only on a higher level, of the periodical *Bikure ha-Ittim* came into being.

[Yiddish page 194]

Kerem Chemed, published by Goldenberg between 1833-1843, appeared first in Vienna then in Prague under the editorship of S. Y. Rapaport (ShI'R). From an exchange of letters with S. D. Luzzatto we learn that Goldenberg planned to publish the periodical in Italy. With the publication of the periodical Goldenberg made a important contribution to our new literature as editor, publisher and patron. The writer Shniur Sachs, who renewed the publication of the *Kerem Chemed* in 1854, was right in writing about him that "... he sowed justice in the field of Israel, his deeds will always stand by him because he performed a great deed in Israel." [24]His respect for learned men and his readiness to serve and help them manifested itself on various occasions: he was one of the mediators, together with the scholar Tzuntz, in the publication of the great work of Reb Nachman Krochmal's *More Nevuche ha-Zman* [Guide to the Perplexed of our Time].[25] He made efforts, together with others, to nominate Reb Shlomo Yehuda Rapaport rabbi in Prague.[26] And when they succeeded, Goldenberg wrote a long letter to his father in which he described the whole matter in detail and added a few poems by Haskalah writers in honor of the event. He ended the letter with the following wish: "If God granted that all Jewish communities in the Diaspora be looked after by devoted and learned 'shepherds', then the light of Judaism would rise as the morning star." [27] He also planned to publish the literary heritage of the Brody*maskil* Jacob Shmuel Bik but his writings fell victim to the fire of 1835.[28] He intervened on behalf of Joseph Perl's grandson that he be accepted at the rabbinical seminary of Padua.[29] In the columns of the German weekly *Der Orient,* he turned to the writers and asked them to donate copies of their books to the library of Perl, may his memory be blessed.[30]

His relationship with the prominent figures of the generation placed Shmuel Leib in the center of Jewish cultural life in those times. S. D. Luzzatto was in constant correspondence with him and in 1833 he wrote the following to him: "It makes me glad that God helped me meet such a pure, dear, kind-hearted person." [31] S. Y. Rapaport wrote him in 1830 that "... My love for you is great, I have found in you a virtuous and pure man who hates flattery and loves the truth, therefore, my soul is happy to unite with you." [32] Rapaport described what he thought of Goldenberg in a letter to the historian Yost: "Goldenberg has profound knowledge and it gives him pleasure to serve learned men and scholars". Yost added that in his eyes, too, Goldenberg was "a pure man and his deeds are just".[33] Everybody praised him highly. Rapaport (ShI'R), noting his learnedness and his literary plans, wrote: "there are scores of men in your land who are learned and thirsty for knowledge... and you, my friend, are one of them". He agreed with Goldenberg's plan of publishing the sforim [religious books] of the Galician Karaites.[34]

[Yiddish page 195]

Shmuel Leib Goldenberg was a businessman but he did not regard his Kerem Chemed as a business undertaking but as an undertaking that required devotion and self-sacrifice. He emphasized that he did not look for profit and he would be on guard despite the temptations because he had a single aim, "to spread the light".[35] It is interesting to note that S. Y. Rapaport argued that Goldenberg was a Jew who observed the *mitzvot*[good deeds], "he has never committed any serious transgressions, such as the desecration of the Sabbath, eating forbidden food, etc.". However, it seems that he did transgress lesser prohibitions. We learn from Rapaport that Goldenberg was not too pious: "he is not a "sedentary person", he is a businessman who cannot observe all the *mitzvot* [good deeds], unlike the scholars who make a living from studying the Torah." [36]

Although S. L. Goldenberg developed his communal and literary activity as a resident of Tarnopol, there is no doubt that he had his roots in Bolekhov. He drew his spiritual force from his father's house, from the atmosphere of the shtetl, and maybe also from his circle of friends and acquaintances, just like his brother Jacob, about whom Shmuel Leib wrote that "I have known you for a long time as a lover of Jewish learning and the sciences, as a diligent student of our old and new *sforim* [religious books]".[37] Like his brother, Shmuel Leib was also well-versed in Jewish learning and the sciences but he also inherited the practical-mindedness of his father, who united in himself the scholar and the businessman, and he supported the community by serving it in the field of culture and literature.

Another personality of the generation of Goldenberg brothers was Zelig Hirsch Mandschein. As we know more about Mandschein, we shall write about him at length. He was five years younger than Shmuel Goldenberg. He was born in Bolekhov in 1812 and died in Jaroslaw in 1872. He also left the narrow circle of the shtetl and lived for a while in Stanislaw in the 1830s. He spent the last years of his life in Drohobycz, then he became a teacher in Jaroslaw. However, he lived the largest part of his life in Bolekhov, where he was one of the responsible movers of the community, he was also one of the community leaders for a while and taught   for many years in the   school of whose founders he was one. Beside   his   activities   in   Bolekhov,   he   taught   a circle of young *maskilim* in Stanislaw. Jacob Bibring (1818-1882), the Hebrew poet of Stanislaw, who was the secretary of the community for many years spoke highly of Mandschein.[38] The historian Dr. Gelber stated that the *maskilim* in Stanislaw were influenced by the *maskilim* of Bolekhov. He wrote: "the influence of Zelig Hirsch Mandschein awakened the youth of Stanislaw to Hebrew literature and he also sent them Hebrew newspapers." [39]

[Yiddish page 196]

Mandschein wrote a few books on science, culture and education and when Peretz Smolensky [40] published his journal *Ha-Shachar* [The Dawn], dedicated to the revival of the Jewish people and its language, he introduced the writer Mandschein with the following words: "The name of the writer is well known to us from his books and articles which are disseminated in the newspapers. And all his books are like a battle field where he fights against Hasidim and darkness. His love of the Jewish people is great and strong is his hatred of those who degrade the honor of Israel. Such books benefit the Jewish people because they are built on strong pillars, on the sayings of the sages of blessed memory. God grant him success in his strivings to bring the light to the hearts of his brothers." [41] Nowadays his books, articles and poems have little literary value but in his time they were important contributions to the Haskalah literature as important journalistic tools in the battle for light, progress and the modernization of Jewish life in his town, in Galicia and beyond its borders. In a book which outlines Hebrew educational journalism in Austria we find the following: "Among the Galician *maskilim* who fought in the first lines excelled especially Zelig Hirsch Mandschein in Bolekhov and Yechiel Meler in Stanislav [Ivano Frankivsk]." [42]

Mandschein, as we have shown, was an important writer and a militant personality. However, he was a modest person and knew the limits of his abilities and possibilities. In a letter to his friend and student Jacob Bibring in Stanislav [Ivano Frankivsk], he wrote the following about himself: "I am a big fowl with little wings which makes futile efforts to spread its wings under the skies." [43] This seems quite true: he had a strong will and was ready for a great swing but he had few possibilities. Maybe we have before us the tragic embodiment of a man of great stature and *bel esprit* whom the atmosphere of a small shtetl left no room to grow in but weighed down and degraded his exaltation. Mandschein complained many times of conditions in the small shtetl. He wanted to break out of it because even though he was spiritually attached to the shtetl, he could not find a place for himself. It remains a fact that he lived almost all his life in Bolekhov, which he saw as his tragedy and perforce also his greatness. In a letter to his friend Bibring he praised the big city so utterly different from the small shtetl: there – excellent educational institutions, nice parks, clubs, libraries, literary cafes for an exchange of opinions and friendly conversation. In the small town, on the contrary, all is petty... the order of studies is not in order... the rabbis and *chazanim* [cantors] do not know how to awake glorious feelings in the people.[44]

[Yiddish page 197]

Sixteen years later, during which life tested him hard because which his literary activity did not reach up to the skies and his communal activities did not bear much fruit compared to the efforts he made, and maybe also because he did not find any satisfaction in his personal life, he wrote to his friend, the philosopher and future thinker Shlomo Rubin who had the privilege to settle in a big city: "Life is delightful in a big city which is full of scholars, where culture and scholarship have their nest." [45] His grief was big but, as we have said above, he perfected the fate of the shtetl man and he was ready to see it even as his greatness. In a letter to Bibring in 1846 he wrote, maybe out of despair, maybe with pride, that "not everybody can be a pillar of light for the whole world, I am content to be of use and to help in one town only and to give them advice to help them not to sink in the abyss of stupidity." [46] He found pleasure in his activities and his studies. The closing words of his book *Lashon Chachamim* [Language of the Sages] (1866) in which he turns to the Almighty are characteristic of Mandschein: "It is not concealed from you that I have loved the truth from my early youth, I have not asked you to give me wealth and the pleasures of the world, I have only asked for wisdom and you listened." [47] In his book *Amudei ha-Olam* [Pillars of the Universe] (1861) he expressed his ideals more clearly: "... Man! If you want to live happily, come into your rooms, close the doors, study Torah and wisdom, perform deeds of loving kindness and do not desire luxury." [48]

Mandschein's life revolved around two axis: literary creation and communal-educational activities, and both of these drew their spiritual nourishment from the same root: love of the Jewish people and care for its improvement. Hence his fight with the Hasidim and "those who rebel against the light", hence also his communal ideals, which he expressed on various occasions: he complained of people's lustfulness for whom "gold is their God and silver is their idol, they worship them and pray to them." [49] He called upon Jews of his town to donate for the benefit of the communal institutions: "Help poor people, give tithe of the goods that God bestowed upon you." [50] He called upon the rabbis to organize communal help. "Perform deeds of loving kindness, support and feed the poor and the paupers".[51] In a letter to Peretz Smolensky on the occasion of the publication of *Ha-Shachar* [The Dawn], he noted that in fact each Jewish community was "full of war and looting". He rose to a symbolic-picturesque image, stating how deceptive the romantic image representing the idyll and happy life of the shepherd was when in fact the shepherd often suffered from hunger and went in tatters.[52]

[Yiddish page 198]

Let us accompany our hero in two spheres of his active life and at the same time learn something about the atmosphere of the shtetl. At the age of sixteen Mandschein devoted himself to literary activity. He confessed in a letter that "when I turned sixteen (in 1828), the spirit of poetry awoke in me... and every day I wrote something".[53] And in a second letter he said: "From the time when my intellect opened up, I sustained myself with scholarship, it was my only comfort in my miserable life." [54] The development of his poetic and artistic spirit was backed by a circle of young people the same age as he. At the end of the 1820s there were a number of young people in Bolekhov who dreamed about changing the life of the Jewish people to elevate the people culturally so that Jews would be equal to other civilized nations. Mandschein's letters reflect the life of the shtetl, even if not the whole shtetl, at least its active part which, indirectly and to a certain extent also directly, laid the basis for the development and character of the shtetl for the coming decades.

Mandschein depicted his inclination to write already in his earliest youth in the following way: "And the friends of my youth regarded me as a model, the daily *Ha-Tzefirah* was successful in our town." [55] In a letter from 1847 he recalled that "... we had a place outside the town where we used to spend part of the summer days, there we used to have long talks, there awoke the love of learning in us, there we thought out noble thoughts." [56] Thus grew the writer and he always found time, even during the busiest years of his energetic cultural activities, for writing an article or preparing a book for publication. The publication of a book was an event not only for him but for the community as well. This is how in 1864 for example people in Bolekhov learned from the monthly *Ben Chananja* that Mandschein had published a book entitled *Goral ha-Tzedakah* and would soon publish a book entitled *Lashon Chachamim* [Tongue of the Scholars] [57] which contained the following chapters: 'The lineage of the Generations', 'World and Man', 'The Torah', 'Torah and Mitzva', 'Torah and Wisdom', 'The Mysteries of the Torah', 'Agadot and Midrashot', 'The Path to Faith'. His most interesting book is the *Amudei ha-Olam* [Pillars of the Universe], in which he talks about a life governed by the "Torah, prayer and acts of loving kindness". We note that Mandschein revealed a thorough and extensive knowledge of the old and new sources of Judaism. He was also familiar with world literature. In his book *Amudei ha-Olam* he cites what the French writer and politician Lamartine wrote about his visit to Palestine.[58]

We will discuss his communal activities as head of the community council and teacher in the Jewish school in detail in the chapter dealing with the history of the school. Here we confine ourselves to describe some of his characteristics.

[Yiddish page 199]

In his communal activities he had only one goal in mind, namely, "to raise the cultural level of the community, to embellish its customs so that we would not be disgraced in the eyes of other nations." [59] He fought bitterly against the Hasidim, but just like Goldenberg, he also sought the middle course between the religious cultural tradition and European cultural values. The ideal man for him was one whose life was governed by reason and whose existence was based on and rooted in true Hasidism. Mandschein's intimate attachment to Hebrew, the revival of which was one of his sacred goals, as he declared it on various occasions, must be noted in particular.[60] His devotedness to education, his love of the Jewish child and concern for his education are also obvious.

Let us now turn to his material circumstances and family relations, and the last years of his life. We have shown already that he was rather badly situated. He himself hinted at it in his writings and his friend who wrote a eulogy of him in the periodical *Ha-Magid* [The Preacher] explicitly said that Mandschein had not had a joyful life... All in all his life was short and miserable. Another friend states that hardship and poverty shortened his life. His last years were very hard. One of his friends paints a gloomy picture in his funeral oration: the remainder of Mandschein's money came to an end with no hope for more. Anger and pain, poverty and distress engulfed him. And beyond all this, he had family troubles as well: his son died young and his grandchildren were thrust upon him. Then his wife died and apparently he was lonely and deserted. We do not know why he left Bolekhov but we do know that he did not find another post at once. He lived for a year and a half in Drohobycz apparently without employment. Finally, his friends, the *maskilim,* found a position for him as teacher of religion in Jaroslaw and his material circumstances improved but he had hardly taught for a year before he became ill and died. Many people participated in his funeral, among them his students who learned "religion and faith" from him.

Two Hebrew newspapers eulogized him. In the weekly *Ivri anochi* [I am Hebrew], which was published in Brody, funeral orations and lists appeared from Drohobycz and Borislaw in the form of a poem written by a Jew from Lemberg. On the contrary in the periodical *Ha-Magid* [The Preacher], which was published in Luk (Prussia) an appraisal from Jaroslaw and Tarnow appeared. His personality and his merits in the battle for progress which he fought courageously and proudly were highly valued everywhere.

[Yiddish page 200]

One of his friends published a mourning poem about his death entitled 'Moonlight' (Mandschein). Below is the stanza of which the first letters give the family name Mandschein:

He who was the pillar of labor, Whose Initiative was great,
Who has struggled with hypocrites, and preached unto them.
He put his soul at hazard as he walked through God's pathways, for the sake
of Hebrew.
Our heart aches, because our moonlight has gone.
From early morning till late at night, his purpose was to help his People.
He established a school that shines like the sun.
His truthful words show the beauty of his wisdom.
Therefore we woe, because our moonlight has gone.

Before we pass on to the representatives of the third generation of *maskilim* in Bolekhov, let us cite the words of Mandschein's friend, the thinker Shlomo Rubin who characterized him thus in his foreword to Mandschein's book *Amudei ha-Olam* [Pillars of the Universe]: "You labored tremendously amongst your brothers – you spoke, you wrote, you even preached – and they were bitter towards you. They saddened your spirit with their deceitful language, with their persistent slander. And you are pure, all the power to you! Bless him with the fruit of wisdom."

(4) The Representatives of the Third Generation of *Maskilim* in Bolekhov

So far we got to know two generations of *maskilim*, let us now turn to the representatives of the third generation: Nechemiah Landes, who was born in 1835, that is, nine years before Shmuel Leib Goldenberg's death, and died in 1899, that is, 27 years after Mandschein's death. While Goldenberg's line of continuation went from Bolekhov to Tarnopol, then to Vienna and finally to Prague and Mandschein's to Stanislav [Ivano Frankivsk] and then to Jaroslaw, Landes' line drew him to Lemberg where he became a permanent resident in 1879. Landes followed closely the renewal and modernization of Jewish life in Galicia. He was especially interested in educational matters, as can be seen from his reports in the periodical *Ben Chananja*, of which he was a permanent contributor. In his reports, Landes complained of the Hasidic camp which, in his opinion, hindered the normal development of Galician Jewry. Landes had a comprehensive education: he attended gymnasium in Lemberg, and most importantly he was an autodidact. His reports were written in an excellent German style, interspersed with Latin and French phrases. Apparently, he did not have extensive Hebrew erudition – this was rather typical of the education of the time, which considered mastery of the language and culture of the nation in which Jews lived the most important and neglected the values which ensured the uniqueness of the Jewish people. However, as we shall see, Landes was devoted to Hebrew.

[Yiddish page 201]

Moreover, he had a splendid mastery of Polish, which was one of the most important factors of the national movement in the second half of the 19th century in Galicia, and which gave a new direction to the Jewish Haskalah as well. Landes' fluency in Polish was acknowledged by such an important personality as the Polish leader Smalka whom Landes visited as the head of a delegation of Bolekhov Jews in order to thank him for his friendly attitude to Jews in the imperial council in Vienna. In his answer Smalka (who received delegations from other Jewish communities as well) considered it necessary to highlight the fine Polish speech given by Landes.[61] In 1866 a communal assembly on the occasion of the nomination of Count Galuchovski as governor of Galicia was arranged in the school building in Bolekhov. At this assembly the representative of the old direction, Mandschein, spoke in German, while Landes, the representative of the *maskilim* of the new direction, gave his speech in Polish.[62] This meeting reveals Landes as a public figure fighting for his people's rights. In his speech he expressed the hope that the new governor will work towards annulling the legal restrictions imposed on Galician Jewry.

Let us depict a few more characteristics of Landes' attitude to the community. In 1861 in a review on a book – speeches about Sabbaths and holidays – written by the director of a Jewish educational institution in London (he read the book in German translation) he remarked that it would be worth translating the book into Hebrew to use in girls' education in Galicia. In the same year he published an article in German that appeared in a Polish calendar which praised the Jewish farmer. On the margins of the translation he stated that in his opinion it would be worth encouraging the development of Jewish agriculture so that Jews would be more willing to turn to agriculture once the legal restrictions which existed vis-a-vis the Jews in Austria would be removed. Pausing on Landes' communal activities it is worth noting that Landes was head of the community council for ten years and he was a member of the city council and the county council.

In 1878 when on the initiative of the Galician maskilim a conference of Galician Jewish communities was organized Landes was elected, together with the representatives of larger communities, to the executive committee.[63] One of Landes' finest accomplishments was the translation from German into Polish, in 1876, of the apologetic pamphlet written by Jacob Menachem Frankel against the attacks of Professor Ruhling, a foe of the people of Israel, on the Talmud.[64] He was especially interested in literary creations which could enhance esteem for the Jewish people.

[Yiddish page 202]

He translated the story entitled 'Zyd' [The Jew] by Kraszewski from Polish into German and the book *Abraham Ezapavitz*, which was originally written by Levande in Russian and translated into Hebrew by Tzitran, from Hebrew into German. This was a clear sign of Landes' absolute fluency in three languages, German, Hebrew and Polish.

It is interesting that Landes tried himself out at writing historical studies. We know his studies on the Jews of Stryj, Stanislav [Ivano Frankivsk] and Zhulkev [Nesterov], and of course, Bolekhov.[65] One of his very important activities was the editing of the newspaper of the *maskilim* of Lemberg. In the last three decades of the 19th century the Galician *maskilim* and Hasidim were fighting with one another for getting control over the Jewish community. The Hasidim reinforced themselves through their association called *"Machsikei Hadas"* [Upholders of Faith], while the *maskilim* organized themselves into the society "Guard of Israel". The members of the "Guard of Israel" were divided on the language question: one party maintained that the activities should be conducted in German, while the other party held that Polish should be the language of culture of the *maskilim*. The newspaper *Der Israelit* was published in German but with the strengthening of the Polish-speaking elements among the Galician *maskilim*, Landes joined the editorial board in order to make Polish the language of the newspaper. He worked as a member of the editorial board for four years and when he left it, the newspaper appeared once again in German.[66]

Landes was an educator first in Bolekhov, where he was a teacher and director, then in Lemberg, where he directed the municipal school for Jewish children called Sztacki.[67] Finally he was offered the honorable high post of inspector of the Baron Hirsch schools for Jewish children in Galicia. As teacher and educator Landes developed a wide range of activities. He published course books for religious education, he served as advisor in educational matters in the Alliance Israelite Universelle, in his reports to various newspapers he frequently wrote on education. Just to give a few examples: in 1859 he asked why the Jewish schools in Jaroslaw and Kolomai [Kolomyya] do not go on; in 1860 he praised the schools in Brzezan [Brzeziny], Fadheytze (?) and Drohobycz where measures were taken to maintain the Jewish schools. He informed the readers about Jewish education in Czernowitz, Jasi [Iasi] and Galati. He called upon the government to raise the Jewish educational budget to make sure that education would not be dependent on the favors of the pious community leaders who sought its abolishment.[68] When a conflict broke out in the progressive camp in 1861, Landes chastised them "because in the hard struggle for the modernization of Jewish life in Galicia, the fighting camp must be united." [69] From the period when he was inspector of the Baron Hirsch schools important information on his relation to Hebrew was preserved.

[Yiddish page 203]

In 1894 a conference of the teachers of the Baron Hirsch schools was organized in Stanislav [Ivano Frankivsk]. The participants expressed their desire to raise the level of Hebrew instruction in these schools. On the conference inspector Landes declared: "a Jewish youth who leaves the Baron Hirsch schools must know Hebrew, just as well as Polish." [70] This statement may surprise us, yet Landes was an opponent of the national movement. He strongly criticized Nathan Birnbaum when he came to Lemberg in 1862 preaching on behalf of "~~Chabad~~Chibat Zion" [Love of Zion], he fought against the nationalist newspaper *Przyszlosc* which was first published in Lemberg in 1893. His opposition to the national movement and at the same time his positive attitude to Hebrew is evident: Landes remained a *maskil* with the concepts of the second half of the 19th century. He dreamed of light and progress but he did not go further. The national movement which wrote on its banner the full emancipation of the Jewish people, not only cultural but also political revival, did not touch his heart, he remained in the circle of the threefold cultural synthesis of Polish, German and Hebrew. But the natural development of the Galician Jewish world reached Bolekhov as well. In 1899, the same year that Landes died in Lemberg, Hebrew courses were organized in Bolekhov – which were regarded not simply as language courses but as tools for the national revival –, speeches were given in Hebrew on public Zionist meetings. We have to note that a year before Landes' death, on the occasion of the opening of the second Zionist congress a telegram was sent from Bolekhov signed by:

1. Dr. Jacob Blumenthal, chairman of the association "Tikvat Israel" [Hopes of Israel];

2. Jewish citizens; and

3. Jewish youth.[71]

(5) The Story of the Jewish school

We have very little material on the Jewish school in Bolekhov and in the literature we encounter contradictory opinions.

As regards Shlomo Rubin's activities in the school, it is assumed that he was active between 1856 and 1861.[72] Professor Klausner in his foreword to the second book of Rubin's writings disagrees with this hypothesis. In his opinion Rubin was in Bolekhov twice: he first came to Bolekhov in 1851 "and established a private school to teach Hebrew and German". His activities were interrupted because he was drafted into military service for two years. After much wandering – in Zurawno [Zhuravne] and Galati (Romania)– "he returns to Bolekhov in 618 (taf-res-yud-khet) and is nominated director of the Jewish school by the government. He held this post for five years", that is, from 1859 to 1864.

[Yiddish page 204]

Nachum Sokolov, who published, in 1899, a collection of the biographies and autobiographies of the writers of his time wrote that in the 50s Rubin "was a teacher in small towns in Galicia", then in 1857 he came to Bolekhov and became the director of the school for five years.[73] We must correct the erroneous assumptions. The *Jüdisches Lexikon* (volume 1, page 1111) says that Jacob Goldenberg who later became editor of the periodical *Kerem Chemed* was active in Bolekhov. We do not understand what the lexicon means by the word "later" as we know that the editor of the *Kerem Chemed* was not Jacob Goldenberg but his brother Shmuel Leib. The editors assured that they would refer to Jacob Goldenberg with the letter "g" but they did not keep their promise. The *Russian Encyclopedia (Yevr. Entzikl.)* (volume 4, page 780) says that the editor of *Kerem Chemed* lived in Bolekhov in the 1840s. *Encyclopedia Judaica* (volume 4, page 921) is of the same opinion. The truth is that Shmuel Goldenberg left Bolekhov at the end of the 1820s and he edited *Kerem Chemed* only until 1843 and died in 1846. So, it is hard to speak in general terms about the 1840s.

It is emphasized in various sources that it was the Mandschein brothers (Leib David and Zelig Hirsch) who lobbied for the permission to open the school. The *Hebrew Encyclopedia* (volume 3, page 808) shares this view. We have no material to either confirm or deny this information. We have not encountered the name of the brother Leib David or his activities in any sources. Zvi Scharfstein in the book *The History of Education in Israel says* [74] that the founders of the school were Shlomo Leib Goldenberg and Hirsch Zelig Mandschein and the permission was obtained in 1847 and it was because of his activities on behalf of the school that Goldenberg had to leave Bolekhov "he went to Tarnopol and then published the *Kerem Chemed* ". We found no confirmation in any of the sources of the view that the efforts to open the school were started at the end of the 1820s, at the time when Shmuel Leib (and not Shlomo!) Goldenberg left Bolekhov. Based on the sources we can conclude that Bolekhov followed the same road as Lemberg, in that the promoters of the school made efforts to obtain the permission to open the school at the beginning of the 1840s when Shmuel Leib Goldenberg had already been in Tarnopol for a long time and these were the last years of his work as editor of the *Kerem Chemed*. And by the way, Mandschein was 16 years old at the end of the 1820s. Scharfstein corrects the historian Balaban who attributes the activities on behalf of the school to Jacob Goldenberg.[75] In truth, Balaban is right – it was Jacob Goldenberg, Shmuel Leib's younger brother, who one of the promoters of the school and not Shmuel Leib, who died a year before the permit to open the school was received.

[Yiddish page 205]

In conclusion, we would like to note that Professor Balaban consulted the archives of the school which he designates 'school archives under Mandschein's name'. The archives are not at our disposal and who knows if anything remained of them, so let us turn to the sources that are at our disposal. As we have already noted a fermentation of awakening and modernization swept through the shtetl in the 1820s. This fermentation bore its fruit in the form of a circle of young people who set before themselves the goal of taking over control over the community in order to carry out their sweeping reform plans. The times favored them because at the very same time *maskilim* gained the upper hand in two large communities, Lemberg and Brody.[76] In 1843 a progressive community council was elected composed of three *maskilim*: Mandschein, Jacob Goldenberg and Zvi Birkenthal.[77]

The young people had elaborate plans but the Hasidic camp put up a strong opposition. Mandschein's words about the new council are reliable: "From the time that I was elected leader of the community, I have been striving to uproot all bad plants which are distasteful to any *maskil*. I and my two comrades will continue our efforts and we will not rest until there is light in our dwellings and, despite the numerous opponents, the nation will be healthy in body and spirit alike." [78] One of the innovations the new council introduced was that in the burial arrangements, the ladder from which the corpse was pulled off with a rope was replaced by a bed with a curtain for the Holy Ark. The other innovation was the founding of a hospital. The council showed great zeal in this latter task. It secured support from the Viennese Rothschilds and from various Galician Jewish communities, as well as a single donation of 500 Florins from the town administration, and it also started negotiations with the administration about receiving a yearly subsidy of 100 Florins.[79] One of Mandschein's important achievements was the introduction of regulations for the benefit of the synagogue, which aimed at preserving the esthetic side and elevating the sentiments in honor of God's house. Mandschein printed the regulations in his book *Amudei ha-Olam* [Pillars of the Universe] and he noted: "I offer you the order of a house of prayer which I made for my community and which hangs by the entrance of the shul [synagogue] so that the whole House of Israel would see it in all their dwelling places and act as our learned men commanded. I greatly rejoice that these regulations will be printed on a special tablet and put up by the entrance of the *shuln* [synagogues] in honor of the "sanctification of the congregation". [80] It is not surprising that in the reports from Lemberg we read words of praise about the small town Bolekhov with its 3,000 souls. "There is an intelligent Jewry, led by an able council, which plans to build a school and has already succeeded in collecting 700 Florins to this end.[81]

[Yiddish page 206]

The council worked zealously on the founding of the school but the council members cherished illusions in this matter. Mandschein talked about a modest institution "where Hebrew language and grammar and also the vernacular will be studied" but in the same letter he also talked about the school as "a school for science and scholarship".[82] The Jews of Bolekhov were, however, suspicious of the school, fearing that the study of the *Tanach* with the *Biur* [Hebrew commentary on the Bible by Mendelssohn and his disciples] and Mendelssohn's translation would be introduced in the school. Mandschein did not rest and appealed to everybody from whom he could still get favor and attention for the school. In his announcements to the Jews of Bolekhov he exposed the low educational standards of the *chederim* [religious elementary schools] from which children came out "without knowing either our sacred tongue or German", at a time when Jewish girls were excluded from education. He called out: "Have pity on your children; heed to my talk; I've opened my mouth with my voice." Although he had only started carrying out his plan, he already saw the school finished and he pleaded with his people: "Send your children to the new school where they will be raised in wisdom and the fear of God." [83] He asked for support for the new task and edified his people: "It is not a marble stone that will immortalize our names... good deeds, charity and mercy will render us eternal and will secure our good reputation in the world." [84] Meanwhile three years passed since the last elections and who could know if the brave reformers would be elected again in 1846. A report from Galicia stated that there a stormy election campaign cold be expected because the reactionary forces would strive to oust the progressive council.[85] The council rushed to hand in a request to the government concerning the permission to open the school, and to defeat its opponents it collected signatures on a petition pretending that they wanted to open a synagogue, "and they made use of the signatures for the request to open a school".[86] In the meantime new elections took place and Mandschein was elected head of the community council again. In 1847 Mandschein thought that his dream would come true because he received the permission to open the school. But fate wanted it otherwise. The opposition of the Hasidim was very strong and it became impossible even to think about carrying out the plan, and the matter came to a halt until 1856. In 1847 Mandschein, who had had some success, still had illusions. He spoke about a dream of his in which the Jews of Bolekhov came to thank him "for your all the good you did to us, for leading us on the right road with your pen and advice". The dream develops: a battle between the rabbis and *melamdim* [teachers in religious elementary schools] on one side and the children on the other, and truth, justice and wisdom also take part in the battle in his dream.

[Yiddish page 207]

Truth demands that the leaders of the community be concerned with vocational training and the development of agriculture.[87] The dream maybe suggests the predicament of Mandschein's plans. As we have already pointed out, Mandschein was forced to put them aside for some years. In the reactionary period which started with the failure of the bourgeois revolution of 1848 in France the prospects of having a progressive council elected were naught. However, the progressive forces had enough power to open the school in 1856 and Bolekhov was the fourth town in Galicia which established such a school.[88] We do not know the organizational and educational status of the school but as we shall see the school budget was based chiefly on the revenues from the *shechita* [ritual slaughter] and *mikve* [ritual bath] tax, and the promoters of the school in Bolekhov managed, with great difficulty, to convince the Galician authorities that they should contribute to the budget of the educational fund. With regard to the educational aspects, the school offered a 2-3-year course to provide the children with an essential basis in general and Hebrew erudition. The promoters of the school succeeded in ensuring school attendance by establishing in the regulations that the school was both for girls and boys, and the parents who sent their daughters to school – and parents were ready to do this rather than "sacrificing" their sons – were obliged to send their sons as well.

The school started off well because it managed to attract two important educators. One of them was the director of the school, Shlomo Rubin, who had been persecuted in Dolina and Zurawno [Zhuravne] because of his devotion to the Haskalah, and who later became known as one of the spokesmen in Jewish thought.[89] The other was the teacher Mandschein. A year later a new and very active person, Nechemiah Landes, arrived whom we have already presented in the previous chapter. The communal forces concerned with the school were reinforced with the arrival of another energetic person devoted to education, Berish Blumenthal, who apparently came from the family Blumenthal, a member of which had been a teacher in Bolekhov in Homberg's time. Blumenthal's appearance on the scene was very important because Jacob Goldenberg, the moving spirit of the school council, had left Bolekhov.[90] The external appearance of the school seems to have been satisfactory. In his book *Amudei ha-Olam* [Pillars of the Universe] Mandschein describes the low standards of the facilities of the *chederim* [religious elementary schools] but praises the facilities of the new schools. "... in the Galician towns Lemberg, Brody, Tarnopol and in my home town, Bolekhov,..." the child comes into a fine building which overlooks the garden and where the rooms are well-lit, the children sit in separate benches in separate classes and are taught by fine and intelligent teachers." [91] Whether the conditions were such in the school in Bolekhov is hard to know for sure but one thing is clear: the school was much better in many respects than the *chederim* [religious elementary schools] and their facilities.

[Yiddish page 208]

One thing is certain, that Mandschein appreciated order and cleanliness very much and he was especially concerned with sick nursing.[92] It seems that the main figures of the school were considering whether the removal of hats in the classroom should be made compulsory.[93]

Despite all the efforts, despite the good teachers, the important promoters of the school, and despite the fact that the *maskilim* saw a "noble flower of culture" [94] in the school, it was built on shaky foundations. The situation of the teachers was hard because the wages were low; the school building required investment and the public was indifferent; the inhabitants, incited by the rabbi and the Hasidic leaders, were hostile to the school and the community council did all in its power to harass the school and its teachers and leaders.

[Yiddish page 209]

The writer and thinker, Dr. Shloyme Rubin (1823-1910), the first ladder of the Jewish school in Bolekhov.

It went so far that when the leaders of the school asked for a certain sum to raise the wages and decorate the school, the community leaders said that it would be more reasonable to donate these sums to the general municipal school in order to strengthen it. The fact that the community council favored Jewish-Christian rapprochement instead of cutting itself off in separate educational institutions was also a hint to the high society of the attitude of the council, it was a sign that the community council was firmly resolved to fight the school to the end until it would die of itself.[95] The fanatics made use of yet another tool to strangle the institution, namely, to ruin the normal school budget. To this end they proposed to suspend *shechita* [ritual slaughter], which meant that the *shochetim* [ritual slaughterers] would not slaughter or open a private *mikve* [ritual bath] near houses of study – the suspension of the revenues coming from the *shechita* and the *mikve* meant a death sentence for the school. And they had an even more important tool, namely, not sending the children to school despite the law on compulsory education. The fact is that in 1858 there were 445 school-age children in the town (250 boys and 195 girls) but only 73 attended the school (51 boys and 22 girls). In 1860 there was a change for the better in the case of girls and for the worse in the case of boys. That year only 45 boys but 46 girls went to school. The year 1864 experienced a clear decline: from the 500 school-age children only 70 frequented the school.

Who were the pupils? Primarily girls, as only poor families sent their sons to the school and even they left the school under the pressure of the *melamdim* [teachers in religious elementary schools] and the Hasidic leaders – after getting clothes and books from the school committee. There was of course a law according to which the *melamdim* [teachers in religious elementary schools] were not allowed to accept children to study Talmud unless they had a certificate that they had attended a school but no decree and no threat helped. They always found a way to evade the law and the decree.[96] Thus, a permanent war was waged in the town. Professor Klausner states "that the fanatics led a stubborn fight". This war embittered Rubin's life so much that he was fed up with teaching in the school and resigned from his post.[97] After his resignation Nechemiah Landes, hated by the Hasidim because of his progressive ideas, took over the direction of the school, and the war reached its culminating point. On the one hand "the school was a progressive center for many towns in the vicinity," [98] and on the other, the opposing forces were trying to destroy it. It went so far that in 1864 the school experienced a serious crisis.

[Yiddish page 210]

At a popular gathering which took place in the big house of study and in which two members of the community council participated the following far-reaching resolutions were accepted:

a. the *shochetim* [ritual slaughterers] would be affiliated with different houses of study and the slaughterhouse, as well as the *mikve* [ritual bath] would be closed until the school ceased to exist;

b. the teachers would be declared lawless and it was also suggested that people of the underworld should be hired to "make a physical impression" on them (in other words, to break their bones);

c. a ban would be proclaimed on the shop of Berish Blumenthal's father if he did not exert influence on his son and tell him not to meddle in the affairs of the school. [99]

Fine words! A life and death struggle! But the school figures were not idle either. Perforce they turned to the government which interfered in the affair and under governmental pressure the community members and the *shochetim* [ritual slaughterers] retreated and the situation returned to normal.[100] It seems that the matter was fixed and the fanatics came to terms with the existence of the school. It is clear that the school and its promoters were not destined to have any easy life. In any case, as we can see, the school struck root. In 1869 there were already four teachers and 160 children in the school.[101] In 1879 a historical note about Bolekhov appeared in a German newspaper and the editors commented it with the following words: "We see a nicely populated community with fine institutions." [102] It is probable that the editor meant among other things the school, too. In due course the institution became a school for boys only, a fourth class was set up and the curriculum improved. It must be noted that the study of Hebrew was an organic part of the timetable which comprised the study of three languages: Polish, German and Ukrainian.

(6) The Beginnings of the Zionist Organization in Bolekhov

Following the Haskalah movement in our town we discussed at length the school around which the socially most progressive forces were concentrated, and in particular the two most important representatives of these forces, Mandschein and Landes. Mandschein died before the first cells of the national movement were formed but there is no doubt that if he had lived longer, he would have surely joined the national camp which found its expression in the "Chibat Zion" [Love of Zion] camp. Landes, as we have seen, honored and respected Hebrew but he was opposed to the national movement and was in the camp of the assimilationists. We are interested in two question. Firstly, which approach determined the character of the youth in Bolekhov, Mandschein's or Landes'; and secondly, what influence did the school have on this formation.

[Yiddish page 211]

It is hard to answer this question and we do not have sufficient factual material, especially about the beginning of the 90s when the first Zionist associations sprang up. We find their echo in the columns of the Zionist weekly *Die Welt* [The World] but we find nothing about Bolekhov: no Zionist association, no reports. However, the news which appeared in the Zionist organ *Die Welt* since it was first published in 1897 give us some information on the preceding years, as well. And the news depict an intensive national life. One of the carriers of the movement was the school teacher Berish Bikl. We learn that the first national association called "Tikvat Israel" [Hopes of Israel] was formed in Bolekhov already in 1895. The answer to the question posed earlier is plain and clear: the youth crossed the bridge of Haskalah and set foot on firm national ground. We do not intend to describe the national movement in Bolekhov, we shall be satisfied – in order to confirm our former premise – with a short chronicler's note about the national activity of the last years of the 19th century.

1897

a) A Reb Yehuda Ha-Levi evening was organized. At the gathering after the evening there was a discussion on the national question and one of the speakers denied Zionism and wanted to show that only socialism would solve the Jewish Question, "but it was not hard to challenge his views". From the style of this report we get the impression that the carriers of the national movement in Bolekhov were the high school and university students.

b) A large public assembly was organized in the synagogue which attracted "more than 2,000 people (!?), the topic of which was whether Bolekhov should join the "Ahavat Zion" [Love of Zion] movement of Tarnow. This movement planned the establishment of a colony of Galician Jews in Palestine beside the regular Zionist activity which was given its organizational framework at the first Zionist Congress in 1897. The chairman of the assembly was Nechemiah Latringer and at the end of the meeting a committee was elected to distribute the shares of the Colonial Bank and Zionist shekels. To honor the people taking a lead in Zionist matters let us publish their names as they appeared in the press of the time: A. Goldschlag, H. Rosenberg, S. Elendman, M. Schuster, I. Pipes, N. Latringer, V. Askreis, A. Spiegel. The enthusiastic writer ends his interesting report with the following words: "There is no Jew in our town who is not a Zionist, the proof is that the day after the assembly merchants, craftsmen and youth gathered to appoint committees which would elaborate the statutes of the various Zionist associations. The women also gathered to establish their own association, the *"Banot Zion"* [Daughters of Zion].[103]

[Yiddish page 212]

1898

a) A Maccabean celebration was organized in town for the third time. At the celebration which made a strong impression the following people gave lectures: Dr Blumenthal, Latringer, Levner and Bikl. The latter gave his lecture in Hebrew.

b) An interesting report relates that the "Gardener Association" which was organized on a socialist basis joined the national camp and its members bought Zionist shekels for the first time.[104]

1899

a) A Zionist association named "Chovevei Zion" [Lovers of Zion] was founded to replace the association "Tikvat Israel" [Hopes of Israel]. Shortly after its foundation 45 members joined it already and it is hoped that the number of members will soon double. The following members were elected into the council of the association: H. Rosenberg (farz?chairman), Landau, Gartenberg, Spiegel, Neumark, Unger, Friedlander, Kornbli, Erster.

b) A memorial service for Dr Ezriel Hildesheimer, rabbi of the "community of Israel" of Berlin and one of the active Zionist leaders, was held in the school auditorium. The following people appeared publicly at the gathering: H. Rosenberg, Latringer and Neumark. The latter gave a speech in Hebrew.

c) A general meeting was organized on which H. Friedlander and H. Rosenberg gave an account of the Zionist regional congress in Lemberg to which they had been delegated as representatives of the Bolekhov Zionists. Not only members of the association participated in the meeting. At the end of the meeting Latringer gave a speech in honor of Dr Nordau's birthday.

d) In the *bes medresh* [synagogue] of Dolina a meeting of the Zionists of Dolina, Bolekhov, Vigode [Vygoda] and Razhnyatov [Rozhnyuv] was organized to report on the last Zionist Congress. Dr K. Lipa, the well-known Romanian Zionist leader, who was a delegate of the Romanian towns, gave a lecture. After the meeting there was a gathering where there were Hebrew speeches.

e) The usual yearly assembly was organized and a new council was elected. The following people were elected: Chairman– N. Latringer; vice-chairman – D. Unger; treasurer – I. Landes; secretaries – S. Neumark and I. Spiegel; librarian – M. Bandler. Members of the council and special functionaries: A. Landau, Ch. H. Friedlander and S. Vilgut. Eizik Shur was unanimously elected honorary member.

[Yiddish page 213]

f) In the apartment of B. Bikl a Hanukah celebration took place and the following persons gave a talk: Latringer, Bikl and Shur. The program also included recitations by Neumark in Hebrew and Friedlander in German.[105]

1900

There are six reports on Bolekhov in 1900 which describe activities similar to the above-mentioned ones. Two new public figures were mentioned that year, A. Halperin and D. Kaiser. "A meeting was organized in honor of the fourth Zionist Congress – says the report – in which the whole Jewish population participated.[106] Despite their dry tone, all these news are explicit. They show that Bolekhov was a Zionist town thanks to its active youth. In those years Zionist activity meant organizational unity, agitation, enlightenment and cultural activity – the study of Hebrew and the cultivation of its literature. In due course self-realization through *aliya* [immigration to Palestine] was to start as well.

(7) Closing words

As Mandschein said about the 1820s, "The ha-Tzefirah was successful in our town." At the end of the 1860s Peretz Smolensky wrote the following about Mandschein: "We can see in his words the spirit of the people among whom he dwells."

I hope that my article threw some light on the new spirit of the young generation on Bolekhov which brought the national revival to the town and its inhabitants. This is but a modest contribution to the monument to the memory of our town and our sacred community, at the bosom of which my parents, blessed be their memory, raised me for the Torah and for fate.

Dr. Mishl Hendel

[Yiddish page 214]

Footnotes from Book Chapter:

1. On Reb Israel Zamoscer see R. Mahler: Divrei Yamei Israel, Dorot Acharonim, book 4, 5716, pp. 26-30; N. M. Gelber: Toldot Yehude Brodi [The History of the Jews of Brody], Brody, 5715, p. 173

2. On Shlomo Chelmer see Mahler's book, p. 173.

3. On Reb Shlomo Dubner see Mahler, pp. 31-33.

4. On Reb Zeev Wolf Buchner see Gelber, pp. 177-79.

5. On Reb Pinchas Eliahu Hurvitz see Mahler, p. 46.

6. On Reb Mendel Lapin Satanover see Mahler, pp. 71-88; Gelber, pp. 179- 80; Klausner: *Historiya shel ha-Sifrut ha-Ivrit ha-Khadasha* [The History of the New Hebrew Literature], vol. 1, pp. 199-225; Tarnopol in the series *Entziklopedia shel Gluyot*[Encyclopedia of the Diasporas], 5715, pp. 88-90.

7. I. Klausner, pp. 202-204.

8. R. Mahler, p. 74.

9. On Herz Homberg see M. Balaban: *Z historji Zydow w Polsce* [Of the History of Jews in Poland], 1929, pp. 236-90.

10. *Bikure ha-Ittim,* 5581 (1821); *Yiddish Shul Anshtaltn in Galitzie* [Jewish Educational Institutions in Galicia], pp. 141-47.

11. *M. Balaban, Dzieje Zydow w Galicji* [The History of the Jews in Galicia], 1914, p. 72.

12. We have no clear information on the process of development of Haskalah ——and the fight between Haskalah and the Hasidic camp in Bolekhov. The ——material became engrossed in the archives and until now it has sparsely —been used in historical work.

13. Gelber, p. 195, footnote 119.

14. *Allgemeine Zeitung des Judentums* (in the following: *Allgemeine*), 1844, ——pp. 545-46, the weekly first appeared in Berlin in 1837.

15. *Der Orient,* 1849, no. 49 – 'Der Valbekante Forshteyer oys Bolekhov' ——[The Well-Known Representative from Bolekhov]. The weekly was ——published between 1840-1857 in Leipzig. The school did not function for –long.

16. *Ben Chananja,* 1859, pp. 469-72, 1860, pp. 458-60. *Ben Chananja,* a scientific-reformatory periodical, was published between 1859-1867 in German in Szeged, Hungary.

17. *Ben Chananja,* 1858, p. 475.

18. *Kerem Chemed* [Vineyard of Delight], 1, pp. 48-50.

19. *op. cit.,* pp. 50-53.

20. Reb Ichak Shmuel Reggio (1784-1855). Rabbi in Galicia, one of the first scholars and scribes of the Haskalah movement.

21. *Sefer ha-Yovel le-Harkavy* [Jubilee volume in honor of Harkavy], p. 487.

22. *Igrot Shadal* [Letters of Sh. D. Luzzatto], published by Sh.A. Graber, 5644-5654, vol. 1, pp. 322-24.

23. *Kerem Chemed* 1, pp. 60-68.

24. *Kerem Chemed* 8 (1854), editorial (?) (be makom hakdama?in lieu of introduction). On the Maskilic writer Shniur Sachs see *Historiya shel ha-Sifrut ha-Ivrit ha-   Khadasha* by I. Klausner, vol. 2, pp. 122-42.

25. I. Klausner, p. 165. – Tzuntz: the founder of *Wissenschaft des Judentums* (Science of Judaism) (1794-1886).

26. *op. cit.,* p. 238.

27. *Kerem Chemed* 4 (q839), pp. 241-259.

28. See Gelber's book on Brody, p. 194.

29. See the letter written to S. L. Goldenberg in 1839, *Otzar ha-Sifrut* [Treasury of Literature], 4th year, 5652, p. 270.

30. Der Orient, 1840, pp. 261-62.

31. *Kerem Chemed* 1, p. 106.

32. *Otzar ha-Sifrut* [Treasury of Literature] 4, p. 268.

33. *Sefer ha-Yovel le-Harkavy,* p. 491 – the historian Ichak Mordechai Yost (1793-1800), see on him S. Dubnow: *Divrei Yamei Israel, ba-Dorot ha-Acharonim,* vol. 2, pp. 65-66.

34. *Otzar ha-Sifrut* 4, pp. 271-73.

35. From a letter to his brother Jacob, in *Kerem Chemed* 3, pp. 189-95.

36. *Sefer ha-Yovel le-Harkavy*, p. 485.

37. *Kerem Chemed* 3. Shmuel Leib had another brother, too, named M. (Moshe?). He is referred to as the leader of the Jewish community in Zulkow [Zhulkev?] and a progressive man in a report On Galicia in 1845. *Allgemeine*, 1845, p. 224. I have not found any more reference to him.

38. See on him in Bader's book entitled *Medinah ve-Chachmeah* [State and its Sages], p. 35. He describes him as "defender of the finest verses". See also in *Sefer Stanislaw* [Book of Stanislaw], 5712, <u>Arim ve-Imahot be-Israel</u> [<u>Towns and Mother-cities in Israel: Memorial of the Jewish Communities which Perished: vol. 5, Stanislawow</u>], p. 33, compare Bibring's letter to Mandschein, in his song book Agudat Shoshanim [Bouquet of Roses], 1876, p. 56.

39. *Sefer Stanislav* [Book of Stanislav], see above, p. 32.

40. Peretz Smolensky (1842-1885), writer and publicist, a spokesman of the national movement.

41. *Ha-Shachar* [The Dawn], vol. 1, 5629, p. 15. His writings appeared between 1861-1866: *Amudei ha-Olam* [Pillars of the Universe], *Imre Yosher, Goral ha-Tzedakah, Lashon Chachamim* [Language of the Sages]. In his last years, he still succeeded in printing one sheet of his book *Imre Noam*, while the rest of the material survived as a manuscript. Apparently he also left behind a manuscript for a book entitled "Pilgei ... Mayim (Fey-lamed-gimel-yud, maym) ["translation?]Water Brooks"].

42. B. Wachstein, J. Taglicht and A. Kristianopoler: *Die Hebräische Publizistik in Wien*, 1930, p. XLII – On Nathan Meler (1822-1893) see *Sefer Stanislav,* see above, pp. 33-34.

43. *Kochave JiYitzchak,* brochure 4, 1846, pp. 27-36. A literary periodical which was published in Vienna between 1845-1873.

44. *op. cit.*

45. *Kochave JiYitzchak,* brochure 25, 1860, pp. 107-112. On writer and thinker Shlomo Rubin (1823-1910) see the preface to all his writings, book 2, of Klausner, pp. V-XV.

46. *op. cit.*, footnote 43.

47. *Lashon Chachamim,* p. 88.

48. *Amudei ha-Olam,* pp. 92-93. Mandschein is nicely depicted by his student and friend Jacob Bibring in his letter published in his song book *Agudat Shoshanim,* stating: "you are endowed with wisdom and morals", p. 60.

49. As referred to, footnote 43.

50. *Kochave ḥiYitzchak,* brochure 5, pp. 20-27.

51. *Kochave ḥiYitzchak,* brochure 6, pp. 21-32.

52. *Ha-Shachar,* vol. 1, 5629, pp. 11-14.

53. *op. cit.,* footnote 43.

54. *Kochave ḥiYitzchak,* brochure 11, pp. 30-38.

55. *op. cit.,* footnote 43.

56. *op. cit.,* footnote 54.

57. *Ben Chananja,* October 12, 1864, pp. 843-46.

58. *Amudei ha-Olam,* p. 43, footnote 21. Lamartine, writer and politician (1790-1869), visited the Orient at the beginning of the 1830s.

59. See Notes 43.

60. *Ivri anochi* [I am Hebrew], 5633, pp. 35, 47, 58. *Ha-Magid* [The Preacher], 5633, pp. 470-71, 498.

61. Balaban's Polish book, *The History of the Jews in Galicia,* p. 187.

62. *Ben Chananja,* 1886, pp. 822-23.

63. *Ben Chananja,* 1861, pp. 58-59, 79-80. It is interesting that writing about the village Neubabylon, near Bolekhov, he stresses that it was not the laziness of the Jews that led to the liquidation of the village but the reactionary politics that dominated Austria after the death of emperor Joseph II (Ben Chananja, 1863, p. 61). *Sefer Zichron le-sofrey Israel* [Memorial book of the Scribes of Israel], Warsaw, 5649, pp. 56-57. Beside the representatives of the Jewish community of Lemberg, representatives of the following communities participated in the council: Kolomai [Kolomyya], Zlotshev [Zloczew], Drohobycz, Jaroslaw, Reishe [Rzeszow], Tarnow, and as referred to, Bolekhov (*Allgemeine,* 1878, pp. 457-58).

64. On the Rohling affair see S. Dubnow: *Divrei YameyiIsrael ba-Dorot ha-Acharonim,* vol. 3, p. 43ff.

65. *Ben Chananja*, 1861, pp. 115-17; 1862, pp. 163-66; 1883, pp. 61-62. *Allgemeine*, 1879, pp. 283-85.

66. G. Bader: *Medinah ve-Chachmeah*, p. 127.

67. (1765-1813) A well-known public figure and writer who promoted Jewish rights.

68. *Ben Chananja*, 1869, pp. 469-72; 1860, pp. 458-60

69. *Allgemeine*, 1861, pp. 521-23.

70. *Przyszlosc*, 1894, pp. 242-46. This report talks about Landes with respect and appreciation, while the newspaper usually talks about him in a tone of contempt; pp. 34-35: "The inspector favored by Viennese bankers"; p. 116: "The assimilated inspector, Mr. Landes" is criticized in 1793 because he reduced the wages of a Hebrew teacher in Stryj because of the teacher's attitude to the study of Hebrew which he did not find proper (1793, p. 224).

71. See the report on the second Zionist Congress, 1898, p. 254. A telegram was sent by the association *"Choveve Zion"* in Bolekhov to the third Zionist Congress (1899) (congress report, p. 260). In the statement on the greeting of the fifth Zionist Congress (1901) by Bolekhov it is stressed that there are 100 signatures on the telegram (congress report, p. 463). The sixth and seventh Zionist Congresses (1903, 1905) received a telegram also from the community council (cultural community, pp. 340-60).

72. F. Friedmann: *Die Galizischen Juden im Kampfe um Gleichberechtigung* (1848-1868) 129, p. 71; See also Balaban's Polish book, *The History of the Jews in Galicia*, pp. 136, 186-87.

73. *Kol Katvei Dr. Shlomo Rubin* [The Writings of Dr. Shlomo Rubin], book 2, Warsaw, 1910, pp. IX-XIII. The designation "on behalf of the government" means that the school was under government supervision. In the first years the authorities did not set any budgetary help. *Sefer Zichron le-sofrey Israel* [Memorial book of the Scribes of Israel], Warsaw, 5649, pp. 102-103.

74. Vol. 1, p. 158.

75. *op. cit.*, note 46.

76. See Friedman's book, p. 146; Gelber's book on Brody, p. 263; Balaban's Polish book, *The History of the Jews in Galicia*, pp. 130ff.

77. Jacob Goldenberg, Shmuel Leib's brother – we already had some opportunity to mention him and know him a little. Zvi Birkenthal, apparently from the family in Bolekhov – we encounter him as rabbi of the Jewish community of

Pisk (Czech lands) in 1863. Both of them are referred to as members of the community council in Jacob Bibring's letter to Mandschein. *Kochave Yitzchak,* brochure 10, pp. 39-42. The preacher of Lemberg, Reb Issashar Ber Löwenstein is also mentioned in the dedication of Mandschein's book *Lashon Chachamim,* (p. 5).

78. *op. cit.,* note 43.

79. *Allgemeine,* 1846, pp. 475-77.

80. *Amudei ha-Olam,* pp. 61-62, 59-60.

81. *Allgemeine,* 1844, pp. 545-46.

82. *op. cit.y,* note 43.

83. *Kochave Yitzchak,* brochure 7, 1846, pp. 18-36.

84. *Kochave Yitzchak,* brochure 5, 1846, p. 20-27.

85. *op. cit.,* note 78.

86. Zvi Scharfstein: *Toldot ha-Chinuch be-Israel* [The History of Education in Israel], vol. 1, p. 158.

87. *Kochave Yitzchak,* brochure 6, pp. 21-32.

88. Take into consideration that the school which was founded in 1830 in Cracow, while it was independent, Bolekhov was in the fifth place (Tarnopol, Brody, Cracow, Lemberg, Bolekhov). On the character of the school in Tarnopol, the most important institution, see *Sefer Tarnopol* [The Book of Tarnopol], pp. 47-51, 55-60.

89. I accept Balaban's view which is based on archival material and he states, as already mentioned, that Rubin came to Bolekhov in 1856. We must remember that Rubin came here when he was already well known in literary circles and in Jewish thought. He had in his literary possessions among other things the translation of the well-known tragedy of Karl Guzkav "Uriel Accosta", as well as the literary-ideological debate with Shmuel David Luzzatto about Spinoza's philosophy.

90. Jacob Goldenberg settled in Czernowitz and died as a landowner there.

91. *Amudei ha-Olam,* p. 46.

92. *op. cit.,* note 78.

93. *op. cit.,* p. 52, footnote 27.

94. *Ben Chananja,* 1864, pp. 843-46.

95. *Ben Chananja*, 1865, pp. 836-37.

96. *Ben Chananja*, op. cit., note 94; *Russian Encyclopedia*, vol. 4, pp. 782-83.

97. *op. cit.*, note 72, p. XIII.

98. Balaban's Polish book, *The History of the Jews in Galicia*, p. 187.

99. *op. cit.*, pp. 187-88.

100. *Ben Chananja*, note 94.

101. Friedman's German book, pp. 150-51, note 6.

102. *Allgemeine*, 1879, p. 283.

103. *Die Welt*, 1897, Pamphlet 18, p. 11; Pamphlet 21, p. 9.

104. *Die Welt*, 1898, Pamphlet 2, p. 5.

105. *Die Welt*, 1899, Pamphlet 23, p. 13; Pamphlet 27, p. 13; Pamphlet 36, p. 12; Pamphlet 37, p. 11; Pamphlet 40, p. 10; Pamphlet 50, p. 16; pamphlet 51, p. 12.

106. *Die Welt*, 1900, Pamphlet 10, p. 11; Pamphlet 17, p. 10; Pamphlet 24, p. 12; Pamphlet 35, p. 15; Pamphlet 39, p. 6; Pamphlet 47, p. 14.

[Hebrew page 57 & Yiddish page 219]

Chapter II. Daily Life
Translated by Jerrold Landau

Words spoken at the annual memorial ceremony of the Organization of Bolechow Natives in the year 5710 (1950) in Tel Aviv.

A Monument to my beloved ones, three generations, who perished in the Holocaust.
"A disaster gathered you together from the four corners of the earth
Its bitter scream you all uttered
And then the great event happened

Tears welled out from their faithful source
The great, the pleasant, the bright, the warm,
We will continue praying for it."
Bialik

1. My Town
by Yonah Eshel-Elendman [1]
Translated by Jerrold Landau

Thirty-two years have passed from the time that I left the home of my parents of blessed memory in Bolechow.

This extended period of time has significantly dimmed my memory of events in the town. This was a period of time full of content and rich in experiences. Despite this, I will attempt to portray the image of the world of its Jews and what went on therein – a world which has now set and been silenced for ever and ever.

Bolechow, a far off corner in the Diaspora in the Carpathian Mountains that support the heavens, in the area of Bubnishche Rocks, the residence of the well-known robber Dowbusz [2] who instilled his fear in the region. Bolechow, enhanced with forests, rivers, mountains and meadows. You were surrounded by villages populated by Ukrainians, whereas Jews dwelt in your midst. They were employed in business, trades and manufacturing, including tanning, salt making, chairs, candle, soap rakes, glue, saws, water wells, which were a mark of water upon it.

As in all places the residents had nicknames. These names portrayed the essence of life, the physical makeup and the source. These included the Dore Mielic, Dodek, Hamgorgel in my soul, Pidgani, Staczyk, Columbuski, Seletsis, Chlapchis, Soike Wielki, Poczaczki, Francois, Eli Bach, etc.

These nicknames stuck with their owners, and the matching was very well.

The Maccabbe Organization.

In addition to the personal nicknames, there was a general nickname, "Bolechower Kricher" (Bolechow Crawlers), perhaps on account of your lethargy and your crawling? No, no. Your sons and daughters did not crawl at a tortoise's pace. On the contrary, they reached all parts of the globe. For they were enthusiastic people, accepting of change and progress. They desired worldly knowledge.

Bolechow, you were alert, revolutionary. Your reality was not sufficient for your children, so they left to acquire knowledge. Glittery Vienna was their place of desire.

Your surroundings had their own charm. Since that was a peaceful part of our lives, they granted us enjoyment and hours of sublimity of the soul. I will write a few words about them.

1. The German Colony.

2. The public gardens.

3. The Hill. The Hill of Shlomo or Salomonova Gurka.

"Heatid" group of Young Zion.

The German Colony: Your houses were small, covered with vegetation, Your yards were clean. There was a barn, chicken coop, and a lodge. On your gates, the milk vessels were neatly polished. Their rims sparkled like crystal. On your long windowsills, there were red apples... tomatoes, desirous food for the "poretzes" (landowners), as yet unknown to the Jewish palate.

The Colony, what jealousy did you arouse in us! You were to us as an example and an emblem for a life of work and redemption.

A. The Public Gardens

You were a living organ in our souls, the delight of our souls. It is impossible to close the grave on Bolechow without mentioning you. Within you, we were able to expose our deepest emotions. The living spirit of the youth was formed within you, the sublime possession, joy and gladness. In you we met, talked, debated, poured out our pure hearts that were overflowing their banks and embracing the arms of the world, with conversation and song. In the summer, many fine festivities were organized in you for the benefit of the Keren Kayemet LeYisrael (Jewish National Fund) and our blue boxes. This too was an eternal victory. Within you there were water fountains, two statues of Mickiewicz and J. Slowacki. In your center there was a pavilion. Near your entrance was the booth of Landau of blessed memory, with cold drinks, sweets and chocolate. The daughter of the aforementioned was Mrs. Soferman, the wife of the veteran teacher and writer Rafael Soferman, was one of the first of those who made aliya to the Land.

The garden, you were a possession of everyone and its center. Everyone who was in need would enter. However the "shkotzim" and "shiksas" [3] did not visit you. They had meadows and gardens, but no problems. For us it was the opposite. In the air of your space, the following songs were heard: "Onward Toward the Jordan", "In my Thoughts", "Raising a Banner Toward Zion", "Let's Go Along the Way", "There is the Place of Cedars". The echoes were heard from afar. You were a refuge to us from the rotten "Rynsztok", in which was gathered every broken vessel, every carcass, and which always exuded a "fragrant aroma" [4]. The Garden! You enriched us with a corner of pleasure, with contentment, with enjoyment.

The Hill. From whence flows our great love and lamentation to you? Several factors are the cause of this: a) my group of friends; b) esthetics; c) salvation to issues of day to day life requiring a solution.

Do you remember? The route to you, how wonderful and enchanted it was. Paths growing wild flowers, meadows, a multicolored checkered tapestry, and above a blue sky – that tell of the honor of G-d.

Groups upon groups streamed toward you. On Sabbaths and festivals, the "aliya" to tradition was overturned [5]. When we arrived to you, with the trees spreading shade over the pleasant grass. There, there were boughs of aromatic, fleshy cherries, whose aroma was like that of the trees.

We sat together in the aromatic air, discussing and enjoying the beauty of the world. The farmers received the visitors graciously, for we were considered to be "customers". There was also a foamy white drink. This enjoyment was not the main thing. Milk and cherries could also be found at the homes of our parents. The purpose was to spend some time in companionship, to grant salvation to our mundane lives, and particularly to liven up reality with song and beauty. Our spiritual world at that time was full of problems. We were oppressed and pined for solutions. The worries searched for a solution, and it seemed as if they would be found in the wide vistas. You, oh hill, served as our vista.

The makeup of the population, which included three nationalities, necessitated the study of multiple languages at school. We had to study three languages: Polish, Ukrainian and German. It was extremely difficult for a poor Jewish child to learn the Ukrainian language. In particular, the study of chapters of its literature was like walking on stilts. It was doubtful if we understood Szewczenko, yet we were required to know it, to quote it.

The child was confused with the multitude of languages, and could not find his bearings. In addition, the youth wished to learn English. Yiddish was spoken in my parents' home. Only in the houses of the assimilationists was Polish spoken. National consciousness which penetrated our city before it opened up a windows on the other cities of the region, obligated the youth to learn Hebrew. With the passage of time, the study of our language became a holy task, and they became dedicated to it with all their enthusiasm. This was a splendid period, which I will dedicate some words. We studied German in school drop by drop. When Galicia was under Austrian rule, the Jewish intelligentsia had a special love for German literature, its writers and poets. Members of the generation that preceded mine knew Germanic poetry by heart. They could not have imagined even in a nightmare what would arise from them, and what they would perpetrate against us.

A proverb circulated among the people:

The Haskalah wished to establish itself well among three cities of Galicia: Brody, Buczacz and Bolechow. In Bolechow, you could find books of philosophy, research and poetry under the Gemaras of those who studied in the Beis Midrashes.

The Maccabee Zionist Organization had its headquarters in the center of Bolechow, in Schindler's house. A library was next to it. Services would also be held there on Sabbaths and festivals. The cream of the crop of the group was centered under one roof. The Goldschlag brothers, the Schorr brothers, the Bikel brothers, Nechemia Lutringer, Herman Blumenthal, Lemel Meir (this was the person who was "crazy for one thing", the zealous Zionist, the dreaming fighter, "the young old man", a one of a kind personality), Shimon Elendman, and many others. The hall was noisy, bustling from the multitude of those who came. Chibat Zion struck roots in it, and spread out its rays from there to the youth. At that time, the group was a workbench, a sign and an example. The settlement in the Land was poor in those days. However, everything that took place there was known from the newspapers.

The settlement was close to our hearts. It warmed our hearts, and gave meaning and taste to life in the Diaspora. There was a strong bond between us and between the best of our sons and daughters.

B. Lovers of Song

These were also not missing. We were involved in song from times of old. We had an established choir. The blind pianist Brukenstein and Avraham Frei were its two pillars. We would learn "songs of the Land" for festivities on various occasions. We were enthusiastic youth, and our hearts rejoiced. "Crazies" were hurrying about in every area. They stood for us at all times and bore the burden. Their concern was the strengthening and forging of the chain. The concern for song enhanced the situation.

As if from a fog, I will attempt to glance back at a communal political event that occurred and left a powerful imprint upon our hearts that will not be erased. This event, which forged our political image, was the parliamentary election.

This took place about 50 years ago. Gershon Zipper was the candidate of the Zionists. Dr. Lewenstein was the representative of the assimilationists.

Both candidates had dependents and dependents of dependents. It was a life and death battle. This was an event for which we lived, suffered, and sacrificed our bread. Each side was convinced of the righteousness of its ideas and stand. Each "voice" was considered complete forever. The hatred of the Zionists for the "prim and proper people" was great. This caused divisiveness, friction, and disputes between parents and children. Zionist activity was liable to weaken the foundations of livelihood, and this was the weapon of the assimilationists. They talked ill about the landowners (poretzes). Thanks to their fawning and their Diaspora-style bent form, they had influence with the authorities, regional and district officials, etc. However, who paid attention to such trivia? On the contrary, the threats added reasons and fuel to the fire. The threats dampened our spirits. Our strong decision was to not pass up on our rights at all, and to fight for our rights and honor. Our one and only aim was for liberation and the removal of impediments.

Haifa, the Festival of Lights 5710.

[Hebrew page 61 & Yiddish page 223]

2. The Hebrew Language
by Yonah Eshel-Elendman
Translated by Jerrold Landau

The first sparks were ignited already 50 years ago. Do you not remember the teacher Shlomo Neimark and the teacher Yisrael Spiegel (Szpigeli). Both of them founded the Tushia School in Bolechow. They did not have fine, practical textbooks. In place of that, they had boundless dedication, love of the language, and a desire to spread it. Their strong desire to inspire the young people to speak and work wonders.

Five decades ago, there was a lack of usable expressions, and a common conversation was extremely difficult. To make a request and to express even the simplest idea was very difficult. The Batalnia academy for language was not yet born. It did not invent expressions, new words, textbooks in all fields of science, technology, arts, song and language, etc. (Who can count them?) Words for many things ranging from kitchen utensils to shepherding terminology did not exist. Therefore, their "holy work" was just commencing.

From amongst our elite youth, a group of girls was formed that made it their point to speak only Hebrew. On the ~~Tylat~~ Tayelet (along the Ringplatz), one could already hear Hebrew expressions, Hebrew small talk, an adage or even a verse from the Bible. These two Hebrew teachers – short in stature but strong in spirit – achieved a great feat. They reached the summit.

[Yiddish page 224]

3. The First Day of Hebrew
by Yonah Eshel-Elendman
Translated by Jerrold Landau

In 1911, three Hebrew organizations – the Organization of Hebrew Culture (Dr. Yehoshua Tahon), the Union of Hebrew Teachers (Rafael Soferman), and the Union of Jewish Schools (Dr. Korngyn) – proclaimed the first Day of Hebrew in Galicia and in the world at large. It was to take place in Lwow. Thanks to this convention, 35 Hebrew public schools in outlying cities and a Teachers' Seminary in Lwow were founded.

Naftali Zigel was among the activists. The Day of Hebrew was a demonstration for Hebrew speakers in the capital of Galicia. That day, Hebrew speakers went out into the street and spoke only Hebrew (which reminds us of the blessed work of Eliezer Ben Yehuda); they purchased a stamp in Hebrew from the post office; they ordered borscht in Hebrew in the restaurant; and they asked to purchase a train ticket in Hebrew from the train station. They argued, chatted, and dreamed in Hebrew. From Bolechow, the following students of Neimark and Szpigeli traveled to the Day of Hebrew: Leika Reiner, Chitzi Shuster, Reizi Landis, Rivchi Elendman, Tzipora Schnur, and Sheindele Tepper. When they returned from Lwow, full of action, impressions and experiences, they never tired of discussing about this impressive event. (I listened to these discussions with great jealousy, and I prayed in my heart: When I grow up, may my lot be among them!).

At a later time, Yaffa (Sheindele) Tepper, today Levanoni-Wissel, worked in the field of the study and dissemination of the language in Bolechow. Yaffa Wissel was the first girl to make aliya. She taught in a school in the Galilee and in the Re'ali School in Haifa. Tzipora Schnurr, a graduate of the Tushia School, served as a teacher in Bolechow at the same time. Later, she made aliya and settled in Jerusalem, where she taught at the Hebrew High School in Rechavia that was founded by Shlomo Schiller.

[Hebrew page 62 & Yiddish page 224]

4. The First Pioneer
by Yonah Eshel-Elendman
Translated by Jerrold Landau

Zeidele Mehering the watchmaker was modest in manner and pure of spirit. To all of us, he served as a symbol of the actualization of dreams. He made aliya to the Land before the First World War as one of the early Chalutzim (pioneers). He, and may she live Yaffa Wissel-Tepper, formed the first connection between us and the Land. They would send us fruit of the Land for Tu Bishvat. We touched, smelled, and lovingly and desirously stared at the fruit with holy awe. The aroma of the fruits of the field of the desired homeland entered our nostrils and our blood. It was passed from hand to hand. I thought to myself: This simple piece of fruit was in the Land, but I, when would I get there?

The counselor Lipa Brill, Hodaya Rozenbaum and Rachtzia Schoor.}

The first group of pioneers, 1920.

In 1916, during the First World War, a Jewish soldier from Stanislawow arrived in our town. His name was Lipa Brill. He was a man of great action. When he took note of our youth, he realized that the situation should be improved.

[Hebrew page 64, Yiddish page 225]

5. Youth Movement
Translated by Jerrold Landau

His first task was to set up groups for the study of Zionism and the Land of Israel. These groups were called, "Tzeirei Zion". The youth who were anxious for action and awakening gathered around these groups.

The number of people who participated in discussions, debates, festivities and excursions grew. The influence of these groups slowly encompassed the youth.

From the ranks of participants of these groups, who absorbed the convincing teaching and doctrines of the gifted teacher Lipa Brill, the kernel of Hashomer Hatzair arose. This was through the efforts of Mishli Hendel, Zeida Mehering and Shlomo Kaufman.

As a result of this education for Zionist preparation (Hachsharah), the first Chalutzim of our city made aliya in 1920.   They laid the foundation for the farms of Cheftzi-Bah and Beit Alfa. These peoples included Berchi Josefsberg, Akiva Fruchter, Moshe Klenbard, Hodaya Rosenbaum, Moshe Reiss, Rachtzia Schorr, Ruchtzia Schindler, and Yechezkel Schlifka.

Before I finish my article, I will deal once again with personalities and events that penetrated our hearts.

Who of you does not remember the "Tzetl Yid" (List Jew) Yankel? It was difficult in those days to acquire all sorts of provisions. The needs and desires grew, and the town could not accommodate them. What could a Jew do, a rich one was in the same position as a poor one? The 'Tzetl Yid" used to accept orders from all the residents of the town, each with his own list. These lists were pasted to the brow of the "Jew" when he returned to us, laden with packages. He received his payment. "Jews earn their livelihood from each other."

At the conclusion of my memoirs, I will touch on other personalities of Bolechow. Among them were the master among his people, "the powerful" the conceited, the refined and the coquettish. Behold! There was the Maskil, the modest one, the scholar who keeps himself discrete, the person of faith, the G-d fearing, the person who knows the Book, the one who knows the square letters [6], the one who studies Ein Yaakov, the one who looks into Hatzefirah, all together. There are the ones who read Shalom Aleichem, Frischman, Peretz, Schnitzler, Zweig, Karelman, etc. And where is the charitable person? And where is the one who gives discretely? One runs into the doer of good deeds at every step. Was it possible not to run into them? These people who do not work regular jobs [7], there is no word to precisely describe these ideas even in a foreign dictionary.

Bolechow! What came across after I left you? I was a wanderer in the final years on a one-legged journey.

Fate was not kind to you. Your dear Jews, comparable to fine gold, drank from the goblet until is conclusion. Where are your elderly and your children? The cruel murderer caught up with you in strange houses, in forests, in hiding, and in bunkers.

The innocent, the pure, those who hoped for good, free of guilt, who can count your number? A world rich in spirit, with many thoughts, sunk into the ground. Dreams and songs were cut off in the middle. Who paid attention to your suffering, and to your last gasps on your final journey?

Dear Bolechow natives, on all corners of the earth and in Israel! The Kibbutz member, the worker on a Moshava, the farmer, the counselor, the teacher, the doctor, the engineer, the housewife! Do you remember your youth in Bolechow, the place of your childhood? The reality that I described to you is like a dream that flew away, taking along our pure dear ones!

With your tragic deaths, terrible beyond terrible, you commended us to a life of struggle and pride [8].

[Hebrew page 65 & Yiddish page 226]

6. From Days Gone By
by Yonah Eshel-Elendman
Translated by Jerrold Landau

Dedicated to the memory of my mother Malka of blessed memory.

Mother told me: Her brother, Yisrael Yosef Szpigeli (one of the founders of the Tushia school in Bolechow, loved by the family and nicknamed "Das Feterl" – "The Uncle") became engaged. The time of the wedding approached.

At the end of the Sabbath, his father (my grandfather) Yoshi sat on a long bench near the stove and studied Gemara. The door opened and the in-law entered in order to decide on the time of the wedding.

"Good week!"

"A good and blessed week!"

Since the in-laws did not like to engage in much conversation, they fulfilled "a word as a stone [9]". The in-law sat on his second side of the bench. They sat and sat, they were silent, and they enjoyed smelling tobacco for enjoyment, until the in-law stood up and uttered:

"With G-d's will, we will arrange the wedding on the week of Shabbat Shira [10].

"It should be at a good and propitious time. Have a good week!"

This ended the mission of the in-law. At the set time, my uncle said the "Harei At" formula [11].

He was a great scholar, and also very wealthy, blessed with possessions. He owned a bank and various businesses. He did not understand the vernacular language, and he wrote the Latin script cryptically, in his own manner of hieroglyphics. As a multi-branched businessman, he related well to people, and he came into contact with institutions. It seems that he had to sign the documents, checks, contracts, letters and other printed items in the language of the country.

The poor man was perplexed. How to do so!

Someone wrote his name as Jacob, and he copied it over verbatim. Dealing with these letters was not simple. It was as if he was walking on stilts.

When he finished Jac, he clapped his hands, shouted for joy, and called out: "I am already at Yatz".

Note: Many other of those who came before him thrust themselves into the true study of Torah. They turned it over and turned it over. Bright vistas and worlds opened up for them, without nullifying their personalities and lowering their stature.

[Hebrew page 66 & Yiddish page 227]

7. A Fire in Bolechow
by Yonah Eshel-Elendman
Translated by Jerrold Landau

It was the middle of the night. The town, with its pathways and alleys, was sleeping a sweet slumber. Its tiny, modest houses were right next to each other. They were covered in a gloomy, dark, wrapping. Nobody was on the streets, and there was no sign of life. There was no sound, and even the dogs did not bark. Sound sleep enveloped the young and the old. Only from one window did a the light of a dim oil lamp break forth into the darkness of the night. The diligent learner was still engrossed in his study, struggling with a difficult section of Gemara, awaiting a solution.

Bolechow was not known for large houses. On the contrary, its houses resembled dice from a game, one being supported by the other, as if each was asking for help from the next. Most were made of wood covered with a material that was quite flammable. If a fire broke out, there was a danger that all the houses would be destroyed. They were fuel for a fire.

"Havdalah" and "Bore Meorei Haeish" [12] were for us portents to a fire. Why was this? Rumor stated the following: There was someone interested in a fire for economic reasons, for that would give the person an opportunity to exchange his poor, rickety house with a good spacious house, on account of insurance money. It is possible that we suspected the innocent. The idea is strange, and nobody can research it. G-d has the answers.

Since fires used to break out at the conclusion of the Sabbath, it was said that Havdalah was the reason.

It was after the third Sabbath meal (Shalosh Seudot), Havdalah, the recitation of Elokei Avraham Yitzchak VeYaakov, talking to a neighbor or a friend, or reading a restful nighttime book. The Sabbath Queen was still hovering over Bolechow. In the dreams of its sleepers there were holy visions, which had not yet given way to the secular – this was the battle between the holy and the secular in its essence. The holy had the upper hand.

The prince was engulfed in his slumber, enshrined in a world that was completely good and sublime. The slumbering prince, the dog's life was for him hence. The burdens of the worries, the yoke, the degradation that he suffered during the six days of the workweek, were all forgotten and erased. Like the thunder from the heavens, suddenly a terrifying voice pierces through the air. "Danger!, Danger, a fire!". From one of the houses, flames leap forth and pillars of smoke ascend. Within moments, a tumult breaks out. Yossel, Eidel, Feivel, Mendel, Yenta, Soshia, Dvosha, scream out with all their might.

Perplexed, desperate, tired men, women, children and elderly burst out from every alley, from every house, and wander to and fro. Here is a woman afflicted with the fear of death breaking down a gate, with her child in her arms.

Ringplatz (the Town Square) after a fire.

Here a dumbfounded young girl wails. There a forlorn elderly person stumbles as he runs to and fro clapping his hands, "Woe that I merited thus!". The disorder increases, and confuses thoughts and action. House after house is engulfed in the flames. Someone throws a wet sack onto a roof. Another one tosses a pail. Suddenly Jerzy Bilinski, the "hero" of the fire, enters into the tragic scene. He is the gentile Jew who speaks a juicy Yiddish, understands the occurrences of the town and its Jews, and displays his power in extinguishing fires.

Bundles and bundles of moveable objects are loaded onto a wagon and transported far from the spreading fire.

The Town Hall (Magistrat.

The domestic animals are aroused from their sleep. A confused cow hurries out from one of the barns, mooing bitterly. A calf hastens to flee. The barking of the dogs, the yowling of the cats, and the cooing of the chickens merge together into a terrifying, tragic symphony. Everyone is calling for help. One encompassing bitter cry ascends heavenward. Even birds smell the fire, and fly about in a frightened, perplexed manner, circling about and moving away quickly from the danger zone.

Terrified images move about, pushing and carrying things. Muffled cries are heard. Broken walls of homes tumble down, accompanied by sighs of anguish. The fire defeated them. The fire bears destruction. It spreads and spreads.

One can see the forms of the chimneys alone, pointing upward, and after a short period, all that is left is burnt out, charred shells. The houses of Bolechow were turned into mounds of ashes, to nothing! Above is the sky, darkened with thick smoke.

What is a fire in the town? An event that is completely terrifying. A painful happening in the chain of suffering, a monstrous event in our early childhood which leaves an indelible impression.

What is it to have your house burnt down? It is to be uprooted from the home of your rearing, in which you were born, from the home in which you grew up and rejoiced, like those who came before you, and who came before them. The house of a legacy! If it is burnt, it is like the uprooting of a tree from the place of its nurturing, growth, flourishing, acclimatizing. With regard to the years of a person, to what is it compared? To embitter his life, to cut him off from his foundation, to cut of his roots and the roots of his roots.

And the children of the fire, to what are they compared? To those nestlings who have had their warmth removed from them, and whose source of life and joy has been taken away.

After the fire, poor indigents were added to our community. This one stayed with a neighbor, this one with an acquaintance or a relative. They sufficed themselves with temporary arrangements.

A few days after the fire, one runs into an honorable couple of the community begging from door to door in the outskirts of Bolechow, or a pair of righteous women dressed up in festive clothes collecting for the needy. "One should not talk about it", or "be discrete with your needy", was an internal command, a voice from the soul.

The more one could give, the more praiseworthy it was.

[Hebrew page 68 & Yiddish page 229]

8. My Rebbetzin
by Yonah Eshel-Elendman
Translated by Jerrold Landau

Who knows four? I know four? Four are the matriarchs [13], Sara, Rebecca, Rachel and Leah. My masters, remove the last two names, and you have the name of my Rebbetzin.

She was called Sara Rivka on the streets of Bolechow. It is a beautiful name that sounds nice. Is it not?

She was a woman of medium stature. Not fat and not skinny. Her face was marked with many wrinkles. Her nose was blessed like a wellspring, and was always dripping liquid. She wore a pair of glasses when she was teaching. The color of her hair? Do not ask, you should not know, for her hair was always covered with a kerchief, tied tightly so that not even one of her hair should ever be seen, G-d forbid. Her thick handkerchief, not white, with which she wiped her nose, was in constant use. Believe me, I remember that handkerchief to this day. Her clothing was not fine and elegant. It was sufficient just to cover up her nakedness.

My Rebbetzin, I did not hate you. On the contrary, you taught me, as a child, how to read my first Hebrew, with those small, square letters. I did not particularly like you, why? Because I had to sit before you as I wasted a thousand and one other opportunities to play with castles, to conduct business, to knead cakes, challas and all types of pastry out of mud – Bolechow was blessed with mud when the snow melted. Bolechow took eight portions and the rest of the world one. Who can enumerate the number of games that were waiting for me at that time? Despite all this, I did not avoid this study, for my conscience was bound with bonds of responsibility for my actions. You were also a progressive teacher for me, and kept me from doing wrong and ignoring the holy work of studying Hebrew. Indeed, the externals of Sara Rivka did not particularly attract me. She did not excite my eye. On the contrary, her appearance was someone bothersome to the esthetic feelings of a child.

With a pointer, you hovered and flew over the Siddur (prayer book), the mixture, the octagon, the blurry and the worn, thick, worn from much use, seeking repose so that the boundaries do not become blurred [14].

In truth, I strongly hoped that the Rebbetzin would get mixed up and skip a page, a line, or even one blessing. But never. She wet her finger with her saliva, which was always plentiful in order to flip through the poor, forlorn Siddur. Thus did she do from early times.

Sara Rivka did not know anything about Pestalozzi, Korzac, or Freud. However, this did not "bother" her. She understood the meaning of the words, if not completely, then partially. I would snatch some Yiddish, some explanation; thus did we drink to our content. My Rebbetzin had her own style of teaching. From where did she acquire it? Don't ask. The youngsters did not ask very much, the main thing was to be freed from this waste of time, from the boring reading of the familiar Siddur that did not interest the hearts of the children. Indeed, do we have to delve into and understand everything? The more knowledge, the more pain, taught our sages. Indeed, there were some words that I could not repeat and understand in any way, for any price. For example, "vehayu letotafot bein eineicha" ("And they shall be as frontlets – i.e phylacteries – between your eyes") [15]. "What are totafot, Rebbetzin?". What is the connection between "totafot" and eyes? I cried out, misery, misery. Do you have to know everything? She answered, "You are still young, when you are old, you will understand everything.". If so, what is "tzeetzaei tzeetzaeihem" [16]? I liked these words, due to the many Tzadis [17], and the strange sound. To my dismay, Sara Rivka did not have an answer to this question of mine. She was stumped. After all, my friends, to this day, believe me, I do not clearly understand the meaning of "totafot" or "tzeetzaei tzeetzaeihem". All this was because of my Rebbetzin. Her soul was refined. I will grant you good if you could give me a clear explanation of these words.

Pure Sara Rivka, the good, the modest of women of blessed memory, even today there are Rebbetzins like you, who are not able to transmit various concepts and ideas to their students. This is despite the fact that they studied some psychology, psychoanalysis, and psychotechnics. Despite this, they are wonderful teachers of Israel.

What is the same of all of you: your pure intentions, your straightforward heart, and above all – your strong love of your fellow Jew that beats in your hearts.

[Hebrew page 70 & Yiddish page 231]

9. Tashlich [18]
by Yonah Eshel-Elendman
Translated by Jerrold Landau

And you shall cast into the depths of the sea all your sins. (Micha 7, 19).

The casting away of sins – this is an unpleasant task for man – into the depths of the river during Tashlich was "technically" straightforward in Bolechow, since we had no shortage of rivers. Tashlich was an extraordinary pompous scene. Before the procession, the diligent would stake out for themselves a comfortable place to stand near the two riverbanks, on a gate, on a roof, near the dam, on a bridge, or on a projection on a house of an acquaintance or a friend.

The ceremony begins. Here is Rabbi Shlomo Perlow – the wise scholar who did not rebuke his daughters if they study Hebrew, and did not worry lest they be ruined in public – with his community of Hassidim, each with a lit tallow candle in his hand. They walked in a long rearward line, walking along jauntily, with importance. When they reached the riverbank, everyone shook out his outer garment, and said with awe, "And you shall cast into the depths of the sea all of your sins".

There was a holy awe surrounding. The last radiant rays of the sun intermix with the lit tallow candles, and they glitter in the slow moving waves of the river. The jokers – they apparently do not have sins and iniquities to cast into the depths – so for them, Tashlich is a different matter. What did they do at that time? They would pile up piles of straw that they had prepared from the eve of the festival, role them into a shape, place a burning candle into them, and float them in the river. Within a few moments, the river was filled with tiny islands, spitting fire, "burning, jumping, flickering". What a splendid site! Fire and water under one roof! And look! The thick bundle does not extinguish. On the contrary, it floats, moves on and on, the light does not dim, for it is very proud.

The ceremony concluded. The rabbi and his entourage head toward the house of the rabbi. The house is noisy with joyful people, exulting in gladness. The community is basking in the presence of their spiritual father. The song breaks forth with enthusiasm. The devotion and the excitement reach the point of leaving behind the physical. The forgetting of the worries of the gloomy weekdays envelops everybody. The sun sets over the treetops. Darkness covers the earth, and on the river, there is fire and water. Around is the joy and happiness of young people and friends, the gladness of the festival, the feeling of calm and salvation. Behold, we are clean of all sin. The waters covered the sins, and the fire burnt them.

Translator's Footnotes

1. This chapter and the next were particularly difficult to translate. They are written in a semi-poetic, dirge-like form. Many of the thoughts in the first chapter appear to be addressed to the town itself and its locations. This style is borrowed from the Zion odes of the Tisha BeAv liturgy, which personify the destroyed Zion and Jerusalem.

2. His full name is Oleksa Dowbusz.

3. Derogatory terms for gentile males and females.

4. The term here, obviously sarcastic, is the Biblical term used to describe the aroma of the Temple sacrifices.

5. This is a cryptic reference. My interpretation was that the younger felt greater spiritual solace at the hill than at the synagogue.

6. I am not sure of the implication of all of these innuendoes. Ein Yaakov is a compendium of the legends of the Talmud, generally studied by the less scholarly but faithful people. Hatzefirah refers to a modern Zionist newspaper.

7. A reference to a person who spends the bulk of his days engaged in holy works rather than pursuit of a livelihood. (In Hebrew, batlan.)

8. I believe that this is a reference to the rebirth of Israel.

9. I am not sure of the meaning of this reference. It seemingly is a term for terse speech.

10. The Sabbath upon which the Torah portion of Beshallach is read. Beshallach contains the Song of the Sea. It occurs in mid to late winter.

11. This is the formula that is declared by the groom at a wedding ceremony.

12. Havdalah is the ceremony conducted over wine, a flame and spices to mark the end of the Sabbath. Bore Meorei Haeish (He Who creates the light of the fire) is the blessing recited over the multi-wicked flame at Havdalah.

13. A quote from a well-known song that is sung toward the end of the Seder on Passover.

14. This sentence seems to be describing a child's view of a worn out, tattered prayer book.

15. A quote from the Shema prayer.

16. A quote from a blessing recited as part of the morning prayers. Literally, "The descendents of their descendents".

17. Tzadi is a Hebrew letter, making the 'ts' sound.

18. *A ceremony performed at a riverbank on the afternoon of Rosh Hashanah, where one's sins are symbolically cast into the River.*

[Hebrew page 71 & Yiddish page 231]

10. Preparations for Passover in Bolechow
by Yonah Eshel-Elendman
Translated by Jerrold Landau

Of all the holidays with which we were blessed, our Festival of Freedom took nine measures or preparation.

It was beloved by young and old. It was full of encouragement, and influenced the manner of life for several months before it arrived.

People would make wine from raisins. This homemade product was the best of the best.Wednesday, October 13, 2004

Our mothers prepared all types of drinks from berries of the forest: hackberries, cherries, and raspberries that were plentiful in the area. These were preserved in flasks. During times of illness, these also refreshed the longing soul.

In the middle of the winter, approximately at the time of Chanukah, they would slaughter fat ducks. The feathers were plucked. (The plucking of the feathers, performed together by neighbors, was a pleasant episode. It kept the children busy on long winter nights). After that, they would melt the fat, separate out the tasty, brown cracklings (gribn [11]) to be used to spice the Passover foods, puddings and soufflés. This task was done with an air of great importance. The fat was preserved in earthenware pots. This was the custom from days of yore.

A. The Borscht

With spotlessly washed hands, wearing starchless aprons (due to the chometz in the starch [2]), our mothers started their work. They drew the water directly from the well into an earthenware vessel set aside for that purpose. They would chop the beets into pieces. At the end of the job, they would cover the vessel with a clear white cloth, and put it away in a far off corner, hidden away so that nobody would approach. This "red, red"[3] became fizzy, and waited to have its turn to benefit people. Until this day, its sweet taste did not leave my palate.

B. The Baking of Matzos

What is the baking of matzos? A communal task.

We did not purchase the "bread of affliction"; we did not get it from nowhere. On the contrary! Every housewife would bake this matzo in accordance with the size of her family, in accordance with a set procedure. Thus was it done: A room was emptied out and whitewashed. The entire room was sparkly clean. They would set up long, smooth tables, as the tables of a Beis Midrash. A flaming oven was in the kitchen beside the room. From where was the staff? Were they hired? Don't even mention that. They were the children of friends and neighbors. When Batya Malka was baking, the daughters of Chava Lea assisted her. When Yenta Soshia baked, the daughters of Chancha came to help. Thus it went around. Thus were the youth willingly enlisted to this communal endeavor, without being commanded.

A pleasant sight unfolded before your eyes when you entered the room in which the matzo was baked. Two rows of girls, gleeful, charming and tall, stood next to the tables, wearing white aprons. They were kneading the dough. The rolling pin passed over the dough and rounded it into the shape of a matzo. It was then placed in the oven. The left over dough was baked into tiny matzos (matzalach) for the children.

This was an activity filled with conversation, joy, laughter and jokes.

The room in which the bread of affliction was prepared turned rich [4]. With gladness and bubbling life. A large quantity of matzo was baked for the holiday. It was not simply baked in accordance with the number of children, for they did not skimp on eating it. On the contrary, it would be eaten even after the festival.

The baked matzos were placed in large, round baskets, covered well with large white cloths, and put in a corner where nobody would go.

However, "stolen water is sweet". Did you pass the test?

C. New Clothing for the Festival

Who of us did not have new clothes for the holiday? Shoes? During the winter, in particular as the snow was melting, shoes tore quickly, for they got worn out, tattered, and softened. They were repaired with patches upon patches, but new ones were not obtained until the festival.

Who other than us us, the children of the towns – towns infused with tradition of many generations that tried through the festivals to improve and glorify the dark, lowly life of the exile, and to grant them grace, beauty and a fine form – felt the meaning of new clothes at Passover.

D. Whitewashing and Cleaning

Now we reach the final stage of preparations. The most important steps were the whitewashing, the thorough cleaning of the home. If you passed through the streets of Bolechow on one of the days leading up to Passover, you would see a different view before you. On Egypt Street [5], Rusaki Bolechow, Shuster (Shoemaker's) Street, there was chaos, confusion, like the overturning of Sodom and Gomorrah. There were household objects, beds and mattresses. Corner beds (small beds that served as a type of bench during the day), shlabenes (wider than the above), taptshenes [6], milk benches, meat benches, blankets, pillow, kitchen utensils, dough troughs, baking moulds, etc., etc. Everything was placed outside.

Mothers and daughters were busy working. They would scrub, scour, scrape, and turn over every object to remove any trace of grime or chometz from any crevice and crack.

At the same time, the vessels were purged [7] with great deliberation and fanfare. During the whitewashing and thorough cleansing, we would sit on overturned pails, crates and barrels, for the chairs were outside. Thus is pleasant and fitting before Passover.

During the course of the year, if a dish broke, one would use a Passover dish. However, from Rosh Chodesh Nissan [8] they would buy new ones, so as not to impinge of the utensils of the festival of festivals.

The new vessel was immersed in the river before use – a proper custom!

The shoemaker, the tailor, the dyer, the whitewasher, the carpenter, and later on the barber and the bath attendant all had their hands full of work. They worked with full steam. The time came, work became greater, grocery stores were busier, prices doubled. The simple folk earned their wages at one time.

At the conclusion of my tour of Bolechow before Passover, permit me to make one point. The conduct, the communal baking of matzo, the mutual assistance – how pleasant was it. It added to the Festival of Spring a longing for freedom and democratic means.

The matzo, which was not produced by a cold, silent machine, was flavored with the energy of the enthusiastic youth, which was poured into it above all ingredients.

All of the proceedings of the Seder, from the Four Questions to Chad Gadya, etc., are they not written in the Haggadah of Passover.

[Hebrew page 73 & Yiddish page 234]

11. Bnot Tzion (The Daughters of Zion)
by Yonah Eshel-Elendman
Translated by Jerrold Landau

In memory of my sister Gitele of blessed memory

My native town of Bolechow in eastern Galicia was numbered among those few towns that were diligent in the study of modern Hebrew at the beginning of the time of the Zionist movement.

This was made possible not because our town was rich, but because it was enlightened and thirsting for knowledge, and the status of the scholar was revered.

Therefore, we found in our town many Maskilim who knew Hebrew language and literature very well. Several of them such as Shlomo Neimark, Yisrael Yoel Spiegel, and others were occupied in the teaching of Bible, not only to boys, but also to girls such as the daughters of the wealthy people: Avrahamele Kurtzer, David Graubard, etc.

Since it was not necessary to bring in teachers from outside, there were no difficulties in founding the Hebrew school, which began to interest the hearts of the finest Zionists of eastern Galicia. The teaching of the Hebrew language in Bolechow, mainly by residents of the town, continued uninterrupted until the Holocaust.

The first Hebrew school, "Tushia", was founded by Neimark and Spiegel. That school produced not only many students, but also teachers.

On the heals of "Tushia", a school called "Safa Berura" was founded after some time. Boys as well as girls studied there.

From 1911-1913, "Bnot Tzion" courses were run by my teacher Chuna-Chanan Hendel. There were only two sessions, since my teacher then moved to Moravia.

In this article, I wish to devote some words to the first "Bnot Tzion" group, of which I was a student. The work of my teacher is fitting to be pointed out in a unique fashion, since his teaching methodology and relationship to us was outside of what was usual and customary.

Our teacher did not suffice himself with merely the teaching of Hebrew language and literature. He devoted himself primarily to the winning over of souls to the nationalistic idea, that is, to turn us into daughters of Zion[9]. He imparted to us the value of Judaism, and tried to impart to our hearts the love of our nation, and our cultural heritage, in order to awaken in us the desire to dedicate ourselves and actualize the Zionist idea.

Since our teacher was one of the prime disciples of Ahad Haam, he made great efforts to instill his Zionist concepts within us. In particular, he emphasized the theory of Ahad Haam with respect to "The Man and the Tent", explaining that the revival of our nation and our Land will not be attained unless we first rectify ourselves and free ourselves from our bad ideas and traits.

This Zionist concept that demanded every Jewish person to rectify himself and to give his share toward the rebuilding of our nation, caught our hearts, young hearts in which the pure religions faith had become weakened on the one hand, and the need for searching for additional meaning in our life was felt by us on the other hand. Therefore, the seed which our teacher planted in us took root and produced praiseworthy fruit.

Most of Bnot Tzion were dedicated to the Zionist idea and were active in the field of teaching or social assistance toward those of lesser means.

During the time of the First World War, Rachel Reis-Hendel founded, along with my dear brother Eli may G-d avenge his blood, a shelter for needy children. She directed this institution along with her friends in Bnot Tzion. Aside from this, she occupied herself with teaching in Bolechow until she left for Moravia when she got married to our teacher. She continued to teach there. She taught in an elementary school after she made aliya.

Rivka Kurtz- Gesthelter, one of Bnot Tzion, taught in Lwow after her parents of blessed memory moved there.

I also was occupied in teaching in Bolechow, Drohowice, Dolina and Danzig. In the Land, I worked with great satisfaction at teaching evening classes, primarily to adults and to those who were learning the language.

Chedva Nimes taught in elementary schools in Lwow, Mezheritz, and Stanislawow, where she was cut off in her prime.

As I mentioned above, our teacher was a disciple of Ahad Haam. Therefore, he taught us his works. Thus, we also studied the poems of Bialik, the stories of Fierberg, and we dealt with "Lon" with great dedication. We did not skip over any important writer, including the nemesis of Ahad Haam, Berdichevsky.

Bnot Tzion

A Hebrew Class. The teacher is Rachel Reis.

I must point that, despite the fact that ourt teacher was a freethinker, he was careful not to contradict our religious belief. On the contrary, he tried to arouse in us a dutiful relationship to tradition, to the heritage of our ancestors, and to that which is sacred to our nation.

It is fitting to point out as well his friendly relations to us. A strong friendship arose between us during the time that he was teaching, that continues to this day.

Aside from Bible and literature, we studied diligently the history of our people. Our teacher knew how to make the history of our people dear to us through his enthusiastic lectures, when the spirit hit him. Such occasions were generally dependent on the presence of Rivka Kurtz-Gesthelter, who also displayed an extraordinary understanding of and interest in history.

We can see how dear this subject was to us by the fact that when our teacher promised to give a lecture to us on a segment of history, it immediately moved us to a straight spirit, and calmed us when we lost our temper on account of the excesses of youth that overtook us on occasion and led us to occasions of wildness.

Our dedication to our studies in our school, which was like a miniature sanctuary to us, was a topic of conversation in Bolechow, for we were seen during most of the hours of the day and evening in the company of our teacher, engrossed in conversation and serious debates. People were astonished at this unusual situation.

Even I, the writer of these lines, am at times amazed at this unusual situation. Even intelligent and sober men can see what this is based upon from two incidents, which are etched among others in my memory.

I recall one winter day, when the snow was very high and covered the entire town. I set out for the class. With difficulty and great effort, as my feet sunk into the snow and reached the level of the ground on the path, I arrived with my last breath to the alley behind the "Small Kloiz" where our class was held. The house had sunk and was buried in mud. The room was covered with a thick covering of snow, and my hands were empty. Should I return? That would be too bad. It was not possible to miss a class! Neighbors saw me, understood my anguish and distress, and cleared off the door so that I could open it.

The following is the second event that I remember. We used to continue our studies until two days before Passover. It once happened that one of the students, Rachel Reis, was sent by her mother to summon a gentile to clean their house after the whitewashing. When she passed by the house in which we studied, she was not able to pass by without coming in for a small moment. She became so engrossed in the topic that she forgot her mission and remained with us.

HaShomer HaTzair, Top 1917, Bottom 1919

Directors and Teachers of the Hebrew School

Opening of the Jewish National Fund in Lemberg 5 Shevat 1914, Shaul Dingot and
Leibish Roter

HaShomaeir HaTzair 1917 Tarnow Cherry Orchard

HaShomaeir HaTzair Leaders and Section Heads

It is no wonder. The studies played a central role in our life in the town. There was always an exultation of spirit in the study hall, which took our minds off of the day to day worries that afflicted each one of us.

A proof that this is not a corrupted idea of childhood memory, refined by the splendor and shine of the past, can be seen from the experience of one of our visitors, a trustworthy person.

We also studied on the Sabbath. This class was like our Sabbath celebration (Oneg Shabbat). One Sabbath, the writer Yonah Gelernter of blessed memory visited us. He was the teacher and pedagogue of Professor Chaies of blessed memory. He sat for a long time and listened with great concentration and attention. As he left, he uttered, "Indeed, the spirit of Jewry dwells here."

As I write down the memories of these words, I must confess that Gelernter was correct.

Indeed, there were set times for classes. However, out teacher never looked at the clock. Of what use is a clock? When the student is engaged, the ears are listening and the heart is open, alert and longing. More than we wished to learn, our teacher wished to teach. He was not satisfied with the set times, but rather continued teaching on past the time. We gathered almost every evening in the "Walking Garden", where we discussed and debated matters that were of utmost importance to us. Thus did we fulfil the commandment, "And you shall delve into it day and night." [10]

Our teacher also concerned himself with our self-completion. To this end, we founded, with his assistance, a library called "Bnot Tzion", which we guarded as the apple of our eye. We devoured the books like a ripe fig before summer. Once, a fire broke out on a street near that library. We all hurried over there to save the library from the fire.

Through the advise of Srulke Spiegel (the brother of Golda who was a student in the course), an enthusiastic Zionist and zealous Hebrew, to our great distress, our teacher was invited by the "Zion" organization to Omelitz to win over souls for Zionism and Hebrew culture.

Our connection was not severed. We continued to study together. Letters from the teacher in Omelitz united us. Joy was at its height when a letter arrived. At times we got wild, and made noise in the outskirts of Bolechow. Word spread quickly that a letter had arrived from the teacher. We ran to one of the members to read it, We turned it over and over as we desired to find out how he was doing, and particularly about his activities.

"Bnot Tzion", where are you? You did not make it to Zion. The hand of the impure murderers, may their names be blotted out, reached you. You were slaughtered along with all who were dear to us:

Lena Gruss, Baltchi Weschler, Sara Neibauer, Gitele Elendman, Ravchi Frost, Feiga Kurtz, Leicha Korel, Golda Spiegel. May G-d avenge your vengeance, and may your pure souls be bound up in the bonds along with the rest of the martyrs of Israel. We three "Bnot Tzion", Rachel Reis-Hendel, Rivka Kurtz-Gesthelter and Yona Eshel, who remained alive and live together with our teacher in Haifa, continue our friendship and will guard your memories in our hearts forever.

[Yiddish page 242]

12. Resurrection of the Dead
by M. A. Tenenblat
(An excerpt from the Lemberger Tagblatt, March 6, 1918)

Is it indeed a holy word, which is used by us only in the specific situation when the principles of Jewish faith are bound up with iron chains? The coming of the Messiah and the resurrection of the dead are bound together like a flame to a candle. The latter without the former is completely inconceivable in the Jewish religious ethos.

Indeed, I witnessed this with my own eyes in the last few days. It is no fantasy, no exaggeration, only simple reality, that matters which a few short months and years ago were considered dead and lost from the body and especially from the soul of the Jewish people – have suddenly sprouted to life before my very eyes.

It is not long ago, I believe, since Bohemia and Moravia gave forth the Half Shekels of Rabbi Yonatan Eibeshitz – the many rabbis and leaders of the generation whose Torah and wisdom lit up not only their own lands, but also far of lands of Poland and White Russia. However, suddenly, the wellspring of Torah of Bohemian and Moravian Jewry became stopped up.

Some time ago, there was a complete interruption of Bohemian and Moravian Jewry from the new Jewish creativity of eastern Jewry and the Land of Israel.

In recent days, I spent a brief time in Olomouc. Since I had heard that there had been a Hebrew teacher from Galicia there for a long time, I naturally wanted to see him. I wanted to join in the despair of an eastern Jewish scholar who finds himself in a strange plase, a foundling who is lost among the gentiles. I wanted to see what the stubborn Galician idealist was doing in half German, half Czech Olomouc, with its 1,400 dead Jewish souls. I wanted to convince him simply that it was a sin to sit in some Moravian town and expend strength, energy, and holy idealism there – futile and fruitless – while

Galicia itself has lost yet another Hebrew teacher, and searches for him with light.

I wanted to convince him, and he completely convinced me. I could scarcely believe my own eyes. I believed that he himself was in a half-dead spiritual milieu. However, I found myself in a place that made me believe that I was in Lemberg, Stryj, Drohobyce, etc. I could not believe that this was indeed Olomouc in Moravia. Stubbornness in general is no small thing. Another case of Jewish stubbornness intermingled with idealism caused him to undertake the first attempt of introducing modern eastern Jewish content to western Austrian Jewry. He persisted, and the experiment succeeded – splendidly succeeded.

His name is Chona Hendel. The young man is from Bolechow, Galicia, where he disseminated Torah for several years, and introduced Hebrew literature to a large number of girls who became readers. For in Bolechow, Galicia, as well, he had his own methodology. He educated only girls, and they studied Hebrew language and literature. His educational methodology was conducted in such a way so as to encourage us to invest all our efforts and energy in winning over the Jewish daughter, the future mother. Without her commitment to Judaism, the Jewish home could not be Jewish. He did this in Bolechow and now he was doing this in Olomouc. He left here already before the war, but he endured the first Russian invasion during a visit to Bolechow. He did not want to wait around for the second one. To him, it was a sin to abandon his work in the spreading of Hebrew in Olomouc, so he escaped back to Olomouc with great self-dedication so that he could resume his activities. He stubbornly persisted in ensuring that there would be a Hebrew circle in Olomouc, where one would read Ahad Haam and general Hebrew literature.

He began working with a few family members. It was not easy. We must realize that even with us in Galicia of today, it is very difficult to convince even one of our Zionist leaders that Zionism without Hebrew, Zionism without Jewish knowledge, is an absurdity, is not Zionism, but is rather at best the first step toward the way of proper Zionism. He began with the county judge Dr. Meisner, with a lawyer, and with Mrs. Barger.

It is impossible to describe the pleasure that I had when I heard the small circle reading Ahad Haam, Hatzefira, Hashiloach, Berdichevsky's Shinui Erchin, etc. The Galician idealist did not succeed by convincing them about the reading of Hebrew literature. He led them to the conceptual world of eastern Judaism in such a fine way that they were convinced that they were no longer Moravian Jews, to whom the eastern Jews appeared strange, comic and tragic, something beyond normal. He simply created there a Galician Jewish milieu of the young idealistic type. He, by himself, affected the many. He won them over, not hiding from them the shadowy sides of the eastern Jew. He taught them only enough Yiddish so that he could show them the spiritual qualities of the Jewish masses in the east through Yiddish adages.

He began with those three, and now he brought them to the blue and white wonderful banner. He worked with the leaders, conducting heartfelt activities. Now they are already learning Hebrew. Their conceptual Jewish world is slowly coming to the idealism of Jewish academics in Galicia. They may not themselves realize that they are the first "Shomrim, Young Zion" in Moravia, the bridge to the ingathering of the exiles.

Can one not appropriately call this "the resurrection of the dead"?

[Hebrew page 77 & Yiddish page 244]

13. Two Bolechowers, Two Different Worlds and Personalities
by Avigdor Ben Leah
Translated by Jerrold Landau

Our town of Bolechow not only made a name for itself in the realm of economics, as men of effort founded two different factories in which hundreds of Jewish employees worked and earned their livelihoods, but also in the realm of culture. Our town was one of the first in Eastern Galicia to establish a secular Jewish school in which boys and girls studied together from Jewish teachers. As well, a Hebrew school for the study of Hebrew as a spoken language was established at the time of the birth of the Zionist movement. Needless to say, a Zionist organization was established at the dawn of the days of the Zionist movement. In short striving and desire to ascend in all areas of life beat in the hearts of the people of Bolechow. This spirit filled up all of the strata of the population, and all age groups.

The youth of my generation who did not yet stream to the Gymnasiums, but nevertheless wished to acquire secular education, used to go out to teach the children of the villages. In their spare time, they would diligently study Hebrew and general studies with books that they purchased from their teaching salary. The skill of these youths of Bolechow spread very quickly throughout the villages. They used to come in to Stryj, near Bolechow, on the cattle market days that fell out during the Intermediate Days (Chol Hamoed) of Passover and Sukkot in order to hire a teacher for a term, which would extend to one week before Rosh Hashanah or one week before Passover. The villagers sought after the youth of Bolechow and offered them good salaries. Furthermore, they would also forego investigating into the qualifications of these youths, as they would do with youths from other places who would normally only be hired after passing a test administered by erudite, scholarly people; for the name of these youths of Bolechow preceded them. From amongst these youths, who would remain in the villages for only a few terms, came people with higher education in Jewish and European culture. They worked in the field of education in our town when they returned from the villages.

I want to dedicate my deliberations to two youths whom I knew personally and whom impressed me. These youths are Yitzchak Hirsch of the village of Zadarovitch near Bolechow and Lamel Meir, a native of Bolechow.

As mentioned, Yitzchak Hirsch was a native of a village that did not even have a quorum of Jews. He finished three elementary school years in the village, and his father taught him some Chumash and Rashi, for his economic situation did not permit him to hire a tutor, as other villagers did. He was diligent and studious, and he acquired for himself some knowledge in the fields of secular and Jewish knowledge. He borrowed books from a young teacher who tutored the children of the lessee of the Jewish tavern in the Hirsch's native village. – Incidentally, it is appropriate to point out that in every village of eastern Galicia, the leasing of the taverns was in the hands of the Jews. They earned their livelihood primarily from Sundays, the holiday of the Christians, when most of the Christians spent their free day at the tavern. – In order to complete his knowledge, Yitzchak Hirsch went to Stryj, like the youths of Bolechow, in order to be hired as a teacher of Jewish children in the villages. Since he was very diligent, studying day and night in order to continue his education, after a few years he had mastered for himself higher education in Hebrew and the vernacular. His name went out in a praiseworthy fashion as a teacher. The villagers competed over him as a teacher for their children. Even though he earned a high salary, he was only left with a few Guilders at the end of the term, for he spent almost his entire salary on books. He was not able to meet even his modest clothing needs. If he had a few Guilders left, he would give them to his impoverished parents when he returned to them for his vacation at the end of his term.

His love of Torah and education knew no bounds. His love of the book was unusual. I revered him as a true scholar, both on account of his wide and deep knowledge, and on account of his modesty, discreteness and his relationship to me, who was inferior to him in years and also in wisdom. At first a teacher-student relationship formed between us, and then a relationship of friendship. Therefore, I am somewhat expert on the events of his life. I now wish to describe two events that will serve as a clear lens into his life.

His parents' home was burnt down during the First World War. Despite the fact that he was imbued with family feelings, he did not lament the loss of his parents' possessions that were destroyed to the same degree as he lamented the loss of his books in that fire. He could not find consolation on this tragedy that overtook him.

Here is another event that typifies him. One fine morning, his mother died suddenly in her prime. As the firstborn son, it was his duty to accompany the coffin to Bolechow for burial. His father, brothers and sisters arrived before he did in order to arrange the burial with the Chevra Kadisha (burial society).

When he passed by my parents' street, he asked the wagon driver to stop for a while at my parents' home, and he entered. When I asked how he was doing, he told me about the pain of the death of his mother of blessed memory. However, as he was speaking, he began to talk about matters of Torah, and asked me for a book so he can look something up relating to a difference of opinion between us, for in the interim, I had matured spiritually, and had my independent ideas. Only after I reminded him that now was not the proper time to delve into such matters while the coffin of the deceased was lying in the wagon outside, and his visit to me was disparaging to the deceased even without taking into account that a gentile was watching over it, and he himself was the only member of the funeral cortege, did he forego the book and continue on with his journey to the cemetery.

Aside from his high intelligence, he excelled in his generous spirit. However, the main character trait of Yitzchak Hirsch of blessed memory was his love of Torah and wisdom. He did not only observe Torah in poverty, but literally abnegated himself in the tents of Torah in the most complete sense of the term. He lacked a sense of reality in an astonishing fashion, and for this reason, he could not find his way in life. All of my efforts to find him a teaching job in the city came to naught due to his exaggerated laziness. He remained a bachelor, and died in his prime while I was abroad. Woe about this fine person who was swallowed up by the earth. May his memory be a blessing!

Lemel Meir also spent several terms in the villages, and obtained a comprehensive education. However, he was forged of a different material than was Yitzchak Hirsch. Whereas Yitzchak Hirsch gave his strength over to Torah, Lemel Meir dedicated himself to the Zionist movement and communal service. After he returned from the villages, he married a girl from Bolechow and moved to Stryj, which was, as mentioned, near to our town. There his wife, who was the daughter of diligent and accomplished storeowners, opened a store. At first, their economic situation was particularly good, for Lemel Meir became an agent for the distribution of newspapers, both Yiddish and in the vernacular. However, due to his dedication to the Zionist movement, which was hated by the Polish ruling authorities – who wanted the help of the Jews in their struggle against the Ukrainians, and the Zionists opposed this – his permit was revoked. Due to the removal of this permit on the one hand, and due to the fact that he was a guest in his store but a regular dweller in the "Zion" organization of Stryj, their economic situation became unstable, to the point that they had to liquidate the store. In the meantime his wife died, and Lemel Meir returned as a widower with several children to Bolechow, where his parents and his late wife's parents lived. A few years later, he married once more to a widow from Bolechow. The couple had children from both sides. They opened a store there as well, but there also, Lemel continued to occupy himself with Zionist and communal activity, and neglected to look after himself and his family. He did not do this out of lightheadedness and out of lack of concern for his wife and children, but rather because of his inclination toward communal and activity in addition to his dedication to the Zionist movement. Work for the benefit of the public, and particularly for the benefit of the renaissance of the Jewish nation in its homeland was the breath of his nostrils and his spirit. There was no communal or Zionist activity in which Lemel Meir did not take part. Everything that he did was done with his full devotion, for he had a warm and enthusiastic personality. From my many discussions with him, I learned that he tried to free himself from his inclination toward communal affairs, but he could not overcome this inclination, for without communal and Zionist activity, his life was not a life. He was occupied with communal or Zionist work at all seasons of the year, such as: the setting up of collection plates on the Eve of Yom Kippur for the benefit of the settlement in the Land of Israel so that those who came to attend the Mincha service would donate to that fund as well; the distribution of Keren Kayemet LeYisrael (Jewish National Fund) boxes to homes; the arranging of Chanukah celebrations; memorial ceremonies on the anniversary of the death of the leader Herzl of blessed memory; summer celebrations in the civic gardens that were called Shpatzir Garten (Walking Gardens). New activities were added each year, such as concern for the pioneers (Chalutzim), their preparation and their aliya. He also played the lion's share in communal activities, and he did not desist from any activity. These activities were numerous, and included: communal elections, the appointing of a rabbi, support of the Talmud Torah for poor children, etc.

It is worthwhile to point out that despite the fact that he was a Zionist and a Maskil, he wore the traditional garb with a tendency to popularity. In addition, he would travel once in a while to the Admor of Dolina, a town near Bolechow, for he was not only an observant Jew, but also an enthusiastic Hassid. He spent most of his time in the mornings in the synagogue that was known as the "Poilishe Kloiz". There he attended services, and he after the prayers, he argued with the Orthodox people who opposed Zionism and conducted publicity for the Zionist movement among the younger generation. As time went on, that house of prayer became a bastion of Zionism.

Lemel Meir was not only dedicated to the national movement and local communal concerns with all his heart and soul, but he became involved in another plan that was very uncommon at the time: civic courage.

This came to the fore in the year 1907, when, for the first time, there were general elections for the legislative assembly in the capital city of Vienna, and the Zionists decided to field their own candidates for the Austrian parliament. As was mentioned above, the government of eastern Galicia was in the hands of the Poles, who opposed the Zionist candidates as they wished that the Jews would vote for Poles, so that they could continue their hegemony in eastern Galicia, where the Ukrainians were a majority. The Jewish population was divided into two camps. Most of the people were attracted to the Zionist candidates, however due to their dependence on the good graces of the authorities for their economic livelihood, they were not so brazen as to publicly go against the Jewish, assimilationist candidates and who were selected by the

Polish authorities. Aside from those groups who were concerned about destroying their economic livelihoods by supporting Zionist candidates, there were also "plate lickers" in Eastern Galicia whose entire essence was to curry favor with the government, so that they would be able to utilize the good graces of the authorities to help obtain a seat on either the town council of the community council. Those Jews who were indentured servants to the Poles at the expense of their self-respect were called by us youths "Ma Yafit" Jews. That is the name of one of the hymns that is sung at the Sabbath table and that Jews were commanded by the Poretz (landowner) to sing for the entertainment of his guests [11]. If they would not do so, they would be beaten, thrown into jail, or have their livelihoods destroyed. That is to say, this was a deed that was completely lacking in self-respect, even if it was done by force. Aside from this, in every town of Eastern Galicia there were Jews who had the lust for power and wished to rule with a strong arm. In our town, the physician Dr. Yaakov Blumenthal was forged of the material of those who lust for power and authority, and had plans for powerful rule. That physician was a native of Bolechow, a fine man who was liked by all strata of the population on account his simplicity, popularity, and the assistance he gave to those in need. On the other hand, he was a polemicist who liked to stand up for his opinions. He liked to instill his fear upon the entire Jewish population of the town. Woe unto the person who would not give in to his opinion. It is clear that he could not tolerate that the Zionists ("the youths") would not dance to his tune, but rather attempted to break loose of his authority and support the Zionist candidate at the time that Dr. Blumenthal was campaigning for – Dr. Lewenstein, an assimilated Jew who was running against the Zionist Dr. Gershon Zipper. The Jews were not willing to publicly cross Dr. Blumenthal, whether out of awe and respect, or whether for fear that it might damage their livelihood. For Dr. Blumenthal ruled over the community even though he was not yet the head of the community, and he did not yet have much influence with the local Polish authorities and the regional governor in Dolina who was all-powerful.

Only one person was willing to publicly go against Dr. Blumenthal. That man was Lemel Meir – even though he was completely dependent on the good graces of the Polish authorities for his livelihood. Lemel campaigned for the candidate with all of his being and energy. It came to the point where Dr. Blumenthal slapped Lemel publicly. However, he was not subdued and did not give in. He continued to campaign for the aforementioned Dr. Gershon Zipper, for in a situation where there was a threat to national pride and the wellbeing of the Zionist movement, it is improper to retreat and to let the battle be won by the opponent.

I know of one more incident in which Lemel Meir did not toe the line, but rather went on his own path without paying attention to the opinion of the community.

The story is as follows. As time went on, he became a follower of Jabotinsky and drew near to the Revisionists in Bolechow, who were for the most part Zionists without any status in life and without any influence in communal affairs. They were also numerically inferior to the other movements. Lemel Meir was at one time the chairman of the local Zionist organization whose members were for the most part people of influence and status. Nevertheless, Lemel did not hesitate to leave the "Zion" organization that was respected by all strata of the people, and to join the Revisionists. Even though he was aging at the time, and concerns of livelihood and education of his children weighed heavily upon him, his enthusiasm and dedication to the Zionist movement in its Revisionist form were not dampened, for a Hassidic soul dwelled within him. Whoever did not see him during the Third Sabbath Meal (Shalosh Seudot) at the Kloiz never saw the sublimity of a soul. His enthusiasm remained with him even as he aged.

An eyewitness told me about an incident that typifies Lemel and his Hassidic soul. The story was as follows. One Sabbath Eve, the leader Jabotinsky was passing through Bolechow on the way to Stanislawow. Even though heavy rain fell that night, Lemel stood on the road for several hours on the street and waited for the arrival of Jabotinsky. When he saw him pass by in a car at the speed of lightning, Lemel declared, "Long live the king".

In summary, it is possible to state that the soul of the venerable Talmudic scholar Rabbi Akiva, who was one of the ten martyrs of the Roman government, was transmigrated and came to life again in the soul of these two Bolechowers. To be more precise, they split the legacy of Rabbi Akiva between themselves.

Yitzchak Hirsch of blessed memory was consumed was on fire with the love of Torah and cleaving to it. On the other hand, the heart of Lemel Meir was consumed with the fire of dedication to Zionism and communal affairs.

Yitzchak Hirsch sacrificed himself in the tents of Torah and Lemel Meir offered his economic wellbeing and the livelihood of his wife and children on the altar of the renaissance of our nation, despite the fact that he was dedicated and faithful to his wife and children, and that he was a man of intelligence and great talents and activity. I myself see the greatness of spirit of Lemel Meir of blessed memory, in that he remained faithful to the ideals of his youth even in his advancing age. This was at a time when he was almost the only one of his contemporaries who remained faithful to the Zionist ideal, for his former friends and co-idealists had turned away from their intoxication with Zionism as they became important people, with well established livelihoods and influence in the community. Furthermore, they trivialized any work that was not related to the earning of a livelihood. In short, they regarded as childish and infantile the dedicated effort of Lemel in the realms of Zionism and communal work, not for the purposes of monetary gain.

A person who works in communal affairs requires support and recognition, as air to breathe. Only few special people are able to labor for their ideal in an atmosphere of self-negation and scorn from their peers, the situation in which the communal activist finds himself.

The situation is sevenfold when the idealist does not find understanding of his situation in his own home, that is to say when the wife does not offer support to her husband. Lemel Meir merited a second time to have a proper Jewish woman, a widow with several children. However, to the best of my knowledge – I did not know his first wife – she was a simple, practical woman, and therefore, she was unable to understand the tendency of her husband toward activism. Not only did she not support him, but she also fought against him, as I have heard from reliable sources. From the vantage point of her weltanschauung, and as a Jewish mother whose first concern is the wellbeing of her children, she was indeed justified in battling against her husband's way of life, and one cannot place blame upon her.

This did Lemel live and struggle from the front and from the back, in the home and outside. His only source of contentment was that his eldest daughter Rivka, today married to a man of a good family, Mr. Kupfertzein, and the mother of two children, made aliya as a Chalutza (pioneer). She spent some time in an agricultural farm to prepare for her aliya. Her father got her in there with the assistance of Rachel Reis of Bolechow. This was a revolutionary thing in those days. After the aliya of his daughter, his son Yisrael and his stepdaughter Tzila also made aliya.

Lemel waited eagerly every day for the opportunity to make aliya. He would certainly have succeeded, for his daughter Rivka worked toward that end. However, in the interim, the Holocaust descended upon our people with its modern day Haman, may his name be blotted out. Lemel Meir perished in Bolechow with the rest of our people.

May his memory be blessed along with the memory of all of our brothers and sisters in all places, our town among them!

Lemel, the illustrious native of our town, did not merit to make aliya to the Land. However, his soul merited to be continued in his two grandchildren Yair and Chaim, the sons of Rivka, who dedicated their lives to fructifying the desolate places of our Land, places in which not only were the living conditions difficult, but mortal danger was lurking every day at all hours, since these places were near the border of our Arab enemies, who infiltrated into the land and perpetrated murder. The young grandson of Lemel, Chaim Kupfertzein, a twenty-year-old bachelor, was murdered in such an ambush within the past few weeks. He was brought to burial in a large funeral in Haifa, the city where his parents live.

May his soul be bound up with the souls of our brothers and sisters who gave their lives for the sanctity of our nation, our homeland and our State, and who labored to fructify the desolate areas of our Land.

[Yiddish page 246]

14. The Song of the Kigel (In the form and rhythm of Schiller's "The Song of the Bell" - A parody)
by N. Lotharinger and Shimon Elendman

Transcribing is forbidden!

* This song was originally published in 1910 in the publishing house of the author.

Jewish food am I, holy Sabbath and I, the Jewish cultivator am I.
The oven is already warmed
Simmering in the noodle pot
For each Sabbath and festival
A kigel is prepared.
The face is hot
Sweat must be wiped off
The kigel must be prepared well
Angels must roast it.

For the food that we prepare
A "cure" for the innards,
We must have good things
And therefore, we ask for the grace of G-d.
For every observant Jew
A good kigel is a good omen
And the young wife is proud
When the husband likes the kigel.
Secrets are embedded in the kigel
A Jewish wife must understand them well
She must know the secrets
That a kigel must contain.
Take the ingredients together
Honey, eggs, chicken fat and apples
The finest delicacies
Are placed into the noodle pot.
Get out the spoon quickly!
And mix the ingredients around!
So it won't get sticky
And the Sabbath won't be disrupted.

All that takes place
In the life in the world

That takes place to a Jew –
Is typified in the kigel.
As soon as the Jew is born
Before he opens his eyes
Once again, not in the lullaby –
The shochet sends kishke kigel.
He is barely out of the crib
He does not yet see his own qualities,
The belfer (cheder teacher's assistant) comes with the father
And takes the child to the cheder.
A dark room, cold and desolate;
The rebbe sighs, the rebbetzin coughs,
A puff, some smoke, dark melancholy,
And Jewish children learn Torah [12]
"Shoham" An'onikel [onyx], "Leshem" Turkois [opal]
"Tarshish" – a yachtshim [beryl], "Shevo" a tirpvais [agate],
"Achu" – gemoizetz [muck], Tzri – triaug [balsam]
"Nachala" an'orb [inheritance], "Negef" a plag [a plague].

Take the splinters, pat them down,
With the poker, quickly, hurry!
Turn the coals over well,
So the fire will not cool down!

Mix the kigel, mix
So it will remain fresh!
So it will be able to bake
And not burn in the oven.
He can barely speak any Hebrew
Yet he is chasing after the Chumash
It will be a joyous occasion –
And a kigel is prepared.
"When a woman conceives and gives birth to a male" [13]
Say it, shout it, dear lad!
Shouts the rebbe in anger
And Rashi explains it in common parlance.

The tefillin are on the forehead
He is already allowed to get married
He can go among people
Get an aliya, and participate in a mezuman [14].
He is already an important person
He can deliver an interpretation of the Torah with reasoning,
Ask a question on the Torah
And answer a question from the Gemara.

From the relatives and the neighbors
They send kigels – only the finest
For the darling, for the fine boy,
For the feast that is being made [15].

The kigel appears done
The oven is already sealed up
It is already becoming calm
Soon the table will be set.
Spread the table, spread!
It is already four o'clock!
Soon it will be the holy Sabbath
An angel is fluttering in the oven.

A fine lad, an important person.
The virgin bride, Miss Dvosha
She has much money and pedigree.
The shadchan [marriage broker] brings joy.

A Jew must get married
Move and turn about
Borrow and lend
Run and hurry
Fraternize and suffer
Bend and sway
Move tortuously and push his way through;
Toil and crawl along
Take oaths and serve
Seek a livelihood;
Smile and lick
Be satisfied and bleat –
And never complain
About the difficulties of being a Jew.

Jews must not prolong negotiations.
An agreement is prepared,
Get married, have children.
Hurray! Hurray! The groom is coming.

The Jew has a woman of valor
The finest strophe and the finest song
Sara, Rivka, Rachel, Leah
The finest portrait of a faithful wife.

Kigels of noodles and potatoes
For Sabbaths at all times

A chicken neck kigel for a change
One licks their fingers from them.

Thinking of the Jew's wandering life
Through the mirror of the dark exile
His opinions, his strivings,
Is it not a mixed up kigel?
Here stands a kigel with an appearance,
From which emanates a fine aroma
A fatty steam blows from it;
The heart is, however, unfortunately empty.

There stands a kigel pale and lean
From the outside it is plain ugly,
One laughs at it like some fool –
The heart is, however, sweet as sugar.

Another kigel well-known
It is not pale and not hard,
Without a face, without a color
It is not sweet and not strong.

Another kigel, well-known
Comes out of the land of exile:

It plays cards, and gathers leftovers
It betrays Jews – and drinks a toast.
Presently a Slav, presently a German
Here an Arab, there a Roman,
Tricking and deceiving the entire world
And selling its people for money.

Lay the cloth on the table,
And cover the holes well
The Sabbath has arrived here in the town
A Jew is already moving about with his streimel.
Lay the cloth, lay!
Finish up already!
Let there be no violation of the Sabbath
The shamash is already knocking, come to the synagogue.
The Sabbath is a day from G-d!
For his holy people, the Jews!
A secret lies within the Sabbath,
The Sabbath is a day of joy!
Alas, the city has no peace,
No unity, no respite,

And the "intelligent" group of leaders
Fight over the cream in the coffee.
About shochtim and rabbis,
Over Gabaim and judges,
Comes a struggle, a battle
And one doesn't rest, day and night.
The kloizes are packed
Thousands stream in.
Long peyos
They state their opinions
About the politics of the town
They clap "Shaaa" from the boards of the prayer leader's podium
Pure boards
Rating their words
About rabbis, mikva, shechita [ritual slaughter]
And not forgoing one coin
They continue to speak in the middle of the marketplace
The discuss, they strongly debate
About whether Getzel Berl
About whether Feivel Shmerel
Are fitting for greatness
To be a rabbi in the community.
Terribly, the Jew becomes angry
And he is prodded on by religion,
Terribly and indeed frighteningly
He delivers blows in the name of the Torah.
A slap, a swat
A smack, a blow [16]
A hand into the eye
A beating on the head.
"You fool, you idiot!
How did you get into this world?"
"You shegetz, you drunk!
I am the most important!!"
For many years it is not calm.
The regional offices are full
With complaints and libels
The community displays might
To the landowner, to the writer –
Even to the wives.
There is no conclusion, no end
In the town of Bolechow [17]

The oven is already opened,
The kigel looks so nice

It was a success, so magnificent
We will have a good Sabbath today!
Cut the kigel cut!
As with observant people!
Whomever does not want to eat kigel
Must forget about the Sabbath.

See how the kigel stands
– The "first' food of the world
It lags behind other food
And lies in a pit.
No air and no light
– From angry people, as is known –
In the oven of exile, oh so bad!
Most of the time, the kigel is burnt.
The whole week he runs and pursues,
The Jew has no joy in eating;
But on the Sabbath, what a joy!
When the kigel is placed on the table...
"This day is honored above all days" [18]
Sings the Jew with great feeling
"For on this day the Rock of the World rested"
Like a king on his throne.
After the kigel, after the meal,
Sleep overcomes every Jew

All worries are forgotten
He sleeps as a weary corpse.

The kigel has been eaten up
A dark bitterness falls upon the Jew
The spiritual feeling has departed
He quietly sings a sad song.
In the house it is lonely and dark,
Mother says from the corner,
"Elijah the prophet, in our house
The holy Sabbath has already departed.
All good things should come to us
Should be with us forever."
And Father, with a sad voice,
Sings, "He who differentiates between holy and secular".

After the Melave Malka [19], late at night
– It is dark, terribly wild –
The Jew lies, scheming, planning
Filled up with worries.

Suddenly, it is three o'clock
A lament, a shout,
Seething and sizzling is heard,
A fire has broken out.
A wind, a storm,
Clanging from the tower,
The sky is smoky
A great confusion.
Wives are shouting
Men running,
Drawing water,
Dragging bags.
Children complain
Oxes moo
And the flames rise high
Black smoke spews forth.
Glass shatters.
Thieves rob.
Feathers fly
Roofs glow
Voices wail
Bitter curses
Merchandise is carried out of the stores
Torahs from the Beis Midrashes
The sick from their beds,
Jews run to save.
People lie on the streets
Outside it is cold and wet.
A hunger, and a terrible need,
A town sends a bit of bread.
The entire town burnt down,
With children, with weakened hands,
Naked and barefoot, without a shirt,
Jews wander around in strange places.
Go Jew, go
Turn your head around, turn,
You know, you will not run for long
And carry the heavy burden.
Beaten in every limb
Dying as a Jew before his time
In his lonely, dismal grave
He lies far from his brethren.
He never lived and rejoiced,
Always only with pain and tribulations,

Must he already leave the world
And eat kigels in the Garden of Eden;
Made from the wild ox [20]
As large as the entire world;
There he eats, sings and laughs,
There, the Jew is a hero.
In heaven he is a king
He eats kigel all week;
Only there are Jews happy
Not bearing the yoke of the exile.

[Hebrew page 82]

15. From the History of the Blumenthal Family
by Engineer Arthur Blumenthal
Translated by Jerrold Landau

When Kaiser Franz Josef II annexed Galicia to the Hapsburg Monarchy, he sent teaching staff from Prague, the capital of Bohemia, to Galicia, including Bolechow among other cities.

His aim was that these educators would instill the love of Austria into the Jewish citizens who had been annexed to the state, and acculturate them.

My grandfather's grandfather, Victor Blumenthal, who served as a teacher in Prague, was sent to Bolechow in this delegation of teachers. Thus was he thrown into it.

Hc was complctcly assimilated. In the style of the gentiles of that time, he grew of plait of hair. IIe was nicknamed, "Victor with the Plait", "Victor mit dem Zopf".

His strange externals, he stood out from the customary manner of the town. Obviously, he attracted attention in our forsaken town.

With the passage of time, Victor realized that Jews of Bolechow were forged from a different material, and that they would not become assimilationists under any circumstances, for they were deeply routed in the tradition, values and culture of the people.

What would this lone Victor, the exception to the rule, do?

He slowly began to acculturate to them, until he married the daughter of Zif, a citizen of Bolechow.

I heard the following story from my grandfather of blessed memory about his wedding.   When the lovestricken lad came to Zif, the father of the girl, to ask his agreement to marry his daughter, he turned as a German speaking Czech Jew to the elder in the following language, "Ich freie um die Hand Ihrer Tochter freien.". (Translated from rhetorical German: "I request the hand of your daughter.") Furthermore, freuen means to "make happy" [21]. The future father-in-law of course did not understand the words of trembling Victor, and asked his daughter in Yiddish, "Vus freit er zich azoi epis?" ("What is he doing for happiness?")

Aside from his role in the school, after the passage of time, he was elected as mayor.

After his death, the school was founded once again by his grandson Shimon in partnership with Nechemia Landis.

Victor had one son named Yaakov, who in turn had six sons and two daughters. From his sons, only Shimon and Aharon remained in Bolechow. I do not know the fate of the rest of them, since they were scattered upon the face of the earth. His grandson Victor the second, my grandfather, was the son of Aharon. The grandchildren of Shimon were Herman and Shimon Blumenthal [22].

Editors's note: Herman Blumenthal lived in Bolechow in his youth. He was an active and vigilant Zionist, and he took part in the movement. Later he moved to Vienna, where he began to exhibit his literary talents.

The following is the list of items that he published: Der Herr der Karpaten; Das Volk des Ghettos; Polnische Juden-Geschichte; Die Abtrunnige; Gilgul, der Roman einer Seelenwanderung; Ahasver in Wien; Junglingsjahre; Der Weg der Jugend; Knabenalter; Der Weg zum Reichtum; Judische Sprichworter; Galizien; Das Ghettobuch.

My father who wrote these words is Dr. Yaakov Blumenthal of blessed memory. As an active student of the Zionist movement, he served as the city doctor when he finished his studies. He founded several charitable institutions, including the hospital, among others. He assimilated as time went on, and at the time of the parliamentary elections, he campaigned enthusiastically for the head of the assimilationist list (Dr. Lewenstein). As a token of thanks, he was chosen by the authorities as an advisor to the Kaiser. He served as the head of the community for many years.

Since he excelled in his traits of generosity and was a popular person, he was recognized and appreciated by young and old. He dealt well with people. He discretely supported the needy. In his latter years, he supported the Zionist movement and the Land. He visited the Land with his wife a few years before the outbreak of the Second World War. He was received very warmly by the natives of Bolechow in the Land. His enthusiasm was very great toward everything that took place in the Land. Like Rabbi Yehuda Halevi, he was blessed with the poetic spirit, and he sang, "Will I not be gracious to and kiss your stones, and the taste of your clods of earth is as sweet as honey to me".

[Yiddish page 251]

3. Love Letters from the Ghetto
by Shmuen Elendman
Translation from the Yiddish by Susannah R. Juni
These letters were published in several printed editions by H. M. Elendman.
The author perished as a martyr (*Kidesh Hashem*) in the year 1942 in
Bolekhov.

A. First Letter
From the author to the Khosn-Kale (bride and groom)

Dear *Khosn-Kale* (Bride and Groom),

I know how very much you're worrying , when you come home from the engagement and you need to write a *mazel-tov* letter. Particularly, the first letter from the groom to the bride and the bride to the groom – who burns so strong and the hearts flutter one to the other – are difficult for you.

The teacher who taught you *tashrak tsfe's* [code system] and *"grizlikh"* writing forgot to teach you about writing such letters. Usually you get the best town writers and for a *sheyne matbeye* (a nice sum of money) he writes the letters for you. In order that you should not need this anymore, I – who for many years have been the town *maskil* [representative of the Enlightenment Movement], and I already wrote a lot a lot of such letters, and the couples live *barukh hashem* (thank G-d) *besholem ubeshalve* (in peace and tranquility) (they even have fine children already) – we enjoy such various types of little letters, each person to express according to his walk of life and his fantasy.

There even exists already little books, which are called "Letter-Writer." But these are old fashioned; secondly not to the topic, but my letters are up to date and very much to the point.

I hope that the kindly bride and groom will buy this book for themselves, and then have great enjoyment and will only be thankful of me.

I wish luck to you and greet you, although we don't know each other.

From me your friend,

Sh. E.

B. Second Letter
(from an artisan to his fiancée - bride)

Oy vey my heart knocks in me like a hammer on the anvil when I take the pen in my hand, to write my first letter to you. Like the sparks which fly out from the piece of iron, my warm feelings fly to you.

[Yiddish page 252]

I beg you that you should write me a lot of letters, because I love you very much and I long for you. You're set into my heart with a lock, for which all the locksmiths from the entire world won't be able to make a key.

From me, your fiancé - groom, whose heart is welded and hammered together with your heart.

Zigmund

C. Third Letter
(Answer from the bride-to-be to the groom-to-be)

Dear Zigmund!

As soon as the mail carrier brought the letter (I recognized immediately that it's from you) so light and happy had my heart become. It seemed to me that the whole room danced. The mirror which hangs on the wall somehow began to shine differently, and the hanging lamp to sparkle like gold. Everything sparkled in my eyes. My heart became warm like a hot pressing iron, my head was spinning so happily like the wheel of the machine... A whole day was like a holiday to me and I wasn't able to work. The needle fell out of my hand and I couldn't anymore thread the needle...

At night I dreamed that the thread had stretched itself out somehow so long, to you, and it didn't even once get tangled... and you, so smilingly, rewound it from you to me... like a seam, which when one sews it through several times it can't rip out and when you press it well, it seems like one piece, thus am I pressed to you.

I send your sister Khane-Beyle very friendly greetings, and an extra greeting for Yenta Royze. I greet your brother Menashe-Chaskiel specially, a greeting for your friend Melekh Godil, who I don't know. When you see Shloyme-Mendl you should leave a greeting for my sake. My mother greets your mother a thousand times, my father greets your father heartily. You shouldn't forget to greet your little sister Pessele, my sister greets your whole family. My brother Shoyl [Saul] for his sake sends over an extra greeting!

From me, your bride-to-be, who greets you with her entire heart,

Roza

D. Fourth and Fifth Letters

[These letters appear to have been written to poke fun at "enlightened" (and therefore German speaking, or pretending to be so) Jews.]

Fourth letter

From a bookkeeper or a travelling sales representative (German)

Dear Bride,

Having just returned home from a business trip, it is with pleasure that I take this opportunity to convey my congratulations to you. I have given you credit in my heart. You have set my feelings going & my love for you is without any deficit. My heart is always at your disposal. On my next trip I'll make a detour to see you.

I am informing you at the same time that in connection with presents I have been in contact with jewelers in Cracow and I hope that my fruit order will be most attentively & promptly executed, whereupon you will be kind enough to confirm to me your receipt of it.

Awaiting an immediate reply.

Sincerely,
Your Josef

Fifth Letter

From a big city Miss to her bridegroom (German)

Dear Josef,

I am happily in receipt of your letter. I am happy that you, the "harnessed Pegasus", can still find time to delight me with your lovely letter.

Schiller says, "The tradesman has no time for love, art, or poetry." It is my good fortune that it is different with you. I love you as Julia [sic] loved Romeo, as Sappho loved Phaon, as Hero loved Leander. Goethe says, "Man cannot live without love anymore than a fish can live without water". Tshoke says, "Love warms a person like the sun in July." Sofer says, "Love is a mad steed, which one must be able to ride well. Otherwise it will hurl the rider into a pit."

Lessing says, "Love and kisses are mighty pleasures." **Kotzebue says, "Hunger and love are powerful urges."**

Yesterday I saw "Madam Butterfly" in the theater. It taught me how to love. I'm asking you also to go to the theater more often.

I have been invited to go to the Sonnenscheins on Sunday for a dance meeting. Three university graduates are to fetch me. What kind of dancing will that be, without you? I am thinking of not going.

Today I bought a pretty cloche hat with a real ostrich feather and a canary. My friends say that I look like the beautiful Helen when I wear it, but alas I haven't the shape.

I read all day long. I read and dream and think of you, for my heart belongs to you alone, all my heart, all of it.

Your Mina

E. Sixth Letter
(An old maid to her groom to be)
Dear dear Leon, my life!

I received your heartfelt letter and it simply delighted me. Dear Leon, my life! I beg you that you should write to me every day. Ay, you should see my trouseau that I decorated from scratch, you would have great pleasure. The small cushions look like two beautiful little ottomans.

You write me, my Leon-dear, that I should pamper myself, in order that I should look good; I obey you and I will always obey you, only you must also obey me; namely you shouldn't go in your overcoat unbuttoned like your nature is, and you should put on a warm-wool scarf in order that you should *khalile* (G-d forbid) not catch a cold and you should drink every morning skim milk.

Dear Leon-dear! You write me that you will buy a piece of bed linen at the fair; I write you that you should get a wide one. The covers for the pillows should be 1 meter 10 in length, the bed covrs 2 meters 10 in length, the feather bed 1 meter 20 wide and 2 meters long, the sleep sheets 2 meters 25 in length, the fabric should be flowered and striped. You should indeed buy 2 good blankets, double width. But you should really see to it they shouldn't fool you, you should haggle... you should watch out they shouldn't pull the suds over your eyes... I ask you Leon-dear, you should see to it to quickly finish this up. I've already finished my things a long time ago.

From me your bride-to-be, who hopes to quickly and soon to see you forever.

Rozalia Altfoter

F. Seventh Letter
A small-town maskl [member of the Haskale, Jewish enlightenment movement] writes a "love letter" to the mekhutin [the future daughter-in-law's father]

Loshn-koydesh [Hebrew] translated af ivri-taytsh [a word-for-word translation, in a second column of the Hebrew into Yiddish, from a traditional method of studying Torah by translating the words into Yiddish without trying to necessarily create Yiddish sentences. The text was laid out in the original Yizkor book in two columns – Hebrew first, on the right, and the Yiddish taytsh (literally meaning) on the left.

The hills and the valleys should bring peace, grace and endless blessings to my dearly beloved future father in-law, the generous and well-known wealthy man. Pinkhas Tzizoger is a shining light and his name is highly respected and glorified.

I cannot suppress inside of me my strong emotions and elation.

My senses and my entire being are swirling like many waterfalls.

Inside of me is melting a flame of love.

Hey, Hey! How good and pleasant it is to sit in the company of a man so highly respected.

One is fortunate to join such a family of good and honest people.

I prayed for such a man and I found one in a million.

I am an innocent and I do not know why I was chosen from among my contemporaries.

This is like a saying of the sages that water as it cleanses the face, it also beautifies.

I have only one wish: that my strong ties to this family will remain strong forever.

God in heaven should cheer these strong ties.

I thank him a thousand times for the gift of a watch and chain. This gift elevates me above my contemporaries.

The chain should bind us together and will symbolize our mutual love.

A hearty greeting to my future mother-in-law and the entire family and to the...

From your future son-in-law who loves you with his full heart.

> Yoel Shmuel, son of Khaim Zeev Tzveilikh.

G. Eighth Letter *)
(From a small-town *maskl* [adherent of the *Haskale* , Jewish Enlightenment movement], a philosophical love letter to his bride-to-be in Linsk [Lesko].)

My pre-established Serafina!

You to the substance-concept evolved in the through attributes to the categorical imperative substrata transendental love cosmologically through complex ideas to the practical postulate in my "I"-ness constellated through relation. Heraclitus and all the other Greek and Roman philosophers and the Talmud with Maimonedes and Mendelsohn agree, that love flows.

Love is a Physic Spirit

That Feeds the Gods

In Goethe's Faust love is an idealistic deduction of the material out of the being of the ego. My love for you is a priori and brings all the ganglias to [the point of] exponential vibration.

As the clasping through often repeats division trunk cells united, my spirit melds with your spirit, my gastrula with your gastrula, my *geyselitseln* [type of cell?] with your *geyselitseln* in infinity.

Es zent zikh nokh dem "ding an zikh"... It is itself after that "the thing in itself" [Kant]

Yours,

Emanuel

*) Over the deep meaning philosophy from the small-town maskl should the dear reader not vesholem khas [G-d forbid] not strain the head.

H. Ninth Letter *

Dear Bride-to-be!

I write you this letter from Tomsk, deep in Russia. The further I roam away from you, the more I long for you, all the more my love burns for you like a glowing fire. Even the big giant cold spells don't have enough strength *khas-vekhalile.*

[G-d forbid] to cool off. The whole day I sit in prison camp, I've forgotten everyone – Pan Feldfebl, the Pan Corporal, even the Major who used to connect with me. I've forgotten about the entire war and Efraim Yosel's little factory and everyone; only one thing lies deeply in my heart, in my mind. That is you, my dear bride.

And as for that report which was spread at home, that I eat and sleep here with a goye [non-Jewish woman] and live with her a gitn tog [all day] is a *shaker-gomer* [an absolute lie], a base lie told by a prisoner of war.

It's true that Yosel Zeigermacher [literally – watchmaker] does have some kind of a *shiksl* who brings him something and gives him a kiss in addition, but only Yosel can do this; he's not better at home; but as for me, what can't witch's tongues invent. In short, it's a *sheker-vkesev* [an utter falsehood], I have only love for you.

Hashem-yisborekh [G-d] should help the war to end and we should get married in peace and it should be good by us in spite of the evil tongues which invent hollow dream-fantasies about me.

I kiss you from the distance a hundred times, a hundred thousand kisses.

Yours,

Rachmiel Vermkroyt

I. Tenth Letter
(A widower to his bride-to-be, a young woman.)

My greatly loved, khosheve [respected] bride-to-be, Sosha life!

Firstly, I write to you that I am barukh *hashem* [thank G-d] healthy, and wish for myself the same to you, *omeyn sela* [so be it].

Secondly, I write to you that my heart is full of love and loyalty to you. I hope that it will be very good for you with me, you yourself won't wish for anything

better. I will hold you like gold in paper;   your children will hold you like a sister. Yet   what   will   the   children   matter   to   you? The   older girl will *bekorev* [soon] be married, they're proposing matches for my boy and the remaining children are very obedient and will go into fire for you.

Dear Sosha my life! I ask that you should not – should not listen to any gossip about me about previous stories... You are by me very loved and appreciated and important. It will be a great honor for you to be Rebbe Shmerl Gingold's wife, with great *nakhes* . We should grow old until 120 years.

I've had the rooms freshly painted, I've also bought new things for the household. I will also add a servant for you; you will come into all good things, already prepared.

From the 5,000 kronen that I'm sending you today you should buy what your heart desires. After the wedding, I will *yirtse-hashem* [G-d willing] set up half a house, because the whole house is in my name, not like you're heard. I'm writing a letter to your father that he should hurry up because the business [or economy] goes to the dogs, and I myself am becoming strongly plagued.

My dear crown! You should be happy and cheerful, you should pamper yourself, you come with G-d's help into good hands, you'll be satisfied with me.

Your *khosn* [husband to be] who waits already for the *gliklikhe sho* [the happy/lucky hour],

Smerl Gingold

J. Eleventh Letter
(A young divorcee to her husband-to-be, Reb Mendel Foyglmilkh, a widower from Podhajce [Podgaytsy])

[The following letter is filled with errors such as might be made by a Yiddish speaker attempting to write German, but who knew the language only imperfectly. I have indicated some of the errors the author has made; there are others which cannot be conveyed in translation.]

Eleventh letter

(A young divorcee to her fiancé Mr. Mendel Vogelmilch, a widower from Podhayetz.)

Dear Moritz,

I ask [sic] you that I am, thank God, in good health. I have looked at your letter with great pleasure but the present did not surprise me. I have already seen such a [she here uses a Yiddish word] presence [the wrong word and misspelled]. You indeed must know that I was truly fleeing to Vienna Prague Gratz to other big cities too [she uses no punctuation here] and that manners today ["heinte" instead of the correct "heute"] are not like they used to be, I thought ["gedenkt" instead of "gedacht"] to marry a cilivizied [sic] person who [Yiddish "vos" instead of German "der"] is not stingy when he wants luxury... For your first wife that was enough, but for a cilivized [sic] woman like me, who ["vos" again] has traveled half a world and has associated with half a world of people and cooked in various committees and popular kitchens, given help to poor humanity – this is a compromise. I have asked you to buy a suit ["Gostum" incorrectly written for "Kostüm"] with matching underwear ["Granitur" incorrectly written for "Garnitur"] and an interesting umbrella.

You should operate and furnish your home and buy yourself an intelligent hat and give support to ["stützen", perhaps written for "schneiden" = cut] your beard; otherwise I will not come. I would never have divorced my first husband if he had not been 'Thodox.

I also cannot understand your letter with holy-ark ["orn-kodesh", for "leshon-kodesh" = Hebrew, with "orn-kodesh" misspelled] words. They said you knew German perfectly, that you were also once in Vienna.

You pester me about my girlfriends who have studied with me and are [she writes "sünden" = sin for "sind" = are] all most cheerfully educated. You must indeed know [misspelled] that I am still just like a girl and college graduates invite me to dinners and to other things.

Yours, Bronislava

K. Twelfth Letter

(A *balebotisher* [a middle class man] war merchant bokher [young bachelor] to his *kale* [bride-to-be].)

Kale love!

I wish you and your father and the whole family a *mazl-tov* . The eternal should help that it should be in a *guter gliklikher sho* [good happy hour]. Our parents should have great *nakhes* [pride] from us and achieve *gdule* [glory/exultation] [i.e., should live to see the wedding]. They should accomplish these things.

The *nadn* [dowry] (in the Polish marks) my father wanted to form a Prague credit-institution but I stopped him from doing it; firstly that bank pays too small a percent and secondly, one can meanwhile until the wedding do a little business with the dowry with various *"skhoyres"* [commodities].

For example, I'm hearing from Lemberg [Lviv] that "turners" are blazing, "colts" are jumping, "tin/ sheet metal" is banging, and "mortor " is shooting upwards... or even German green and red marks, or true German-Austrian, stamped and unstamped, or even Czechoslovakian, Yugoslavian, Bohemian, Hungarian and Rumanian, all of the stamped and unstamped and everyone can earn a pretty penny.

Reb Moyshele Goldreich advises me of all things to buy a little *"tsarski"*, *"dumski", kerenski", seminski"* , really, even a little *grivnes, karbavontses*, or *denikintsis* ; that fool thinks that I will do what he says. My own preference would be to buy a little American or Canadian dollars or actually shillings or *Lea'* [?] and with that I hope *im yirtse hashem* [G-d willing] to earn a lot.

I already know how we will *yirtse-hashem* [G-d willing] have the business. After the Russian retreat, Schmerl Kutsermacher had a stone building [house] built for himself with 2 storefronts. I *shmuest* [schmoozed] with him and he answered me that he won't rent it out to anyone else. The house will be finished between the *yomim-neroyim* [Days of Awe, days between Rosh Hashonah and Yom Kippur] and our wedding won't be until *shabos-brevshish* [Sabbath after Simchas Torah]. So, the business won't need to stand empty for long.

I greet you and your dear father lovingly.

Your *khosn* (husband-to-be),

Yisocher Honikvax

[Hebrew page 84 & Yiddish page 261]

16. Personalities and Events [23]
by Manes Weisbard
Translated by Jerrold Landau

Editor's note (only appearing in Yiddish section on Page 261)

The name of this Gabaila was Hershele Wohl. He was named thus as he stemmed from the family of Shaul Wohl, who was King of Poland for one day. He was called Gabaila because in truth, he served for a long time as the Gabbai of the Russian Rabbi Padwa of holy blessed memory. Aside from being the newspaper distributor, he served as the shamash of the Zionist organization during the time of the Zionist movement. He used to serve a buffet there, ensure that there was a minyan, and often served as prayer leader on Sabbaths and festivals.

Light is Sown for the Righteous (Or Zarua Latzadik) [24]

As was his custom each year, one Sabbath during the years of the First World War, the Rebbe of Gliniany (Glyn) visited the large Kloiz. On the Sabbath eve near sunset, the Rebbe and his entourage prepared to greet the Sabbath Queen. They had already completed the Mincha service, and the Rebbe started chanting "Lechu Neranena" is his clear voice. He finished the first Psalm of the Kabbalat Shabbat service, "Arbaim Shana Akut Bedor...". He also finished the Psalm "Shiru Lashem Shir Chadash", and concluded it with "Yishpot tevel betzedek veahim beemunato".

The congregation commenced the next Psalm, "Hashem malach tagel haaretz". As the Rebbe neared the end of that Psalm, he succeeded in saying "Or Zarua Latzadik", and then slumped to the ground and died.

Everyone, old and young, indeed believed, "Light is sown for the righteous".

A. Kanfas

Thus would a child count in Bolechow: one, two, three, four, five... to ten. Twenty, thirty, forty, fifty... to one hundred. Two hundred, five hundred, one thousand, a million, and kanfas.

Kanfas was the largest number we could imagine. From where did we get this idea? We used to hear from our elders that so and so gave a dowry to his daughter of "Kan Reinesh" (300 Crowns). We understood that this was a jar filled with Reinishes. If this jar "Kan" is many, then a kanfas (a jar and a barrel) is that much greater. This was how did we invented this strange number.

Editor's note: In the "Yada Em" group, the explanation is that the aforementioned kan is 150 measures of pure gold.

B. Appetizers
(From Avrahamche Strassman of blessed memory)

A miser died – thus said Avrahamche Strassman – when his mouth was filled with appetizers. As long as he was healthy, and requested that the work from the wealthy people in town, they would push him aside with a straw, adding the known adage "A Jewish worker". Having no other recourse, he was forced to go from door to door requesting donations. Then they would reprove him: "What? Are you too ill to work?"

However, when he was lying on his sickbed, righteous women would come to him with desserts and beg of him to taste something, for it "revives souls". However, at that time, the sick man was preparing for the way of all flesh, and he did not pay attention to their entreaties. Having no other option, the women forcefully opened his mouth and fed him the appetizers and desserts that he had brought – and thus did he breathe out his soul.

C. Advice
(From my brother Avraham Meir of blessed memory)

When Dvora Hirsch came to my brother's house in order to take leave of him before she made aliya to the Land, he told her a story about the meeting of two wagon drivers who had not seen each other for many years.

They asked about each other's wellbeing – and both complained about their bitter lot and the backbreaking work. Before taking leave, they entered a tavern, and over a glass of drink, they wished each other health and a long life, and added: "Would it be that we would already stop working". "And to you" – my brother finished his story – "I wish you that you should go up to the Land and start working there."

D. Abale

Three times a day, morning, noon and evening, he would leave his home with a running gait and go through the Rynek toward the Magistrate, proclaiming, "I do not want to be a Kaiser, a king, a president, a vice president, a regional head, a Starosta, a mayor or a communal leader. I want just to be Abale and nothing more."

E. Gabaila

I did not know his name, and I was never able to find out why they called him Gabaila. He was short, thin, with a wispy beard, and wore boots in the summer and winter. He was the sole representative in town of the Reuters, Fett, Jutte, and other agencies.

Every day, he would go to the train station with slow, deliberate steps, with a leather satchel hanging from his front like Laiganarsky the mailman, in order to receive the newspapers and distribute them to the residents of Bolechow. We waited impatiently for him every day, for we were curious to hear and read the news, and in those days only a few people had radios.

His customers were divided into four groups. The first group paid him in advance, and added his travel fees. To them, he delivered the newspapers to their homes. The second group consisted of those who came to his store that was located in his home near the small bridge. They bought the newspaper from him each day, and on the Sabbath they received it as an inclusion [25]. The people of the third category had to pay him even on the Sabbaths. To the fourth group, non-regular customers, he did not want to sell a newspaper at all. He claimed that they should request it directly from the editor.

Once, an elderly German from the German Settlement came to him and asked to purchase a German newspaper. He found an old newspaper that described the German attacks on France in 1915. The German read what was written and began to angrily curse: "Donnerwetter - die fangen schon wieder an" ("Thunder weather - they are starting again").

F. Foregoing
(From my mother Rivka Leah of blessed memory)

My mother would say that there were three things she was willing to forego without hesitation:

1. Wealth after a fire.

2. Regaining health after a difficult illness.

3. Having a successful match for the second time.

G. A Wife of another Man

We started to study Gemara with Reb Eli Berel Boshes. His stringent face judged frivolity harshly. We did not act up in front of him, for his facial expression made it clear that seriousness was in order.

His seat in the kloiz was near the door. He did not feel himself deprived on account of this. On the contrary, he was someone who respected his place. On Simchat, he was honored with the "Ozer Dalim" Hakafa [26] – whether he requested this himself, or whether it was given to him as being suitable for his position. On occasion, he told a joke, but even then, a smile did not come across his face.

When we came to the segment in the prayers "And say to them, make fringes", and we kissed the Tzitzit (fringes) of his tallis, he did not stop us. However, after the prayers, he told us, "He who kisses his friend's tallis is as if he has kissed the wife of another man".

Now, we are permitted to reveal it. We tried not to touch his tzitzit to the point where we almost passed over this mitzvah – not because of fear of being involved with someone's wife, but we were not so brazen as to do this publicly in a holy place.

Translator's Footnotes

1. The fried fat skin of a duck or goose.

2. Chometz is the term for leavened products forbidden on Passover.

3. A reference to the soup that Jacob served to Esau.

4. A play on words, for "bread of affliction", can also be rendered "bread of poverty".

5. The word here is Mitzrayim Gasse, which would mean Egypt Street – although it sounds unlikely that there would have been a street by that name.

6. Perhaps shoemats.

7. A halachic procedure whereby vessels are passed through boiling water or fire (depending on the vessel and the circumstance of use) to render them Kosher for Passover. (In Hebrew, batlan.)

8. The New Moon of the month of Nissan, two weeks before Passover.

9. Bnot Tzion means Daughters of Zion.

10. As a Mitzvah, this refers to Torah study. The adage here is used more generally.

11. I suspect that there is a double entendre hear, as Ma Yafit literally means "How fine" – and could here have the connotation of "Fine and dandy".

12. The following words are various words from the Torah, with Yiddish renditions, as would be taught in cheder. I included the English translations in square brackets. The first four words are the names of four of the twelve stones on the breastplate of the High Priest.

13. A verse from Leviticus.

14. A mezuman is the call to recite grace, which must be recited only in the presence of at least 3 males over the age of Bar Mitzvah. I suspect that the reference to marriage here refers to the theoretical fact that a boy of Bar Mitzvah age can get married (and very young marriages did take place amongst European Jewry on occasion).

15. A reference to the Bar Mitzvah feast.

16. The next two lines contain four other synonyms which I omitted.

17. Spelled here as Bolechof.

18. From a Sabbath table hymn.

19. Post Sabbath meal.

20. The "wild ox" is a mystical creature (along with the Leviathan), which, in Jewish lore, is on the menu for a feast for the righteous in the Garden of Eden.

21. This is a play on words of a word in the sentence.

22. Note, there seems to be an extra generation here. At the outset, it was stated that Victor Blumenthal was the author's grandfather's grandfather. From this paragraph, it seems that he is the author's grandfather's great-grandfather.

23. The Hebrew and Yiddish sections are equivalent, although there are some discrepancies in order of the subsections. The Yiddish section also has an editors note on the Gabaila section that is not in the Hebrew.

24. A verse from Psalms, forming part of the Kabbalat Shabbat (Welcoming of the Sabbath) service. The next few lines contain other verses of the Kabbalat Shabbat service.

25. No business would be transacted on the Sabbath. The Saturday paper was given free to those who paid for their newspapers during the week.

26. Hakafot (singular Hakafa) are the seven circuits made around the synagogue with the Torah scrolls on Simchat Torah. Ozer Dalim (literally, He who helps the poor) is the segment of the hymn recited during the sixth Hakafa.

[Hebrew page 86 & Yiddish page 264]

17. Memories of My Childhood Years
by Isser Eshel-Ichel
Translation from the Hebrew by Jerrold Landau

A. The Thin Meilech

If there ever was a lean, thin, emaciated Jew, it was Meilechl.

This thin Meilechl was a tailor with the relatives of Yeshaya Leib Gertner. He frequented our home. He would especially visit us in the winter to snatch a conversation with my father about some topic or another. On the evenings of Chanukah, he would join us for the eating of grieven (cracklings) that was left over from Passover.

It was warm in the house even though there was a snowstorm outside. Probably, a "gentile" hung himself in the forest. When it came time for Meilechl to go home, my father, who loved jokes, would innocently say to him: "Meilechl, do not forget to put heavy stones in your pockets, for there is a storm outside."

Those in the house, including Meilechl, would burst out in hearty laughter.

[Hebrew page 87]

B. Wolf Diengott's "Heder"

Wolf Diengott was a *Cohen*. He was bad-tempered, quick to anger, and grumpy. When his wife Sprintza would irritate and vex him, complaining and grumbling, Rebbe Wolf would stuff his fist into his mouth, chew it, get all red in the face, and shout in Yiddish:

"Don't provoke me Shprintza, because anger is idol worship."

She would answer. *"Never mind. Idols, shmidols, just stop chewing your fist."*

And when the quarrel began the lessons stopped, and we little folk would break outside with joy, running around, moving mountains, and playing until the storm blew over.

C. The Cheder of Yosel Kahut

In the cheder of Yosel Kahut, if a boy misbehaved, played a trick, or hit someone, the custom was to punish him.

What was this punishment? They would flip his coat to the left, put something on his back to make it look hunched, turn his hat inside out, and put a feather on his head and a broom in his hand. His face would be covered with soot, and he would be made to sit on the oven for an hour or two.

This did the poor misbehaving boy expiate his serious crime.

D. Hurray, I Started to Study Chumash

In memory of my father Daniel and my mother Reizel Rachel of blessed memory

I studied in the Cheder of "Shlomo Haszower". When I reached the age of four, the Rebbe began to prepare me for the awaited day when I would start to study Chumash.

In addition to the first section of the book of Vayikra (Leviticus) that I studied with all of it commentaries, I also had to prepare a "discussion" off by heart, and tell it over in my parents' home on the Sabbath after the sweet afternoon nap. As was customary in those days, this was a "discourse" that was appropriate for a four-year-old boy who was starting to study Chumash.

I wish now to tell you about this "discussion".

In the afternoon, the students of Shlomo Haszower's cheder gathered in his home, wearing festive clothes, along with the belfer (the cheder assistant). I, the honoree of the party, appeared wearing a chain and my father's watch. We walked in pairs through the marketplace (Rynek) to my parents' home. The house was filled with relatives, neighbors and friends who had come to hear my "discussion" of the first chapter of Vayikra.

The "discourse" took the form of a series of questions and answer. The rabbi asked, and I answered, sitting on a high chair.

"Come to me, oh young child!"

"I am not a young child, I am already a fine youth!"

"If you are already a fine youth, what have you succeeded in learning?"

"Chumash!"

"What does Chumash mean?"

"Five."

"What? Five bagels for a 'greitzer' (a type of coin)?"

"No, five holy books of our holy Torah."

"Bereshit, Shmot, Vayikra, Bamidbar, Devorim" (twirling my thumb around).

"And which are you learning?"

"This" (I showed my middle finger).

"What? You are learning about your middle finger?"

"No! I am learning the third book of our holy Torah."

"What is it called?"

"Vayikra!"

"What is the meaning of Vayikra?"

"He called."

"Who called? Did mother call father? Perhaps the Shamash (beadle) called the Jewish community to come to the synagogue?"

"No! Vayikra – he called. Hashem – G-d. El – to, Moshe – to someone whose name was Moshe. Leemor – saying as follows. Daber – tell. El – to, Bnei – the children. Yisrael – the Jews…"

Thus did I continue to read the entire first chapter, as the people around melted with contentment [1].

When the "discourse" concluded, the Belfer (assistant) and a family member stood at the door, and every child who left received a bag of goodies. The children spread through the city, running with joy. Then the gathered guests sat down with the Rebbe to enjoy food and drink, as we celebrated the event with great importance and with an exalted spirit – that four year old Isser started to study Chumash at a propitious time, and became attached to the yoke of Torah.

[Hebrew page 88]

18. My Town Bolechow
by Yocheved Vinitzky (Eva Altman)
Translation from the Hebrew by Jerrold Landau

If the bonds of love and longing for the landscape of one's hometown, enveloped with a radiant bright halo, winking from the foggy past, are so powerful – then the soulful longing and anguish in the recesses of the heart is sevenfold greater regarding the memory of a hometown that has vanished and is no more; and seventy-seven fold for the memory of our dear Bolechow, a significant Jewish city, which went – with its elders, women, and children – to the fiery furnaces and the great streams of blood, through which six million of our brothers and sisters traversed, may G-d avenge their blood.

At the time that I pick up the pen to write my memories, my heart is perplexed and my emotions are stormy as I asked myself, not about what to write, but about what not to write. For there is a great deal about which to write regarding this city – but the couch is too small to spread out.

Should I write about its wonderful Jews, Torah scholars, and businessmen, who continued to weave the tradition in the mire of the exile?

Should I write of its wonderful youth, particularly of the dear youth that were close to my heart – those of the Betar group of Bolechow, about its faithful activities and events that were conducted on the stormy winter nights of the harsh and bitter exile, with golden dreams of a Jewish state, of a great future for our people – they dreamed and did not merit in witnessing the realization of their dreams, for they went on their final eternal journey with the song of "Ani Maamin" on their lips, as a sort of self-eulogy, with the splendor of faith and belief in the eternity of their people fluttering before their eyes?

Behold, they pass before my eyes as if in a play, a long, variegated procession. With whom shall I start? Whom shall I pass over? I will only bring forth a few sparks from that great flame, warm and bright, that was – and has been extinguished.

A. The Rebbe

Our town had its own Rebbe, Rabbi Shlomo Perlow may G-d avenge his death, the scion of holy forbears. His image comes before my eyes from the fog of childhood. He was great in Torah (he wrote a commentary on Psalms). His Hassidim streamed to him from afar to benefit from his Torah and splendorous wisdom. People would come to him primarily on the High Holy Days. We would then close our home in the village of Przebrodz and travel to Bolechow in order to worship with the Rebbe on the holy days. The Rebbe himself would conduct the services, and his sweet voice would attract the hearts. Through his words to his Hassidim, he succeeded in encouraging them and instilling in them a spirit of faith and belief despite the difficult life that pervaded in the towns of Galicia. His heart was open to listen to their worries and to advise them about all of their concerns. My father of blessed memory, Reb David Wechsler, was one of his enthusiastic Hassidim, and a frequent visitor to his court.

He did not abandon his flock until the end. He accompanied them on their final earthly journey – until the end. He was tortured to death by the Nazi enemies, and returned his soul to his G-d.

May G-d avenge his blood!

B. The Betar Group

Behold, the images of male and female friends float before my eyes – participating in the great dream of a free Zion that would unite the sons and daughters of all groups and strata – from the wealthy homes and the houses of the poor, in accordance with the words of the song: "With us is the worker, burgher, and farmer, attracted to the common front."

The group on "The Road of the Shoemakers" was small and discrete – but at night it turned into an enchanted palace that contained everything – vision, scenery, imagination, and youthful enthusiasm. Hebrew classes were interspersed with study of the homeland, episodes in the history of Zionism with lessons in training practice. On top of everything – there was a Hachsharah farm [2], which was a required hallway to the salon of the homeland. Few were they who merited to pass through the hallway and enter the salon. They partook of the bitter lot of Polish Jewry, of whose salvation they had dreamt all of their life, and those who did merit – died the death of the brave with weapons in the hand, in forests, fighting the Nazi enemy, avenging their children, and there were many victims.

Betar.

Betar.

C. Among the Wolf-like Men

Our family tasted the taste of being the lone Jewish family in a village of Ukrainian gentiles. Father owned the only store in the town, from which we earned our income. I will never forget that frightful night, at midnight, when there was a sound of the knock on the door.

"Who is there?" asked my father.

When father opened the door, he was immediately stabbed in the face and started bleeding. Twelve masked hooligans burst into the house. Some of them stood guard over myself, my mother, and the maid, with revolvers pointed to our heads. "If you open your mouths – your blood is upon your head", they said, as their friends emptied the house of money, jewelry, etc. I attempted to jump out of the window to call for help, but they grabbed me and beat me over the face. "One more such attempt and we will kill you!" they said. After they finished their job, they threatened, "If you take one step, we will kill you. We will be guarding outside."

The police searched and investigated for two weeks until it found the head of the band of thieves, who refused to reveal the names of his accomplices in crime.

"Wait, wait", he threatened father after he was sentenced to five years in jail, "I will get out of jail and settle accounts with you!"

He was not able to settle accounts. I made aliya to the Land two years after that, and brought my parents three years later.

However, the gentiles "settled" the "accounts" with the rest of our family – my sister, and all of my relatives, friends and acquaintances, who ascended heavenward in fire.

May their souls be bound up in the bonds of the holy and brave, who through their deaths bequeathed to us life and the assurance of the life of honor for coming generations.

[Hebrew page 91]

19. The Wedding of Rabbi Perlow's Daughter
by Dvora Ichel-Adler, Kvutzat Kiryat-Anavim
Translation from the Hebrew by Jerrold Landau

More than a quarter of a century has passed since the celebration of the wedding of Rabbi Perlow's daughter took place in Bolechow.

Obviously, this long period of time has gnawed at my memory, but I will nevertheless attempt to describe briefly my personal experience, and the general impression that this event left upon the population in our town.

The "wedding week" began on Thursday. Festivity and a spirit of joy rested on Bolechow and enveloped everything.

That day, the groom arrived from Warsaw. Young and old – also non-Jews including the policeman Jerzy Bilinski, streamed to the railway station to greet him.

Bahn Gasse (the street leading to the railway station) was bustling with a crowd of people.

Some by train, some on foot, some dressed up, crowds streamed to the railway station. The landscape of the street changed. Everyone wanted to see the groom's family who arrived from Warsaw and from various cities and towns. The whole community of Hassidim of our Rebbe arrived in a special train car. Various types of personalities were among the arrivals – rabbis, children of rabbis of previous generations, some wearing kolpacks and some wearing barzulkes, all in fancy clothes with their faces exuding nobility. Everything exuded honor and glory. All around, there was a sublime spirit. Here and there, there were the peaked caps that typified the Jews of Congress Poland.

With great feeling and extra pomp, accompanied by music, the crowd of relatives led the groom to the house of the Rebbe.

The many guests were accommodated in the houses of the Hassidim, friends and neighbors of the rabbi. A large "shalas" [3] was built in the courtyard of the Rebbe, and nobody said that there was not enough room.

For an entire week, the onlookers experienced joy, pleasant melodies, dancing, and food provided by butchers and served by waiters.

The wedding ceremony took place in the courtyard of the Rebbe during the day on Friday, accompanied by musicians. Echoes of the sounds of joy, mirth and glee reverberated through the town: "The sound of joy and gladness, the voice of the bride and the groom" [4].

Bolechow, could you have imagined that you would no longer exist on the face of the earth? Indeed, did you preserve anything from the proper hour of joy and gladness? For when the satanic Holocaust arrived, full of agony and suffering, you added a drop to the sea of blood and tears.

You did not lead your sons and daughters to the wedding canopy.

[Hebrew page 92 & Yiddish page 267]

20. The Kapliczka Church
by Sima Pohoriles (Shindler) [5]
Translation from the Hebrew by Jerrold Landau

On the route to Stryj, in the forest to the left, was the church. Grandfather told me thus: A Jewish woman once was coming home on the eve of the Sabbath. The sun was setting, and it would be too late for candle lighting. What did the woman do? She took two candles, lit them, and continued on her way.

A farmer and his son stood from afar and saw the lit candles. They quickly distanced themselves from the place. They told the farmers that they had seen the "Holy Mother" from afar, with the two burning candles. The rumor took on wings and spread. The farmer and his son were brought to Stryj to be interrogated.

The Jews were silent.

The place was sanctified in the eyes of the gentiles.

Epilogue: When pilgrims came and went to the monastery, they would turn to this church to draw water from the holy spring beside it.

[Yiddish page 267]

21. The Wedding at the Russian Rebbe's
by Dvora Ichel-Adler of Kiryat Anavim [6]

A full quarter of a century has passed since our rabbi, Rabbi Shomo Perlov, married off his daughter. Obviously, the long time that elapsed has blurred my memory. Nevertheless, I wish to write about it, for the wedding was an important event for the entire town, as well as for myself in particular.

On Thursday, the groom and his relatives arrived from Warsaw in a special carriage. Young and old, children and adults, even non-Jews such as the policeman Jerzy Bilinski, streamed en masse to the train station to greet the groom. Dressed in festive garb, some by foot, some by wagon, with the appearance of a Cossack [7], like a wave rolling down the mountain – thus did the people crowd in to the railroad station. The train is arriving!

"Fine Jews" in Reszvelkes, kapotes, kolpacks, "silken youth", rabbis from the previous generation, with the appearance of spiritual aristocracy beaming from their faces, The town took on the ambience of the "extra soul" [8]. The joyous mass of thousands of people from Warsaw and other places accompanied the groom to the Rebbe's house with song, dance and musical instruments.

The Rebbe's Hassidim, neighbors and acquaintances provided accommodations for the guests. A large shalas (tent or canopy) was built in the courtyard of the Rebbe, so that nobody would be lacking space. The ceremonies continued for an entire week. Each day, Hassidim from a different city celebrated the wedding [9]. The Jews of Bolechow had a great deal of pleasure watching all the customs, and, above all, fulfilling the commandment of gladdening the bride and groom.

Bolechow, did you imagine that you would not exist for much longer?

Bolechow my town, did you know that the cruel executioners would turn you into a heap of rubble?

Yes, my town, your daughters, sons and grandchildren were to have no more weddings.

Your drop was added into the sea of tears and blood.

[Hebrew page 93 & Yiddish page 268]

22. My Path to Zionism
by Meir Gottesman
Translation from the Hebrew by Jerrold Landau

During my early youth, when the Zionist youth was still in its early development, it was considered "non-kosher" by the orthodox zealots.

In those days, a Zionist was considered as a "transgressor" in their eyes. In their opinion, it was forbidden to precipitate the end by actual deeds. We were obligated to await the coming of the Messiah, and nothing further.

From this perspective, Dr. Herzl of blessed memory was a thorn in their eyes. Their fundamental principle was, "If G-d does not build a house, the workers toil in vain" [10].

My father of blessed memory forbade me all contact with the "transgressors". Day and night, he warned me not to enter into their confidence, for I might fall into "bad company".

I recall that during the times of the elections to the Austrian parliament, Zionist activists approached my father to my father to urge him to vote for Dr. Zipper. Of course, their efforts were in vain.

The Zionist "Maccabee" movement headquarters was across from my parents' house. Once, as I was playing with children, I approached the door of Maccabee. My father saw this and beat me soundly in his burning anger, as he threatened me, "I will starve you and expel you from my home if I catch you in your transgression a second time."

This was the prime factor that kept me from joining the Zionists, and attracted me like a charm to the ranks of the "apikorsim" [11].

As I got older, I would secretly enter Maccabee, and I became a member at the time of the Balfour Declaration [12].

From that time, I donated to the Jewish National Fund, purchased the shekel [13], and participated in the festive gatherings that were arranged by the Zionists in my town.

[Hebrew page 93 & Yiddish page 269]

23. Memories from my Childhood (5693/1933)

by Ada Machvov-Berger
Translation from the Hebrew by Jerrold Landau

When I was five years old, my mother took me and said, "Come my daughter, the time has come to go to school". She led me to the house of Freda Brenner on Kilinskaga Street, near my house.

The orphanage (Ochronka).

A meeting with Fishel Werber.

Ochronka

That house was once a grocery store. Its windows were broken, and a pillow had been placed in one of the windows to prevent the harsh cold from entering.

As I entered the cheder, I was met by a gaze of pity and surprise. This was my first teacher, Rachel Reiss, now Hendel.

My mother of blessed memory pleaded with her to allow me to stay, not as a student, but rather just to remain in the class. She refused, and said, "She is still too young, and I have no room for girls of her age." To my ill luck, there was no kindergarten then.

Mother sighed bitterly and left, but I remained within the walls of the cheder. A desire was awakened within my heart to remain there no matter what. The picture book in the teacher's hands, which she raised up to show the class, attracted me. I was the only one who put up my hand to answer the questions. When the teacher saw this, she immediately agreed to accept me.

However, my joy was not for long, for the shelter was moved to Ruski-Bolechow near Yankele Mapes, far from my house. I often rolled along the slippery road that was covered with ice. When I reached the shelter, I put wood onto the fire, for the school had no janitor. The wood, which was provided by the "leader" of the city, Yeshaya Gripel, heated the cheder.

There was no parents' committee. The overseer of the institution, Eli Elendman, concerned himself with everything, as a father to his home. He distributed tasks to the grown girls. The teacher was Rachel Reiss, the gym teacher was Chaika Halperin, the music teacher was Hinda Delman. Eli also concerned himself with providing food and clothing to the needy children, and even toys and recreational items.

We once performed "Tofilei Totorito" in the Sokol auditorium. The performance was crowned with success, and the income was donated to the benefit of the public kitchen. The women of Bolechow would work in that kitchen on a voluntary basis. They cooked, served the food, etc.

The first kitchen was opened on Wiziltir Street. After words of dedication and speeches, the children were given their first meal, rice and milk.

[Yiddish page 271]

24. From the Kloiz to Israel
by Yosef Tishenkel
Translation from the Hebrew by Jerrold Landau

The Chevra Tehillim Kloiz was on the road to Ruski Bolechow.

The house belonged to a Bolechow family in Vienna, David and Beila Wohl.

For many years, the prime activists and gabbaim were Itzikl Weilgot (the rope maker) and Baruch Rotter, who was also the gabbai of the Meir Baal Haness charity boxes. Itzikl made his way to the Eretz Yisrael. His sister settled in Cairo and used to visit Bolechow. She was referred to as "The Egyptian".

There in the kloiz, I along with a few cheder and schoolboys often discussed forming a youth organization, so that we would not become like the adults of the kloiz.

Over a game of dominoes at the home of my friend Yitzchak Wolf, we decided to found a Zionist youth group. We asked our parents for a bit of money, and we rented an attic room from Chaim Beriche.

We collected from among the members a half-broken table, a 2-½ foot long bench, and a few pictures for the wall.

A short time later, we invited two veteran Zionists who took interest in us, Mrs. Itta Krebs (Shalom Reisler's daughter) and Getzel Weisbard (Izi Prive's son) to talk to us.

In his first lecture Mr. Weisbard clarified to us what we should be striving for. Then Mrs. Krebs discussed with us some educational problems in our plans to promote aliya to the Eretz Yisrael.

Following their suggestion, we began to call ourselves by the name Tzeirei Zion (Zion Young).

We invited many young people to our meetings and discussions, including those who already belonged to Hashomer Hatzair. A youth by the name of Shlomele Weitzner gave much of his free time to us. Unfortunately, he suddenly became ill with dysentery, and died young.

We continued our work with sadness and pain. The number of members grew. We invited various older members to conduct activities and discussions. We also began to study Hebrew.

In a discussion with the Hebrew teachers Rachel Reiss and Tova Elendman, they suggested that we change our name to Hechalutz Hatzair.

We were no longer able to remain in the small, cramped attic room. In order to be able to rent a larger place, a few of our members decided to work in a tannery a few days a week. We were able to pay our rent and expenses from the proceeds.

We then got in touch with the central Hechalutz headquarters in Lemberg (Lwow). Then, we all registered with them. We visited a member of the central organization, who gave us directions regarding the upcoming work.

A little later, we founded a committee called Ezra Lemaan Hechalutz (Assistance for the Pioneers), which took part in the activities of the Keren Kayemet (Jewish National Fund) committee, in the Eretz Yisrael Workers' League, and the like. The Hechalutz headquarters demanded that each of us learn a trade, so that we would be productive participants in the upbuilding of the Land when we arrive there.

The Hechalutz movement developed well. Its members went to Hachshara (activities for preparation to aliya). Among them were the member Yitzchak Wolf, who unfortunately died young with his goal unrealized.

Hitachdut-Gordonia.

A group of Chalutzim.

The Union of the Hitachdut and Poalei Zion groups.

Hitachdut-Gordonia

The dedicated chalutz Shimon Tennenbaum, who worked day and night for the benefit of the public despite his poor state of health, also died suddenly.

We will always recall their dedication. May their souls be bound in the bonds of eternal life.

A while later, chalutzim from other cities began to come to our city for Hachshara. They were employed for the most part in the ale factory of the Meisels family. The local Zionist organization supported them with credit, etc.

The member Moshe Hausman (Eshel) was very active in educational and cultural activities of the youth movement. He never declined to become involved in any responsible, public work. He set up educational courses and interceded with the masters of the studying youth that they be freed from their work one hour earlier so that they would be able to participate in the evening courses.

At the same time, a Chalutz group made aliya.

Gordonia was one branch of the youth movement. Its chief activist was Feivel Schindler.

Government politics led to persecutions and a critical material situation. It was with great difficulty that we raised the funds needed to pay the expenses of the group.

Two people from Bolechow became energetic and dedicated members: Yitzchak Hirshhaut and Ben-Zion Rottenberg. They succeeded in bringing Gordonia to life, and with the passage of time, they founded "The United Poalei Zion", and "The United Groups". Many new forces were attracted, which was evident in the work of Keren Kayemet LeYisrael, Keren Hayesod, Ezra, and the League of Workers of the Eretz Yisrael, etc.

At a regional convention at Synowocko near Skole, we, together with the groups from Stryj, Drohobycz, Boryslaw, and Skole, developed a comprehensive plan of action. We mainly concerned ourselves with Hachshara locations for chalutzim.

It is worthwhile to point out that, despite the differences of opinion among the various Zionist organization and movements, we conducted ourselves with tolerance, and never denigrated each other.

In 1932, we succeeded in organizing for the chalutzim of Bolechow and other places many workplaces in the tanneries, factories, sawmills, etc. Until they made aliya in 1933, their influence in the town was quite noticeable [14].

That same year, a "Haoved" group was founded from among the members of the workers' circle. A number of them succeeded in making aliya in the years 1934-1935.

The rest perished along with all the other victims of the Hitlerite murderers. May G-d avenge their blood.

Gordonia.

The Hitachdut regional convention in Synowocko.

Hechalutz.

Dramatic club.

[Hebrew page 95 & Yiddish page 283]

25. "Hanoar Hatzioni" in Bolechow
by Aryeh Reichman [15]
Translation from the Hebrew by Jerrold Landau

In mid 1930s a branch of "Hanoar Hatzioni" came into existence. The branch developed quickly and in a short time the majority of young boys and girls in Bolechow joined its ranks.

As in other youth movements, we learned Hebrew, history and especially the history of Zionism.

Our aim was to broaden the horizons of our comrades through educational classes, debates and literary discussions, etc.

The Achva Hachsharah.

Achva.

"Hanoar HaTsioni" was a synthesis of national and humanitarian elements. In accordance with Professor M. Buber, we dreamed that the freedom of the Jewish people in our homeland would save all humanity from moral decline.

Together with other Zionist youth movements, we slowly came to dominate life in the Jewish Bolechow. On the Sabbath we arranged excursions to the accompaniment of Hebrew and Zionist songs. On national holidays, we had impressive celebrations. On Purim, bands whose members were dressed up in nationalist costumed passed through the streets of the town in song and dance.

Locked up in our own world, we prepared to continue in the Land. [16]

The Russians entered the city in September 1939. A few days after the conquest, we were asked to give over the keys to the headquarters and its property. After the first blow, organizational activity began once again slowly and in secret. We conducted meetings in private homes to welcome the Sabbath, to mark national holidays. That year, we were certain that the war would pass over quickly, and that we would be able to realize our desires.

I was drafted to the Red Army. In the many letters that I received, there were innuendoes about the continuation of the educational, Zionist activity, and the strong faith that was not broken despite the difficult circumstances. After that came the Nazi conquest and the destruction of the city.

We were 120 boys and girls in the chapter at the outset of the war. Only 3 survived.

[Yiddish page 284]

Hanoar Hatsioni 1938 On the way to a summer camp

"Ahava"

[Hebrew page 97]

26. The "Hashomer Hatzair" Chapter from 1920-1930
by Isser Eshel (Ichel), Kiryat Ata
Translation from the Hebrew by Jerrold Landau

The first Shomrim [17] made aliya in 1920. Crowds of people accompanied them to the train station with joy and special festivity.

The first letters that arrived from them to Bolechow testified to the difficulties in acclimatization and work conditions. Despair overtook those who were about to make aliya. The chapter maintained itself for a year and then disbanded.

The chapter no longer existed as a separate body, but individuals and groups of its former members became involved with Zionist and communal work in the city.

The lovely library turned into a communal library. After some moving around, it became headquartered in the office of the school of which Dogilowski was principal. This became a meeting place for many members of the chapter. Its leadership was drawn from members of the chapter. They developed it and raised the level of the library.

The members worked in many areas:

For the leadership of Jewish National Fund, they collected and emptied charity boxes; for the Keren HaYesod they canvassed many groups; for "Ezra", an organization that helped those of meager means when made aliya to the Land. They were involved in the founding and the leadership of an evening school for the study of Hebrew. They organized celebrations, parties and plays by amateur troupes, the income of which was dedicated to the funds.

Hashomer Hatzair.

Hashomer Hatzair.

Hashomer Hatzair 1925.

Hashomer Hatzair.

They were involved in the election campaign for the Polish Sejm; Zionist activity prior to the elections to the city council; the organization of a garden party in the public gardens; and in the founding of the Yad Charutzim workers' organization.

In order to maintain contact, the members of the chapter would meet in the home of the Sheps sisters or in the civic garden. They were engaged in song. Some of the members completed their schooling in Poland or outside of Poland. The gymnasium students traveled to Stryj each morning.

It is appropriate to mention Shaika Zeiman. He was a jolly, intelligent boy who possessed organizational talent. He was a member of the chapter in Stryj. He organized several of our young people into a group.

We rented a room in the old match factory on the way to Hosiv. We decorated it and set it up in a manner fitting for study, recreation and games. We turned it into a pleasant place.

We lit a bonfire outside the city on Sabbaths and festivals, and lived our life secretly. The chapter was reconstructed thanks to the efforts of Shaika Zeiman. It moved to the center of the city and established links with the nearby chapters in the region, with the central leadership in Lwow, and with the regional leadership. They took part in summer retreats, summer vacations, leadership retreats – in short, in all activities of the movement.

Once again, you could see in our city boys and girls, members of Hashomer, in their uniforms, emptying boxes, arranging role calls, parades, and excursions. We would accompany the members who lived in Salina home with song.

The community of the chapter was from among the workers. There were times when the chapter attracted the finest of the youth. The older members studied trades such as locksmithing, carpentry, plumbing, blacksmithing, etc. The evenings were dedicated to the study of Bible, history, Hebrew, and the Jewish and general workers' movement.

We would conduct stormy debates until past midnight. There were issues that engaged the world of the workers, the improvement of the work conditions, justice, problems with the Kibbutz, the group, the Moshav, A. D. Gordon and his teachings, and Borochov. We experienced and suffered the "pangs of the world" (Weltschmertz).

The group was particularly bustling on Saturday nights, on holidays, as the sounds of song and dance broke forth.

The elder members prepared themselves with agricultural Hachsharah.

The Hashomer Hatzair alumnae who made aliya were centered in two Galician Kibbutzim: Kibbutz Hashomer Hatzair and its Moshav in Nes Ziona, and Kibbutz Hashomer Hatzair Gimel in Bat Galim.

The chapter was still functioning when I made aliya in 1930, and I remained in contact with it for a long time.

[Hebrew page 101 & Yiddish page 285]

27. Tanneries in Bolechow
by Michael Schneeweiss

We distance carcasses, graves and tanneries 50 cubits from the city. One only makes a tannery east of a city.

Baba Batra 25a [18]

28. The Tanners "Di Garbn"
by Michael (Mekh) Schneeweiss
Translated from Yiddish by Susannah R. Juni

One of the principal branches of industry in our town was the tanners. The largest part of them was owned by Jews. The agricultural region and the developed livestock farming supplied the rawhide. Apart from that, the great big rich Smerekine in Dembina [Debina] Woods supplied the bark, which contains a large percentage of the composition of the tanning substance.

Thanks to the tanning industry, a lamb and a camel-factory developed in connection with it, as also did the serst [hair from the hide] business.

Already in the beginning of the 19th century, tanneries existed in the little town on a small scale, all as a cottage industry. Furthermore, the first big leather factory was founded by Yisroel-Leyb Hauptman, who was also one of the first Jewish mayors. He was also one of the founders of the Chamber of Commerce in Lemberg. It's worth mentioning that in the time when the Kaiser Franz Yosef the First came hunting in our region (that's where the name comes from "Kaiser-Aykhe – Kaiser Oak, on the way to Lisavits) he was *mkabules-ponim* [he represented the town in welcoming him].

The Dervinte Factory actually became founded in 1814, as a Christian firm because [persuant to] the then contemporary law, Jews were not allowed to occupy themselves with industry. When in 1844 they lifted off that law, the firm became known as: The Kaiser and the Royal Privileged Leather Factory Yisroel Hauptman and Co. – The subsequent owners of the firm were: Moyshele Hauptman, Arie Goldschlag, and their descendants.

The firm was in its time the only one in town, which enjoyed credit from the "Austro-Hungarian Bank" in Lemberg. Years later, other factories arose, like: Gershon Kurtser (his descendants – Avramele Kurtser and Avramtsi Kohn), Rechter, Kurts and Eisenstein, Weissbart and Frey, Kimmel, Kaufman,

Reizle and also two Christians – the German Pfeifer and the Polish Shlatshits Lubatshtevski.

After the First World War a lot of tanneries became founded, T. A. Feder, Rotfeld, Adler, Gottesman, Roth, Karchin, and others. Apart from that, two modern factories of Chaim Frisch, and the Landes Brothers, which manufactured soles and goat leather.

The tanneries and those with connected trades provided employment to a large portion of the population, both as workers and also as brokers of hides, finished leather, merchants of bark, horns, tallow, soap etc.

Primarily they manufactured in the tanneries two types of leather: cowhide and sole-leather. They sold the cowhides for uppers for shoes, which shouldn't leak in the seams in wintertime, as opposed to soles of *hadekes*.[1]

Several of the above mentioned factories supplied leather to the Austrian and later the Polish military. Jews worked in most of the tanneries. One had to labor very hard, especially because no machines existed and everything had to be completed by hand. In spite of that, here one must refute the *goyishe* charges that the Jews are lazy and not capable of hard physical labor.

It's interesting to note that there was a special *minyon* of the tannery workers in which the old preparer, a *Talmud-lehokhum* [learned] Jew, Reb Yankl Schnee, taught the tanners each *Shabos* or Friday night a *blat ayen-yankev* [Yiddish page from "Eye of Jacob," a religious book].

In the year 1941 during the Soviet regime, they nationalized all of the tanneries. And when the Nazi murderers destroyed our town, they murdered the owners and the workers from all of the operations, and so made an end to such a useful trade in the town that was so dear to all of us.

In "HaMagid" from the year 1878, issue 44 from November 13, page 379-380 is a correpondence from a Drohobycz [the Galician town now known as Drogobych] Jew about his trips in a lot of countries. He was also at a trade show in Paris. There he became interested in the origin of Galician Jews. He wrote there: "I heard that they say that they manufacture splendidly beautiful colored leather in the factory of my in-laws, the well known *gevirim* [wealthy people], the likeable and God-fearing brothers *mu-h* Israel-Lieb and Reb Notar Hauptman *n-r* from the town of Bolekhov. The factory was called "Israel Hauptman and Company." They received an award at the arrival of the show in Vienna and later in *Kroke* [Krakow].

[Hebrew Page 102]

Wood and Other Industries
by Abraham Weber

The translator of this chapter wishes to remain anonymous. The translation was donated by Karol Schlosser in memory of her father, Joseph.

Like the other towns around the Carpathian mountains, (Podkarpaty) in Bolechov, too, one of the main livelihoods among the Jewish population was in the timber industry. This was due to the huge areas of forest which surrounded the town. In the Northern parts, – towards Satri [?], Pacharsdorf [?] and Tniw(b)a [?] – , there were mainly forests of oak trees, which were used for furniture production all over Poland and were even exported to other countries.

Some of those oak trees had grown for hundreds of years and were often one and a half meter wide. The high grade of their beauty and quality was reason enough to exhibit them at the annual exhibition, called "The Eastern Fares" (Targi wschodnie), which took place at Lwow.

Oak trees also grew in the East, near Czulani. But there the trees were thinner and served rather for wooden base parts and the construction of buildings, train rails or fences. The forests at the South-Western side , which covered the bigger areas along the Carpathians down to the border with Czechoslovakia were entirely different. Those forests were full of pine, which are called in Israel more familiarly "the white tree". The beech tree was also well represented.

The pine tree was prepared in special factories both in the town itself and in its environs. Tables and shelves were produced most of which were exported. As far as it was possible, the beech tree as well was prepared and cut into shelves for the further production of furniture in local factories and in other towns and cities. The remaining wood was cut to pieces of one-meter-length and used as heating material, of which large quantities were sold during the winter months throughout the whole country.

Field Transport

Carpathian Scenery

The exploitation of the forests, the lumber industry and its different branches were almost entirely under Jewish patronage. The factories of different size were owned by Jews, except for one. In one of the bigger factories, owned by Grifl, worked up to 2000 men, most of which were Ukrainian peasants or inhabitants from the nearby towns. Those who came from a town were craftsmen. They were often wandering from place to place and lived in the shelter of the factory for the duration of their work. Their nickname was "Barber". Among them were but a few Jews. They predominated rather in the administrative and leading positions. In the management of the big factories were Jews, who were doing their task their whole life, from their youth. They were engaged in the construction of the factory's building from the very beginning. In the surroundings they were well known as specialists in the wood-profession. The following should be mentioned : Mr. (Reb) Moyshe Bin, who to emigrated to Israel and died here; Zaynvl Rapaport; Aharon Shor and the Shtrasman-brothers. Especially the most responsible person of the factory, Leybtshe Shtrasman, was highly respected for his knowledge, justice and work. Two of them survived and are living with us in Israel. One Mr. Meir Shmuel Shtrasman, living in Petakh Tikva and the second Mr. Meir Fridlender in Hadera.

The territory of the factory included thousands of dunam. Preparation and production were handled by machines, which were quite modern for that time. Big pieces of wood, transported in little wagons (kolejka) from the forests were used almost entirely. Tablettes and shelves were cut in order to be exported as material for ship-construction. First it was brought to Danzig, there it had to be collected in containers and could finally be sent abroad. Grifl himself owned such containers in Danzig, where several men from Bolechov were employed. (Zelig Shtrasman, Leyb Shtrasman, Moyshele Altman and others.)

The factory had a department of box-production as well. For this purpose pieces of wood could be used, which would not be useful for other purposes. These were used mainly for boxes for eggs. There were even orders from orchards in Palestine for boxes in which citrus-fruits were to be kept. The smallest parts, not useful even for the box production, were used as heating material. The employed workers got portions of such heating wood and the rest was used for running the factory's machines.

Rails leading to the factory itself guaranteed a comfortable transport of the goods straight into the wide world. Trains left regularly, day by day.

As already mentioned, there was a wagon in which wood was brought in from the forests near Polnice, Brzeza, Bsarwow [?] from one direction, and another wagon transporting from the other direction of Cerkovna, Sloboda, Lurzki and Lipa.

Five trains ran twice a day, leaving from the factory and returning to it each of which had between 15 and 20 wagons for goods. In addition to that, there was one wagon transporting the workers from the forests and, during the summer, people who participated in organised trips. Those were set up by the youth movement and took place on Sundays. The rather symbolic fees for such trips couldn't really finance them.

This factory was successfully run by our Jewish experts for 20 years. In 1931 the contract between the factory and the State, which regulated the rent of the ground on which the factory was located, but which belonged to the Polish State, ran out, and the State refused to prolong it. This caused the passing over of the entire factory to the patronage of the Polish forest ministry. The first change, undertaken by the new directive, was to dismiss all the Jewish employees from work, with only a few exceptions.

Those who remained were forced to work on Shabbat. The newly employed workers, declared as "specialists" came from the so called "Szkoly lesnicze" (forest schools) and didn't have either experience nor knowledge of what they had to handle. Their "specialized skills" were the reason for more limited and worse production, even up to a partially closing down of the factory. The main "achievement" was indeed the exclusion of Jewish workers. The few remaining Jewish craftsmen – who stayed thanks to interventions by the writer of this article among the new leadership - finally had to go because of the pressure of the non-Jewish majority.

Aside from this big factory, existed some others, which were far smaller and less important. One of them, which was located near the petrol refinery, belonged during the last years to the owner of the refinery, whose name was Baknbart. There all kinds of woods were prepared for further production. They were sent by a number of foreign "wood tradesmen", who paid the owner for working their wood.

In the grounds of this factory a little branch of barrel production was founded, shortly before the Shoah. Oak trees were mainly used.

Near to the railway station were two other factories. One, located between the station, owned by Buchman, and the known villa of Dr. Reifeizn, also specialized in work on woods, which had been brought by different tradesmen. The second, half way from the station, was a cooperative, "spolka stolarska", which belonged to the partners Bunum and Shnur. In this factory the prepared wood would be exported in the same way as it happened in the big factory. A carpentry was founded, here which mainly produced home furniture, especially chairs and armchairs.

Continuing on the way from the station to town was a bridge leading above the river Sokal [?]. On one side was a rather spacious building, sheltering a mill station, a little factory owning one machine and a branch for furniture production. The factory prepared the woods for the furniture factory. The products were of high quality and the furniture of both factories mentioned above, made them famous throughout the whole country. Those factories were concentrated in one huge building in one court. The owners were the following: Kremer, Altman, Loyfer, Shnayd.

On the way to the market place of the town, on the right hand side, was a factory for vinegar and [?], run by the Rand-family. Although the size of this factory wasn't extraordinary, its success was known, as was obvious because of the quantity of filled [?] which were transported all the time to the railway station.

Another little factory was located on the way to Horzow [?] (Dunki), near what had been once the mill owned by Neuert [Neuoyrt] (Olinik). The last owner had been a German named Rach, "may his name be erased".

Little factories were maintained also in villages, from which goods were brought to town and sold to the Jewish merchants.

To complete the description of the timber industry at Bolechov one further factory should be mentioned: that of cork production for barrels. The corks were made of birch wood, which could also be found in the woods of that area. This factory was owned by the Roznboym family which employed a dozen workers.

The main season for the timber industry was in winter. Wide areas covered by snow facilitated the transport of big pieces of wood even through areas, which were not that accessible for any kind of vehicle. Winter was characterized by traffic jams of thousands of wagons arriving from the different forests at the railway station and making urgent an immediate handling of the goods. Day by day hundreds of train wagons were loaded with beech and oak wood either as heating material or for the furniture production in the factories. The workers were busy at night and even in the worst weather conditions. At the same time other industries, like the leather or candle industry were not less represented by business activities at the station. The latter was concentrated around two factories, one run by Yoel Halpern and the other run by Zishe Vaytsner.

Deliveries of wheat and flour for both mills and shops also took place at the station.

The best known deliveries were those of coal for the salt refinery ("Haslina") and of the salt itself which were brought in the very same wagons. The most responsible persons of "Haslina" for those tasks were for many years Abramczik Shtrasman and Yudel Rat.

Several of the most skilled carpenters who were widely known for the high quality in the field of furniture production or the construction of buildings remain to be mentioned. Among them was Moyshe Goldman who died a few years ago here in Israel and whose furniture was praised in the whole area.

[Yiddish page 106 & 287]

29. The Printing Shop
by I. B. M.
Translated from Yiddish by Judie Goldstein

In memory of my eldest brother Israel Joel hy'd

The only printing shop in the shtetl started on a small scale until our printed material went to all the cities in the area, even Stanislov.

We worked it virtually by ourselves: a father and his seven children. All together we built and developed it. The printing shop of my father, Hersch Mordchai Elendman z'l, was founded in 1884 and was located on Station Street.

Whoever came to or left the shtetl went by the print shop. A lot of good friends would come daily to the shop. The seven children had sixty friends.

There were always two standing at the machine or the font case: a typesetter, the printer and his friend. These friends would come not really to place orders, but only to talk to Israel Joel, Shimon, Yantsi, Rebtsi, Eli, Gitele and Taubele.

The social, cultural and private life of the shtetl was reflected in the print shop. In the printing shop was everything that happened in the houses of study, synagogues, charitable institutions, unions and the like.

It heard "betrothals", a wedding, a circumcision, without an invitation?

Even women giving birth were "clients" because so long as she lying in the delivery bed, in each corner of the room there were four childbirth notes hanging. These were "amulets" against devils and ghosts, may the merciful God save us! The women giving birth, poor things, did not understand these "amulets" of course. Also the *"ketubah"* [Jewish marriage contract] was not clear to the brides. Apparently it is better this way.

[Yiddish page 288]

Celebration with Fishel Verber

Hebrew School. Teacher: Yonah Elendman

From *Tishri* to *Tishri* [first month of the Jewish year, from one year to the next] the print shop was swarmed, just like a beehive.

Before the elections for the Jewish Community Council, Town Council and so forth, there was a great tumult – The candidate lists were a closely kept secret. During the printing, party members stood "watch", even though this was excessive. They did this so that none of us God forbid would betray the "secrets in the room".

Landowners, priests, teachers and so forth were constantly in contact with the business.

Years ago, before there was electricity, the gentile Jasz turned the wheel of the machine by hand. He worked for us for a long time. This is one of his "witticisms": "tea without margarine does not vote". Well, so be it!

Also yearly events were reflected in the print shop:

Here comes Passover and the "proclamation" demanding people to give "wheat money" [given to poor people to buy matzah]. During the summer the billboards for festivals and performances in "Sokul" Hall. Before and during the Days of Awe [from New Year to the Day of Atonement] was "high season": people ordered masses of custom printed New Year greeting cards, also ready to sell [mass produced].

On the table in the shop were little boxes with greeting cards of all kinds: see! There is a bird; in its mouth "Happy New Year". Look! There is a basket of roses bringing you *"Leshona toyve tikoseyvu"* [may you be inscribed for a good year]. Two hands sending forth "peace" and wishing you a year of blessings. Perhaps you would like a "Holy Ark". Here the little doors open and a Torah scroll looks out! One card is plain and the other bronzed. One is smooth and the other cropped, zigzag. In short, whatever your heart desires you can get.

Were the thousands of blessings fulfilled?

To close, an oddity:

The peasants from the area would come to the market place in the shtetl on Mondays. Those who knew how to read would confuse *"drukarnia"* [print shop] with *"drogeria"* [pharmacy] and coming into the print shop they wanted a mercury ointment for their boils (it is not for us to say). Often they would get excited because their wish was not realized.

Translator's Footnotes:

1. The Hebrew / Yiddish word "Nachas" – literally "contentment", but has nuances that do not translate well.

2. Hachsharah is a training session for aliya, with a focus on farming skills.

3. I am not sure of the meaning of this word, but it seems to imply a large tent or canopy.

4. A quote from the wedding benedictions.

5. A Kapliczka is not actually a church, but rather a commemorative altar in the Polish countryside, that is constructed as evidence that someone has seen a heavenly sign.

6. The Hebrew on page 91 is evidently a slightly abridged translation from this Yiddish section. I believe that the Yiddish would have been the original.

7. The implication is probably "with the appearance of a Cossack invasion".

8. According to Jewish tradition, a Jew obtains an "extra soul" on the Sabbath.

9. A "Sheva Brachot" ceremony, where the wedding blessings are recited after a festive meal, takes place for the seven days following a wedding.

10. Psalm 127.

11. Heretics. The Hebrew term comes from the name of the Greek philosopher Epicurus.

12. 1917.

13. The token of membership in the Zionist movement.

14. I believe that this sentence refers back to the two individuals mentioned four paragraphs earlier

15. Translated in full from the Hebrew, although the analogous section appears in the Yiddish, due to a few additional paragraphs appearing in the Hebrew. I used the translation from the Yiddish, with minor alterations to match the Hebrew idiom, for the equivalent parts.

16. This is the end of the part that was equivalent with the Yiddish translation.

17. Members of Hashomer Hatzair.

18. This Mishnaic quote from Tractate Baba Batra introduces this Hebrew segment. Aside from the quote, the Hebrew and Yiddish are essentially the same, with minor differences.

[Hebrew page 109 & Yiddish page 289]

30. Memories
by Frimke Braver-Fordes and Abraham Weber
Translated from Yiddish by Judie Goldstein

Twenty-one years ago I was present as children from all the kindergartens in Tel-Aviv celebrated *Shevuos* under the open sky, on a large square, outside the city. Dressed in white, with wreaths of flowers on their heads, they sang and danced like angels. It did my heart good to see them.

The elite of the city and a representative of *Keren Kayemet* [Jewish National Fund] were sitting on a dais. A child went onto the dais in order to bring the *KKL* the offering. Vegetables, fruits and ears of corn, even white doves, from all the good things that this country has been blessed with. At the time it did not occur to me that these dear children would years later be our fighters and free us from a foreign yoke.

נוף

בובנישץ (Bubniszcze)

Top: Scenery

Watching the ceremony reminded me of the *"Majovke"* [May outing, picnic], the former outing of the Polish school in Bolekhov.

I will describe the *"Majovke"*, because it opened our eyes, it ended our way of life.

The class teacher told us about the *wycieczki* [trip, excursion or outing] and it meant we were lucky! A *wycieczki*! With joy and anticipation we waited for the "great day".

Dressed up in our Sabbath best and paired off, we left the city with the Solina band. The sun was hot. Somebody decided, no matter what, to march especially when the drumsticks hit the drums to give the beat and were audible.

After marching for about an hour we were at the chapel of the holy [?] we ate and drank. The forest that we were in hid the sky and we did not notice that it had become dark. There was thunder, lightening and hail. Confused and frightened we ran to hid in the chapel. The gentile children drove us away and the hooligans beat us with sticks.

Wet, in despair and embittered we stood and waited under the wet, storm tossed trees until we could run home. After the storm, offended, with wounded hearts, we went home. This was a blow to our morale. But it showed us that we had to get organized.

We had already made a decision in school. Even at that time, girls older than us, had founded a Zionist union "Rachel".

[Yiddish page 290]

We decided to do the same, but in secret, because we did not have permission. We immediately subscribed to the Polish language children's newspaper *"HaShakhar"*. We used a small room and every free hour was used to read the newspaper, happy to have our little corner and this is how weeks passed.

On a beautiful day when we were engrossed in reading the *"HaShakhar"* the door opened and an unexpected quest came in, the academician Nachman, an ardent Zionist, who profoundly influenced *gymnasia* [high school] students.

Jewish National Fund Committee

Suburbs of the town

The guest told us that he was surprised by our initiative and was prepared to help us. So a teacher was provided to teach us about Zionism. We read Herzl's writings. Our eyes and hearts opened and a couple of years later we created courses and organized the youngsters.

I remember a children's Hanukah celebration in Brukenstein's hall. The author of the presentation, on a theme from the *Tanakh* [Five Books of Moses] was my unforgettable comrade, Eli Elendman.

The scenery was ready, the rehearsals with the children all done. Shortly before the presentation, the gendarmes arrived and declared the presentation illegal. What did Eli Boch do? He immediately went for advice. He quickly ran to the printing shop and brought prepared invitations. At the entrance our volunteers were distributing invitations (according to paragraph two) and so we were for appearance's sake "kosher". The hall was, in spite of the enemies, packed. The children acted well and the cash box was full. Our goal was reached. The funds were destined to be used to paid the expenses of getting to Israel for our first, dear pioneer, Zeydale Mehring *z'l* [*zikhronu librocha*, Blessed by his memory]. Shortly thereafter he made *aliyah* [immigrated to Israel] bringing greetings there from us.

The realized dream of Mehring did not last long. During the First World War he was in a Turkish prison as a volunteer when he died of typhus.

In the name of the Kibbutz [?] near Petach Tikva, we are perpetuating his memory and two other comrades from Turka and Kolamei, for their sacrifices and ideals.

May his soul be bound in the bonds of life.

In 1913 the first pioneer from Bolekhov arrived in Israel. This was Sheindali Teper, now Yafa Lvnoni-Veisl.

She was a Hebrew teach in Bolekhov, Sambor and Drohobitz. Arriving in Israel she worked as a teacher in Safed and Haifa.

[Yiddish page 291]

A winter outing on Bolekhov mountain 1916

The Small Puddle

Forty-three years ago under the Turkish government, the living conditions in Israel were very difficult. She did not have an easy time of it.

Year later, when a lot of our Bolekhovers made *aliyah* she helped in every way possible. Her house was open to every new Bolekhover immigrant and she helped make our acclimatization much easier.

The connection of our work in the shtetl was the *kk'l* commission under the guidance of Mendali Landau, the rabbi's son. No holiday or community activity, family celebration took place without us collecting for *kk'l*. Besides them, the festivals brought in a large income.

Now I would like to share the memory of one such festival.

A couple of weeks before the festival we worked hard: the formalities at the sheriff's and town hall to make it legal, pledges to collect, from the women cakes, tsiastes? or bokhtes? and so forth. Also a gift to order, booths to be put up and for all of them "oracle". The promenade garden had to be decorated with various ribbons, the orchestra hired and lanterns attended to. We did not spare any effort so that the guests, who were also coming from the surrounding area, would be well entertained and also leave with lighter pockets.

The Sabbath before the "great day" (Sunday) was beautiful, not a cloud in the sky, we were lucky to see the sky clear: may it be God's will, the same tomorrow, Master of the Universe.

There were no weather forecasts on the radio at that time. We hoped and "prayed" that the Most High would have pity us and not mar our celebration.

Three o'clock was the opening. The Solina band with drums and trumeyters [?] called the people to the festival. The train brought guests from Strij, Dolina, Rozshniotov, etc. There was great joy here for the Jews.

Suddenly, the blue sky was covered in dark clouds. The clouds sped across the sky faster than a train. It was pitch black. There was thunder, lightening and fat merciless hail destroying our beautiful buffet. Embarrassed, we look at each other. Why? Why now? In order to frighten the guests and to punish us. The tables were wet. Rain dripped from the trees. Oh, all our labor.

The sun came out after the rain. Like a miracle! As quickly as the storm arrived, it left. We recovered our courage, wiped the tables, put back the beverages, the sweets, good refreshments and everyone came back to the promenade garden as if nothing had happened. It was warm, cozy and the program started.

[Yiddish page 293]

The music thundered in the air. Couples walked around. People threw confetti. People were please with the good, homemade sandwiches. The police for once had made themselves scarce. And now people were pushing through to get to the oracle. In a booth sits the "prophet", masked and "prophesized". The children wanted to know "the future". The people were having a good time. Who can this be? I know who. My friend, Eli Elendman (Eli Boch). He told the "truth" without protection, only the truth. It got a little warm in the booth. What wouldn't one do to reach our goal?

Sha, quiet, here comes the mail. The "libespost" brings "love" letters. On every letter a JNF stamp. Real mail, with all the seals.

And here comes the group of harvesters. They carry ears of corn from the fields and they symbolize the young farmers in Israel.

Attention! Attention! Announces the drum beat: Two beautiful women are waiting. The first prize goes to Leah'tche Korol, the gray eyed young girl who speaks fluent Hebrew (Chana Hendel's student).

The guests are heard talking proudly and they are in a jolly mood. Time flies, people push and shove and laugh. They walk in the garden here and there until nightfall. The moon, the colorful rockets light the garden.

To finish properly, everyone sings *"Hatikvah "* [the National Anthem of Israel] and the garden empties out. Only the members of the JNF committee stay behind, to count the cash. It is more that we expected. Full of hope and with new plans we go happily home.

During the First World War we were cut off from the world. A lot of Bolehovers left as refugees and went to Vienna or Bemn. Our worked was lighter. The JNF commission worked.

Then Meilech Braver,a soldier from Turka (near Sambor), wandered into Bolekhov. He quickly became accustomed to the town. As he had theatrical experience he gave us a piece to study, "The Jewish King Lear" by Jakob Gordin. Braver brought the players together. In Moshali Teper's confectionery shop was where rehearsals took place. There people snacked on a *"lodi"* "Tzaluskes" (a kind of macaroon), etc.

Braver had the starring role. After a lot of rehearsals and enough tickets were sold, we amateurs were ready to go on stage. The audience did not expect a lot. They knew that the group was made up entirely of amateurs. However, they had a great time seeing Moshe Hauzman (in Israel known as eykhel-Aschl) as Shmai the servant, Yona Elendman – Aschel, Sabke Gertner, the merry laughing maiden as an old Jewess, Yehaskel Shlipka, Frimke Braver, Hersch Kleinbort, etc., on stage. The actors clutched flowers on the stage.

[Yiddish page 294]

It was a great success, especially the moment when the evil, old king supported by a stick, begged for a donation. Which Jew did not shed a tear? We were even asked to make an appearance in the neighboring towns. But our parents would not give their consent.

A. Winter Memories

The windowpanes were frosted, fancied up with artistic, beautiful flowers. The fields, gardens, fences and roofs were snow covered. The ground on which nobody walked was covered with perfectly white snow and what fun it was to make a snowman or snowballs. We threw snowballs, to keep our hands warm, our faces burning, we were warm all over. A flock of birds flew by. "Black on white". We went sledding. Oh how wonderful it was! There were a lot of hills around Bolekhov and so there were plenty of places for us to sled.

Hills, mountains, forests, fields and rocks encircled the shtetl and in the spring and summer called us to outings.

In one of the forests where Kaiser Franz Yosef came to hunt, an oak tree was planted in his honor. The place was called "Kaiser *Eiche* " [oak]. The first time I saw it, it was fifty years old. Strong, wide roots and around it an iron fence. That is where we went for our outings.

Two years passed. During the First World War, after we had returned home, I went to the Kaiser-*Eiche* and what did I see? Everywhere there were graves of those killed in the war.

Now a couple of words about our water Sokel. The Sokel cut the shtetl in two. The large bridge and the Lauke tied the two parts together. The water was calm, still, clean and clear. Every small stone could be seen. We bathed there. We sat on the banks, being warmed by the sun and getting a tan.

But after heavy rain storms or when the snow melted, it was terrible, frightful! The Sokel went wild, spilled over its banks and took everything in its path. It destroyed fields, homes and drowned animals. Like a wicked beast it swallowed everything. We stood far away and watched the misfortune, the destruction.

[Yiddish page 295]

After causing all that trouble it slowly calmed down and once again was still, quiet.

It is said that we were fortunate to have the topographical situation of Bolekhov that allowed us such interesting outings. Each outing was adapted to the previous one. Once to the *"bergl"* [mountain] where our friend, Eli Elendman already waited with red and black cherries. Once to Marshin, the watering place that was renown for its sulphur springs. Sick people in need of a remedy came to Marshin. The good, pine tree air, the calm, beauty of the area were exactly what they needed. They lived in small villas in the forest.

We also walked to *"unter shtein"* (Fadkamien). On both sides of the road were stone mountains. Their color looked like the setting sun. A little further from there was Bobnishtch. It took a whole day to get there. From early in the morning until night.

The area was wild, beautiful, just as God had created it. We took provisions. In the dense forest we discovered a rock, a cave and in it two beds made of boards. On the walls and ceiling were signs of carpentry. Whose hands hewed out these? The legend is that the famous robber Dobosh made the beds. He lived there and from there he attacked suddenly. Was any living person was able to do such work? I doubt it. It is possible that his followers, other robbers, began to quarrel. The robbers were killed. Their diligence and perseverance were perpetuated. Tourists from every part of the country would come to Bobnishtch to live the legend.

At the foot of the high rocky mountain one hears water flowing. Look and see: our Sukel murmurs here. It wrestles with the mountain and finds a road, a waterfall! Until the Sukel reaches Bolekhov it is of course tired and weak. Who can only look at the waterfall? Sweaty from the climb up the mountain, we jump into the ice-cold froth and stand under the waterfall. Refreshed and happy we had home.

B. Koleyke

That is what the small forest railroad from Griffel's sawmill was called. The railroad carried wood from the forests to the sawmill to be worked. We used the *koleyke* on one of our outings to Brzoze and Besarabov and traveled the so-called *"Schweytz"*. A day prior we received a permit from the sawmill and the next day early in the morning we were sitting in an open train car. The *koleyke* was entirely steam driven. It was even pleasant because we were able to see the enchanting countryside. The forests, the greenery, you only had to stretch out your hand to touch the branches. The greenery brushed again our faces. Before we turn around the landscape changes and we cannot satisfy our eyes. Here and there we hear a stream and in it are fish.

An outing with the *koleyke* was wonderful. After a couple of hours it returns loaded with wood to the sawmill and we are loaded with what we saw, impressions, happiness and merrily arrive home.

C. The Parting

I bid you farewell wild forest, your close air that melted us.

I bid you farewell meadows, cornfields, on your paths we walked and picked flowers.

I bid your farewell dear tree that grew in my garden, in your shadow I sat, dreaming about my future. The richest fantasies cannot describe what kind of tomorrow was waiting for us.

I could not imagine how shocking that last dark night would be that our dear, loved ones would be tossed into the abyss. As our neighbors, with whom we had lived for years, with hatchets, hammers, scythes and knives, like wild animals, dragged our dear ones, in the dark of night, from bed to the cemetery and buried them alive.

Row after row the executioners, like ears of corn, cut them down. And as the last scream from the last Jewish slaughtered child faded away, the devilish laughter of the murderers shook the air.

Was this a theatrical presentation? No! On stage as the curtain comes down, the victims stand up, the murderers and their victims (who for a minute played these roles) hugged and kissed each other and it is only a play. This was not a play. The moon crept into the mountain and the hanging sun shone. Were you able to see the victims and on their bloody, tired faces the question: why? why?

But the murderers, looking up to the sky, satisfied with their work, went back to the shtetl to rob and steal, everything that our dear ones had with sweat and blood in the course of generations, earned by hard work.

The blood of the thousands of martyrs ran to the Sukel, from the red Sukel this blood flowed to the Shvitze, from the Shvitze that had become purple-red to the Dniester. Fiery red it swam to the Black Sea, it did not stay black. From the red-Black Sea it continued to the Dardanelles and the Mediterranean Sea. Suddenly a small ship is notice, large as an eggshell balancing on the sea. It was tossed here and there, like a small flag. And once it caught site of the shores of Israel. With joy and full of hope the little ship approached the shore, knocked on the gate in vain, no answer. The gate was locked. Very bitter and with a broken heart the small ship distanced itself from shore. Where now? Suddenly there was a heavy storm and a mighty voice was heard: Jewish children! Do not despair! I will gather you up! With me you will have peace. Immediately the little ship was smashed and disappeared without a trace. After a couple of days a small piece of the destroyed ship with the word "Struma" was found.

I bid you farewell, graves of my parents, relatives and friends.

Desolate, you are destroyed. The road to you is cut off. I cannot even lay a flower or shed a tear for you on your grave.

In "the city of the martyrs" in the Bolekhover forest in Israel we erected for our immortal souls a *matzevah* [a gravestone, memorial]. I come here, fathers and mothers, sisters and brothers, friends and good comrades, to my parent's grave.

May their souls be bound in the bonds of life.

[Yiddish page 298]

Branch of "HaShomer HaTsair"

HaShomer HaTsair

[Yiddish page 299]

Chanukah 5697 [1937]

The Hebrew School – 3rd grade – 1938, Director: Pesakh Lev

[Yiddish page 300]

The Hebrew School – Purim presentation – 5698 [1938]
School Director: Pesakh Lev

Hebrew School – Purim presentation 1939

After the Balfour Declaration, Jewish youth throughout the world organized in pioneer movements and some of them, by a variety of means, made *aliyah* [immigrated to Israel].

The youth who remained behind were the mainstay of Zionist cultural and community life in the shtetl until its destruction.

Every Sabbath the representatives of all the parties gathered at the *"Maccabee"* [Zionist sports club] Union where they held their weekly meeting of *KKL* [*Keren Kayemet l'Israel*, the Jewish National Fund]. At the *KKL*meeting they run up against the left and fanatical orthodox circles.

To the Zionist consciousness a lot had carried the election to the Sejm [Polish parliament] and Senate, municipal government, *Kultusgemeinde* [Jewish Community Council] and as representatives to Zionist congresses.

Five parties participated in the congresses: General Zionist, Revisionist [militant Zionist group], Labor, *HaShomer HaTsair* and *Mizrahi* [Zionist party for observant Jews].

Middle-class and working class young adults belonged to *"Hitahdut"*; [Labor Party]. The party worked on a wide scope in various fields. Those in the *"Gordonia"* organization were given help by the Labor Party so they could go to *Hakhshara* [Zionist agricultural training center] in the Bolekhov factories and work places or in other cities in Poland.

The activists in the *"Hitadut"* movement were Herschaut (Ortman's son-in-law) and Ben Tzion Rotenberg (Hirsch Mordchai Elendman's son-in-law). Thanks to their energy and enthusiasm for the party and Zionism in general, they were delegates at various institutions. They left their mark on every public effort.

The Revisionist ranks were organized as follows: adults in *"Hatza'r"*, the young workers and students in *"Massadah"*. The youngest were sent to *"Betar"*. Thanks to comrade D. Rapaport (Eli Weitzner's son-in-law) the movement grew. They had interesting programs and summer camps that were also used for military exercises (along the model of P. W.).

Besides developing cultural activities, there were also Hebrew classes under the direction of Hinde Delman. The mainstay of most Zionist activities was Yosali Shindler *hy'd* [*Hashem Yinkoym Domoy*, may the Lord avenge his blood] (Yitzhak Shindler's son). Because of his noble character and devotion as a volunteer, all the comrades were drawn to him and had great respect for him. Without his advice nothing important would get done. He wanted very badly to make *aliyah*. But unfortunately he never had the chance. He was murdered as a martyr.

[Yiddish page 279]

Betar

Betar

[Yiddish page 280]

"HaShomer HaTsair" [Zionist group, no political affiliation] and *"HaHalutz"* [pioneer movement belonging to *Poalei Zion*] members were the best youngsters in the city. They were brought up in the spirit of the scouts and socialist ideas. They were involved in every important Zionist activity in the shtetl, staring with teaching Hebrew, collecting money for the Zionist funds, Hakhshara through to aliyah. The majority of them had the honor to make aliyah. Their pride and joy was the library that was used by everyone, regardless of their affiliation.

Some of the HaShomer HaTsair comrades unfortunately went over to the extreme left wing.

The living spirit of the *HaHalutz* was Shimon Tenenbaum who with all his strength and devotion organized the *Hakhshara* locations for various cities in Galicia. But, unfortunately he died very young.

The head of "Mizrahi" activities was the scholar, [8 Hebrew words], Reb [Mr.] Chaim Kremer z'l [*zeykher livrokhe*, may his memory be blessed]. In order to wake the pious Jews from their indifference, every Friday afternoon he taught a chapter of the Pentateuch at his home. They came from all corners of the city, young and old, to attend his lessons. Rain, wind, snow, nothing could keep the people from going to hear Torah from Reb Chaim Kremer. Given the opportunity, he also lectured on world affairs, with enthusiasm about life in Israel and informed us about the political situation in Israel.

These lessons, full of Torah and wisdom, had a great influence on the youth, and made it easier for them to do their work collecting for the national funds. The Orthodox circles had because of him ceased their persecution of us.

The rabbi, Reb [Mr.] Mendeli Landau *hy'd* served *"Mizrahi"* with advice and deeds, as well as other Zionist youth movements. Officially he should not have been present because of the government and also because opposing *"Agudat Israel"* [against Zionism and based on absolute rule of the Torah] always stirred them up against him. All of us profited from his Torah and wisdom.

The above mentioned library was in the Jewish school. The director, Y. Dogilevski z'l, contributed to its development. Thanks to him it was masterfully organized.

Eli Elendman (Eli Boch) developed the Hebrew-Yiddish section. His knowledge and skillfulness amazed all of us, especially his ability to write so quickly with his left hand.

An important factor in public life was the artisan union *"Yad Harutzim"* [Hand of the Diligent Men]. Its comrades participated in all Zionist and community affairs.

[Yiddish page 281]

Gathering of HaHalutz Hatza'ir

Betar

[Yiddish page 282]

Betar

"Yad Harutzim"

[Yiddish page 283]

During elections they would present their own independent list with its best activists: Shmuel Valik, Zelman Kesler, Shmuel Yeger, Wolf Hofman, Zishe Gertner and so forth.

Once before the municipal elections, their top candiate Shmu Valik was present at a meeting in the Polish meeting halls on behalf of *"Yad Harutzim"* Saturday afternoon wearing a straymel with 17 *shpitzn* [points of fur] and began his speech with the words: "I, as the *shpitzncandidat* [top candidate]..." Since then he was called the *shpitzencandidat*.

Hanukah and Purim and so forth they gave lovely presentations and the people were always well entertained and as a matter of course the material success was always assured.

[Hebrew page 117 & Yiddish page 301]

Chapter III. The Destruction

1. Bolechow and its Jewish Population under Soviet Rule (1939-1941)
by M. Reisman
Translation from the Hebrew by Jerrold Landau

The Polish-German war that broke out in September 1939 did not last long. There were no almost victims in our town until the last moment. The fact that Poland was fighting for life or death against the Nazi beast was not noticeable in our town.

After fierce battles that lasted for approximately three weeks, the German army conquered almost all of Poland.

In the final phase of this bloody clash, Bolechow served as a passageway for the routed Polish troops, for the officials of the administration, etc. Refugees from the breadth of Poland fled via Bolechow in the direction of the Hungarian and Romanian borders. Here and there, one would run in to infantry soldiers; thousands of civilians in cars, bicycles, and wagons – some on foot and some in vehicles – everyone going through the city in the aforementioned direction.

Those starving refugees purchased and depleted all of the food stores in the city. Some had to stay over in the city, since they were too weary from their great wanderings to continue on their journey.

Many of them requested financial assistance from the municipal authorities, since they were destitute.

There were many Jews among these refugees. The Jewish committee set up a soup committee as a temporary measure in order to meet the needs of the suffering people. Some of them remained in the city until it was captured by the Red Army.

At that period of time, the Germans approached Bolechow. The German troops captured the city of Stryj, which was near Bolechow. The troops would retreat to Stryj in order to fortify themselves and take a stand against the last garrisons of the Polish army and the civilian refugees. A small number of Bolechow officials succeeded, during this confusion, in escaping Bolechow through roundabout routes.

Nervously and sadly, the Jewish population waited for what was to come. A miracle took place. The German troops who stood at the gates of Bolechow retreated to Stryj in order to fortify and strengthen the Stryj River, which was of great strategic importance.

Apparently, the Germans did not attribute great strategic importance to our town.

That day, the German-Soviet agreement was announced on the radio. That agreement allowed the Soviet Army to capture a portion of Poland – that is the regions of Tarnopol, Lwow, and Stanislawow. Despite this, the German army did not retreat, but rather left its troops in Stryj and nearby towns. Bolechow was caught between both alternatives, since the civic administration had left, and no army had conquered it.

The citizens awaited their new rules impatiently. They gathered together in groups and deliberated about the fate of the city and its future. One group was the Ukrainians, who were convinced that the Nazis would conquer the city, for that was their desire. The second group consisted of the Poles and a small part of the Jews, who were neutral. The third group, consisting entirely of Jews, awaited the arrival of the Soviet Army.

The Ukrainians decided to send a delegation to the Germans requesting that they hasten the conquest of the city. When they realized that the Germans were not inclined to this, they took advantage of the lawless, anarchistic situation. They organized the farmers in the surrounding areas, and sent them in to pillage the city. The wild mob fell upon the stores and houses as they pillaged. As a result of this anarchy, the Jews took turns standing guard in order to prevent the pillage and plunder.

Within a day, the Soviet Army conquered the city and took control over it. The Jewish population breathed a sigh of relief, in the hope that a German foot would not trod upon the town. They believed in the power of the Soviet Army, which was mighty.

On the other hand, the Ukrainians did not have faith in the power of the Soviet Army. They protested publicly to prevent them from maintaining a stand, in the hope that they would be forced to retreat.

After a brief period of military administration, the military officials turned over the reins of power to the civilian officials from Russia, to whom they added local Communists. Bolechow became the regional capital. The office was in the house of Gross. A Ukrainian native of Russia was appointed mayor.

Various laws and decrees altered the landscape of the city. The merchants were forced to sell their products at the former prices, despite the fact that the value of the currency was severely reduced, and it was not possible to obtain new merchandise.

They restricted the sale of bread, and a food shortage slowly began to be felt. Obviously, a black market was created, from which it was possible to purchase foodstuffs at inflated prices.

Queues formed outside the stores. Many woke up early to stand in line to purchase bread and other food necessities, for not everyone had the means to buy food at black market prices.

The situation was similar with regard to the purchase of clothing, woven goods, shoes, haberdashery, etc. The officials who had come from Russia purchased everything with Soviet currency, which had no exchange value. That is to say, they emptied the stores with the cheapest of cheap prices.

The merchants were forced by the authorities to sell their merchandise and liquidate their businesses. They would pay government taxes with the money they received. The taxes imposed upon them were unbearable, and the payment timeframe was short. Those who could not pay the taxes were imprisoned by the militia.

The factories and workshops were nationalized. Only in rare circumstances were the former owners permitted to serve as workers in them.

Former workers and owners who were able to prove that they were Communists were appointed as directors of the enterprises.

However, not all of those workers and employees were able to remain at their posts, for they were not experienced tradesmen, and their lack of experience would impede the manufacturing. Since the salary of the employees was low from the outset, they pilfered the merchandise in the storehouses and sold it on the black market.

The government found out about the shameful situation. Instead of confessing its own guilt on account of the poor and inadequate administration, they suspected the factory directors of sabotage. The era of imprisonment and court cases began then. Many directors who were suspected as being enemies of the revolution were imprisoned and sent to Siberia.

During a later period of nationalization, the Polish currency was exchanged for Soviet rubles. Obviously, from that time, the zloty was no longer legal tender, and it lost its entire value.

Instead of private factories, workshops and stores, government workshops and stores were opened. The prices were inflated.

Fundamental changes also took place in the administration of business. Instead of experienced, contracted officials, only Soviet officials were hired. Despite this, the civic administration remained in the hands of local Communists. Moshe Hauftman, who was well known in the city from the former court cases against Communists, was appointed as mayor.

The first activity of the mayor was to arrange a group of workers to uproot trees in the forest. Former small-scale merchants or non-organized workers were engaged primarily in this work.

A short while later, an edict was issued demanding that residents of houses with many rooms be evicted.

These decrees injured the burgher class. (For example, the owner of a cigarette kiosk was considered to be a burgher.)

Since approximately 90% of the Jewish residents of Bolechow were employed in business and trade, it would seem that these decrees primarily affected them.

In the eyes of the Soviet authorities, the land was not conquered, but rather liberated. Every subject automatically became a citizen of the Soviet Union. In order to add force to its authority, every subject was given an identity card. This certificate not only served as an identity card, but also as a certificate of validation: that is, it testified about the behavior of its owner, his past, honesty, etc. Great importance was attached to those cards, since a person was evaluated based on the information contained on it when he would turn to the government for various administrative reasons or when he would be looking for a job. This document also noted the place of origin and nationality of its holder.

Notes and paragraphs were added to the certificates of the former manufacturers and merchants. Obviously, a citizen possessing such a certificate was restricted and limited in his freedom of work.

At a later date, the civic militia arrested former wealthy people in accordance with a prepared list. They also arrested many refugees who were suspected of fleeing from the Germans to take refuge under Soviet authority.

A special train was prepared for all of these people to transport them to Siberia. Zionist activists were also judged and sentenced to many years of imprisonment. Later, they were drafted as "volunteers" to sell coal, etc.

The Jews slowly accustomed themselves to the situation, despite the oppression that pervaded in the town. They preferred this to the German boot, a government of cruel tyrants. Thus did they live until the end of June, 1941.

[Hebrew page 120 & Yiddish page 305]

Chapters of Destruction

Translation into English of the chapter dealing with the annihilation of Bolechow Jewry, out of the Memorative (Yizkor) Book dedicated to the Martyrs of Bolechow, published in Hebrew and Yiddish in 1957 by the Association of Bolechowers in Israel.

Translation by Josef (Jusik) Adler

I

Some preliminary remarks: Certain important details then unknown or intentionally ignored are added, mainly from sources such as testimonies by competent survivors given in Poland after the war and from data based on material in the Nazi archives, or the like, provided by Dr. Thomas Sandkuhler, a German historian.

A number of explanatory notes will be added as well as a short chapter on the Soviet rule from September 1939 until June 1941.

It should finally be noted that some mistakes occurred when printing the original edition of the book. In the present translation this, naturally, is being corrected, along with some modifications in text and style.

II
Bolechow Under Soviet Rule 1939-1941

In the aftermath of the German invasion of Poland and the Ribbentrop–Molotov agreement Eastern Galicia, including Bolechow, was annexed to the Soviet Union. Whereas the attitude of authoritics toward anti-Semitism shows a clear improvement in comparison with the former Polish rule the economic situation, already difficult, further deteriorated.

There were no more private shops, workshops, or small industry such as in the traditional Jewish trades. Most people had to work in nationalized enterprises. This meant they were given very meager wages. In order to subsist one had either to resort to stealing or to other dubious practices.

Some young men were enlisted in the Red Army. Several were sent to the Finnish front. Most refugees who fled the Germans and settled in Bolechow were deported to Siberia along with some members of the Jewish upper class. Apparently those were the ones who rejected the proposed Soviet citizenship. This applied to refugees only. One such family was the Sobel family, co-owners of a small oil refinery. Ironically, in most cases, this saved their lives. The same goes for a few dozen Jewish communists and others who fled to Russia after the German attack on June 22, 1941. Regrettably, conditions and the state of mind were such that not many people could, or wanted to, escape.

2. Chapters of Annihilation
By Joseph Adler

A few days before the Soviet forces left Bolechow several Ukrainian activists approached the Soviet military command with the purpose of allowing them to organize a neutral militia force. This, they said, would ensure the safeguarding of the inhabitant's lives and property during the expected period of chaos resulting from the withdrawal of the Red Army. Permission was granted and soon one could see groups of 2-3 Ukrainian militiamen patrolling, bearing rifles, in plainclothes and wearing armbands.

At the same time, many villagers and Bojki mountain dwellers (Ruthenian tribesmen) along with local Ukrainians gathered in yards. Many brought sacks. The Russians opened the bakeries, well stocked in meal, and also the "Univermag" (department store) on the Rynek, the main square. The mob soon plundered everything and started storming warehouses at the railway station and elsewhere.

At this stage, Jewish property was left intact. However, this picture of an omnipresent, plunderthirsty and bloodthirsty mob would repeat itself with every "action."

Somewhat later Soviet engineers destroyed some facilities of the oil refinery. During the Nazi occupation no attempt to reconstruct it was ever made. Some amount of carburant was distributed to the populace. The reminder was drained into the stream ("Potok") and incinerated. As a result the town was draped in a thick black cloud. An unsuccessful attempt was made to destroy the "Great Bridge" and some other installations. As the last Russian soldiers left Bolechow the Ukrainian intelligentsia established a new administration. Dr. Harasimow was appointed Head of the District and Simkow, a former police inspector, as Mayor.

After several days, a regional meeting was convened with the participation of representatives from nearby villages. They gathered at the "Magistrate," the town hall, and were joined by members of the clergy wearing ceremonial garb. There they proclaimed an autonomous Ukraine. The neutral militiamen then changed their white armbands for blue and yellow ones. After a week or so, the German authorities issued an instruction abolishing the Ukrainian autonomy and imprisoned the government with its head, Stefan Bandera. The local administration did, however, remain in Ukrainian hands until Mayor Simkow's arrest and execution by Germans along with some Jews. He was accused of collaborating with the Jews although being a notorious anti-Semite. However, another Ukrainian mayor had him replaced. During the first days of July, Ukrainian nationalists ran wild. Apart from minor anti-Semitic incidents, neither the Slovak nor Hungarian army brought harm to Jews at this stage.

On July 3, 1941 in the afternoon a Slovak army patrol of three infantry soldiers appeared on Dolinska Street. Somewhat later the Hungarian forces entered Bolechow and its surroundings in great numbers and disarmed the militia. But, prior to this, the latter succeeded in levying bloody advances on the Jews of Bolechow. Among their atrocities best known are as follows:

A. On the night of July 24th, twenty Jews were exterminated. Most were ex-members of the Komsomol, the communist youth organization, headed by Lea Schindler. They shot them dead under the "Great Bridge." Leaflets were distributed in Ukrainian saying more or less, "Young Jewish communists murdered their decent brothers, etc."

B. The killing of a number of Jews, mostly collaborators with the Soviets in nearby Dolzka village.

C. The cruel assassinations of Soviet Jewish soldiers who either deserted or became cut off from their units. These men were trying to reach their homes west of Dolina. Some were caught at Hoszow, tortured and brutally murdered. Then they were thrown into the Swica River. The exact number of victims is unknown, There were, supposedly, dozens.

During the relatively calm period from August through October 28th, there were no human losses with the exception of the suicide of Dr. Reifeisen, Judenrat head, who hanged himself in his orchard following maltreatment by the Germans.

However, Jewish life became deeply affected by administrative and legislative measures along with the annexation of the ex-Soviet Western Ukraine to the "General Government" as "Distrikt Galizien." All the racist laws prevailing there entered into force. One had to wear a white armband with a Star of David in the center. No public institutions were permitted. Elsewhere signs appeared saying, "Entrance for Jews Forbidden." This included cinemas and theaters, shops, hairdressers, parks, etc. Walking on sidewalks was not allowed. Jews had to step aside when passing German soldiers and take off their caps when greeting them. All their radios were confiscated under threat of the death penalty. Until the summer of 1942, Jews were given separate food cards, allowing them meager rations of poor quality.

All furs, even the smallest fur fragments were requisitioned one day. The transgressors were, again, exposed to capital punishment. It was later written in the Lwow newspapers, notably in the Polish collaborating "Gazeta Lwowska," that the Jews voluntarily donated their furs to the German army suffering from the cold on the eastern front. The closing of all Jewish businesses and transferring of all industry to the German army brought further economic hardship. These, later, mostly passed into the hand of German firms. All of this had already happened under Soviet rule. A strict night curfew was imposed. Also, during the day, there were movement restrictions. It was forbidden to leave town limits.

Soon all these measures became unbearable and there was practically no way to survive without bypassing them. The Ukrainian police was created by the Germans consisting of ex-militiamen subordinated to the gendarmerie (the Germans). They arrested and cruelly beat the transgressors.

The Bolechowers were witness to tragic migrations of Transcarpathian Jews. The Hungarian authorities chased tens of thousands of them into Galicia, some from the direction of Skole. First they were seen moving in a southerly direction by foot bearing their scant belongings. They vainly hoped they would be allowed to return home at another place near Wyszkow. After some time, the survivors again crossed Bolechow toward Stryj. Others perished in a horrible massacre at Halicz and elsewhere. The Jews of Bolechow helped them greatly by giving them food and clothes. About one hundred of them remained in Bolechow until the very end, as also happened with a number of ex-German Jews. Most of the unfortunates who tried to go back home were murdered in the mountains of the Skole frontier. These events deeply shocked the Bolechowers.

The creation of the Judenrat on the premises of the former Jewish public school on Szewska Street, became an important event. Its first task consisted of sending scores of Jews to maintain the roads, railways, or the like, without any remuneration whatsoever.

Later, a huge tax was imposed consisting of a million Soviet rubles, four and a half kilos of gold and a large amount of various commodities. After Dr. Reifeisen's suicide, Dr. Schindler was appointed as the head of Judenrat. Jewish police (or militia) were, as well, organized under the command of the lawyer Dr. Pressler. Initially their role was quite modest and restricted, as for instance, the safeguard of order in the public kitchen of the Judenrat. Later on their importance increased. They got a special cap with a yellow band and an armband they wore on their lower forearm that read, "JUEDISCHER ORDUNGSDIENST" in red embroidered letters. A kind of cooperation developed between them and the Ukrainian police. Jewish policemen helped in the forced mobilization of Ukrainian labor for compulsory work in Germany. For some time the Ordungsdienst was much feared by the Gentiles in the neighborhood.

In the autumn of 1941 all Jews living in nearby villages were forced to move into Bolechow on short notice. They were allowed to take with them only a few belongings. That meant the deportation brought hundreds of deprived people, most of whom would soon starve to death.

Many inhabitants started working in tanneries and/or leather factories. There were dozens of them in Bolechow. Most were small operations. This enabled the people to subsist by thievery of the products, continuing the "tradition" of Soviet days.

Working Jews got some wages until December 1942, although the wage was extremely low. Most people had to sell their possessions of every kind.

Often these were bartered for food, with a very cheap exchange rate. A new class of Christian merchant was born specializing in the trade of Jewish belongings. Many traveled to the agricultural region of Podole in order to sell there while acquiring food.

Since the early autumn one could see dozens of men, women and children begging for food from door to door. Most were horribly swollen from hunger. They also picked nettle and other supposedly edible plants in order to prepare something to eat. These people came mostly from the poorer element as well as from the expelled. The Judenrat kitchens supplied hundreds of meals but, unfortunately, these only consisted of thin soup. Typhoid and hunger played havoc with scores. The mortality rate started with several deaths per day and gradually rose to more than 40 deaths a day in the winter of 1942. Then there was a decline. Almost daily, Jewish policemen had to break into dwellings and pull out dead bodies. The total number of victims was then estimated at between 600 and 800.

In contrast, some relatively well-to-do Jews still managed to lead more or less normal lives. Some even had Gentile housemaids and their children got private lessons. Some problems could still be solved by money.

Both the Ukrainian and Polish press, notably the Lwow "Gazeta Lwowska," was filled with anti-Semitic attacks of the lowest and most venomous kind. The same is true for the many pamphlets, wall posters, etc. in the "Der Sturmer" style, often warning of the danger coming from the dirty Jews, spreading typhoid and lice, and advising how to avoid contact with them.

From time to time new anti-Jewish regulations appeared. The infractions often threatened death. Most were signed by the "SS and Police Commander in Distrikt Galizien," F. Katzmann. In 1942 they were also signed by Friedrich-Wilhelm Kruger, the Superior SS and Police Commander in General Government.

It goes without saying that Jews were deeply depressed by the situation. But even after the most horrible news of huge mass executions in Lwow and Stanislawow, some still showed optimism, perhaps as a denial mechanism.

Religious activity was then intense, with prayers held in private houses under tight guard. People were ready to disperse immediately. This was in spite of the prohibition against gathering in groups of more than ten.

Within the framework of a new administrative division Bolechow was put under the jurisdiction of the "Landkreis" Kalusz, later Stryj, headed by Victor von Dewitz. So-called commissaries were appointed in smaller towns to be in charge of the civil administration. This was in accordance with the already existing model in General Government. The commissary of Bolechow was named Kohler. He was a drunken ex-school janitor from Breslau who sadistically attacked Jews on the streets. He had continuous requests from Judenrat for various commodities for his Polish mistress and himself. He also completely arranged everything in a luxurious manner at his large, former

Jewish villa. He and Aldak, the "Judenreferent" from Kalusz, dealt with several extortions, mainly in order to completely furnish several houses for German functionaries and an especially lavish hunting lodge for Dr. Hans Frank, Hitler's crony and governor of what remained of Poland. Their cruel ways directly caused the suicide of Dr. Reifeisen because of a delay in his fulfilling one of their excessive demands. Dr. Reifeisen was the first head of the Judenrat. He was a decent and respectable man. Aldak, a former theologian, spoke some Hebrew. He used to "collect" Jewish religious artifacts and books.

In Stanislawow, today's Ivano Frankivsk, there was the outpost of the Security Police and Particular Services, (Sicherheitspolizei und Sonder Dienst) commonly known as Gestapo under the command of the fanatically anti-Semitic SS Hauptsturmfuhrer (captain) Hans Kruger. The infamous Stanislawow prison evoked horror. Unfortunately, Bolechow was included in their sphere of action until the end of March 1942.

During the fall of 1941, a shortage of food prevailed in Galicia owing to floods and plundering by German troops and their allies. This furthered the will of the Germans to hasten the "final Solution" in the region. Earlier than elsewhere in General Government in the Distrikt Galizien, the mass murder of the Jews began in October.

For this end, policemen, Schutzpolizisten, from Vienna and the 133rd Nuremberg Reserve Police Battalion arrived. This unit took part in the October 12th killing at the Jewish cemetery of Stanislawow of at least 10,000 people under Hans Kruger's command. This massacre, known as "bloody Sunday," was done wholly in public. News of it spread quickly.

In Bolechow, with the addition of the grizzly details, such as about people who had been wounded and who crept out of the mass graves, the effect was terrible. It seemed, however, that most soon adapted to even this. Some tried to acquire poison. Later there were attempts of suicide and successful suicides by dozens and often involving whole families. In many cases, poison was ineffective. This continued until the end of the occupation.

For the moment nothing happened. The Polish population as a whole was rather sympathetic to the Jews of Bolechow, in contrast to Lwow, the "Distrikt" capital. The worst anti-Semitism came from the new class of "Volksdeutsche," i.e.: people having some ethnic German roots.

A. The First Action - October 28-29, 1941

At dawn on Tuesday, October 28th, several covered trucks arrived from Stanislawow with uniformed SS men and gravediggers with their tools. Ukrainian police and members of the Ukrainian youth organization, "Sitch" from Drohobycz, as well as reinforcements of German police from Stryj, and probably other formations, started arresting Jews beginning at about 10 A.M. They had lists with hundreds of names of intelligentsia, merchants, rabbis, and so on. The first stage was silent. They took most of the victims by surprise. There were no arrests of women and children until the afternoon. The apprehended were instructed to dress well, since they "will have a long journey." During the arrests searches were made in order to loot valuables.

In the next several hours many people on the lists succeeded in hiding and by this means, it was believed, other Jews were indiscriminately caught instead. It appears, however, that both kinds of actions were applied: the "intelligentsia action" (also in practice against the Poles) and the mass extermination action.

In the afternoon many shots could be heard along with the commotion caused by the omnipresent, looting crowd. One could see the Jews being dragged out of their hideouts in attics and basements. No one could see or hear how these bands were raiding streets and houses, capturing, beating and extraditing Jews. On the other hand, many found refuge in their Christian neighbor's houses, often due to heavy payments or costly presents. But quite often these "trusted friends" chased out or denounced them after receiving the money or like. Then they participated in robbing their victim's houses or worse. In general, Christian houses were not subject to searches, especially in the first action. As there was a pause toward the night, hiding Jews profited from it. They brought food, warm clothes, etc. In the early morning of Wednesday, October 29th, the intensive searches resumed and continued until noon. The action was stopped at a predetermined time and those caught afterward were released. At the same time, some 800 – 950 Jews kept in the hall of the former D.K.A. (Red Army House or "Catholic House") were about to begin their last way, after being subject to horrible physical and mental suffering, suffering beyond description.

A certain Polish book dealing with the Holocaust says the D.K.A. episode was unique and extraordinary in the whole of Galicia, for the horrible methods applied.

Here is a typical story of the action as told by survivors: "At eleven a.m. three strong knocks were heard at my door.   "Who is there?" An immediate answer came, "The Gestapo."   I opened the door and four people entered.   A German in an SS uniform with a skull and cross-bones on his cap, a Ukrainian policeman in his black uniform, and two Ukrainian civilians.   The German was armed with a Parabellum pistol and the policeman had a rifle.   Both civilians held thick sticks.   The German greeted me with "Guten Tag" (good day) and asked whether I understood German.   Following my positive answer he asked if I was Mr. ..... then he instructed me to be ready in ten minutes to go with them. My wife started begging the German to free me.   He calmed her by saying, "Your husband will be back. But he has to go far away.   Prepare warm clothes for him and give him lots of money."   Suddenly the Ukrainian policeman started shouting,   "Give me the Red banner and weapons.   Show me your clandestine communist printing press."   I answered that I never was in possession of such things.   "We will find them," yelled the Ukrainian. As

I dressed myself they made a search while yelling, threatening and breaking glassware and furniture. The German, who suddenly completely changed his conduct, mainly looked for jewelry and money, while the Ukrainians filled the baskets and bags found in our house with utensils, clothes and shoes. When they discovered a page from an old Soviet newspaper in a drawer they started beating and kicking me numerous times.

The SS man then threatened my wife with his pistol for some time but suddenly removed the wedding ring off my hand and put it in his pocket. After leaving the house, I had to carry the bags and baskets of the looted goods.   As we passed the Rynek, the town's main square, I could see many acquaintances escorted, as I was, in the direction of the "Great Bridge," some of them bleeding as a result of their copious beatings. The mob began to concentrate. We were accompanied by shouts of contempt and derision. However, there also were many looking at us with compassion, some eyes filled with tears. Nearby, at the D.K.A. house, tens of Jews were about to enter the hall. Most of their faces expressed fear and suffering. Others were apathetic. But some even smiled. In order to enter the hall I had to run the gauntlet of young Ukrainians with their sticks, horribly beating every entering Jew. Some people died as a result. Almost unconscious, I reached the hall where many people were lying on the floor. I lay down in expectation of what would happen next. In a few hours the hall became completely filled. Windows were closed and the iron stove turned almost white hot. People sweated and suffocated.

Each attempt to remove some of the warm clothing was met with terrible atrocities by the SS men who threatened to kill the offenders.

The Germans spread a powder in the hall that caused coughing and suffocation.   They stepped on the bodies, kicking them with their heavy boots and beating them indiscriminately.   No one was allowed to sit.   All had to lie down.   From the stage various instructions were given.   At sunset Fridman, a teacher in the Jewish public school was ordered to climb the high glowing stove. His horrible screams joined the incessant laments and moaning of the wounded.

Above all one could hear the cries of many women who became hysterical. Many fainted. Several did not recover consciousness and died.   Occasionally, from the balconies, the Germans shot into the crowd. The number of wounded and dead increased.   One woman suffered a miscarriage and died too. An order was given that everyone must immediately hand over their money and valuables. The great majority complied.   Many later endured an extensive search of their person.   Eleven people who failed to deliver their valuables were shot to death on the stage, while the others had to watch the execution.   The bodies of the dead remained in the hall among the living, who were suffering from hunger, thirst and suffocation.   Gradually they became more and more apathetic. Bruckenstein, the blind pianist, had to play the piano. The

Murderers were dancing with naked girls to the merry tunes among the agonizing and the dead.

The rabbis Mendele Landau and Yossele Horowitz had to go up to the stage. Two yellow candles were lit and the old men had to preach nearly this, "Heavy sins have we committed so God brought upon us the punishment we deserve." Afterwards holy books were desecrated the rabbis were crucified. They died after being horribly tortured, their eyes pulled out.

A surprising announcement about dinnertime was made. Some begin to rise. They did not get the cruel joke. Bursts of machine gun fire followed, accompanied by satanic laughing and shouting, 'This is your meal."

When compelled to visit the toilets, again I had to run the gauntlet and be beaten with sticks. Some paid with their lives. At sunset the flow of captured Jews intensified, as many were caught by villagers. Often the victims were brought in horse carriages. They were tied with ropes like wild beasts. For these despised acts the Germans did not pay much; fifty groszy and a small jar of marmalade or a honey substitute ("miodoslod," a cheap surrogate then widespread). In the evening, delegates of various firms arrived and read the names of needed employees from their lists. In this way hundreds were saved. The employees of the Judenrat were also released.

This night of horror passed with extreme slowness.

In the lit hall people were dying, the others fainting or were in a state of semi-consciousness. As far as possible, people helped each other by sharing an apple or candy or by whispering encouraging words. A few more were executed on the stage and everyone saw this.

In the morning, the "joke" about breakfast was repeated. Soon many new victims were packed into the D.K.A.

Toward midday, people were pushed from the hall into the yard. Then a sort of parade was mounted with bayonets and rifle barrels literally on our throats for hours - or on empty stomachs. Later trucks arrived. Groups of people were loaded onto them and headed to an unknown destination. After some time the trucks came back for new human cargo. Finally my turn came. I climbed into the crowded covered truck with dozens of mostly broken and indifferent people, and was placed next to the rear door. The two guard's rifles were aimed at our heads. We could hardly move because of the density of people packed into the truck. Out of the guards sarcastic remarks I understood we were being transported to the site of execution. With thoughts about my wife and children whose fate was unknown to me, an enormous desire for life suddenly overcame me. I gave a cautious glance upwards. I could see the treetops with falling leaves on the background of gray skies. I thought, "Forest. Jump!" I leapt from my place, pushed the German aside and jumped off the truck. I landed with a strong blow to my leg. But immediately I stood up and ran into the woods. I could hear shots and cries from behind me. Soon weakness forced me to fall. But I could hear from far the truck's engine turning over again and concluded they had stopped searching for me. While still lying, after some time, mainly bursts of machine guns but also the shooting of rifles and pistols could be heard in the distance.

I reached Bolechow at night. The Jews I met told me that the pogrom was over. My wife and children were in the flat out of which many of our belongings had "disappeared."

And so the gloomy story ends.

The number of people murdered in the Taniawa woods by six machine guns was estimated at between 850 to 1,000. Many Gentiles were witnesses to this mass extermination, either from the forest or treetops. Some Jews tried to escape from the mass grave, which was dug beforehand, but they were shot dead. The only one who succeeded was Ducio Schindler, of blessed memory. He reported many details regarding "the last moments of the Taniawa martyrs." Many were beaten on their heads with stones by members of Drohobycz Sitch.

The Ukrainian policemen partly decided whose turn it was to be executed. The ones who cried or implored mercy were punished by being killed first. By contrast, some old "non-communists and decent" merchants were given the "privilege" of dying last. Many fell into the grave while wounded and in full consciousness. Some were shot again and died; the others were buried alive.

Many died proudly, cursing the murderers and telling them about the expected punishment of the German nation.

It seems that the killers celebrated the action's end by getting drunk. A bill was submitted to the Judenrat specifying the number of bullets used and other "expenses" incurred in the action. The Judenrat was also ordered to send Jewish women to wash the blood off the walls and floors of the D.K.A.

The bodies of the 28 victims who died in the D.K.A were buried in a particular lot of the Jewish cemetery. The body of Rabbi Horowitz, however, was not found and no one knew where it was. Only after a year or so his remains were discovered during the cleaning out of the latrines.

The impact of this first action defied description. It can be said with certainty that all the further disasters did not shock the Jews in the same manner. For many months after the action, one could hardly be found smiling. There were endless stories in Bolechow about the action. So it was told how the supposed Gentile friends proved to be traitors, and how in contrast, sudden salvation came from complete strangers. There were tales about some Germans with human hearts, making efforts to let the Jews go free. To this end, they told the Jews in German to escape and then simulated shooting at them, where in fact they fired into the air.

This had to be done in order to mislead their Ukrainian "aides" who showed unlimited energy and enthusiasm for the dirty job. Again, many, in spite of blatant facts, did not want to believe that many hundreds were massacred. There were persistent rumors supposedly spread on purpose about imaginary labor camps in nearby Vienna or other places where one or another Jew captured in the action was allegedly seen.

Even after fixing the grave of Taniawa for sanitary reasons, by many of Jews, the illusions remained. It was believed that only a part of those captured perished.

Due to the fact that, in the nearby town of Dolina, Jews still did not suffer an action, the head of the Bolechow Judenrat was blamed for his lack for ability to properly bribe the authorities in the manner of his Dolina counterpart. Such naïve assumptions were spread, mostly among the common people. But the educated were not entirely free of various illusions, perhaps as a way of escaping the cruel realities. The saying of Antek Zuckerman, one of the renowned commanders of the Warsaw Ghetto uprising, was, "In the Warsaw Ghetto the Jews had two enemies, the Germans and the illusions," fits Bolechow perfectly.

Some weeks passed and the life of Bolechow Jews apparently returned to "normal," as it was before the action. In the looted houses, locks were changed. People got used to sometimes seeing their Gentile neighbors wearing the clothing of the massacred, or even their own. Many started looking for work, since they learned that many saved their lives during the action because they had jobs in greater enterprises. There was a great decline of morality. Many felt their days were numbered so they decided to have a good time. At the same time preparing hiding places took premier importance. Valuables were hidden in secure places or buried in the soil. Furniture and households were transferred into Christian-true or imaginary friend's houses. The purpose was to avoid robbery or securing an "advance" or payment for future help. As later proved, this caused more harm than utility with only a few exceptions. The poorer element further suffered from hunger and disease. The Jewish burial society had their hands full with work. A large lot was assigned in the cemetery for the hundreds who died of typhoid and starvation. The destiny was such that soon most mass graves of various actions would be close to it.

The spring of 1942 brought the almost total eradication of the backward and the poor. More German functionaries were arriving. The greatest factories became German companies except for the leather industry, which was directly working for the German army. Lesser enterprises, such as the flour mills, now belonged to the municipality and were named United Town Industries (Vereinigte Stadt Industrie). A labor exchange was created, also for Jews. A Railway Guard (Bahnschutzpolizei) composed of the locals and a "Forest Guard," under the command of aged Germans, was being organized in Bolechow. Those bodies too, in the future, would fully contribute to the annihilation of the Jews.

The Jewish police (Ordnungsdienst) then consisted of several tens and had ties with the Ukrainian police. German directors of some factories seized the most beautiful Jewish houses along with furniture, etc. Megoff, the hypocritical criminal from Vienna and manager of the barrel factory, lived in the Bornstein (veterinary surgeon) villa. The manager of the "Great Sawmill" occupied Dr. Reifeisen's house. Krauthammer's house was chosen for a siege of the municipality. Its former premises in the "Magistrate" (town hall) became a Ukrainian police station, a place of torture and murder. During the spring and summer of 1942, the Germans intensified their various demands from the Judenrat. One asked for twenty kilos of cocoa, another wanted 50,000 zlotys and 500 kilos of white flour. Every hooligan or passerby seized the opportunity. As usual the blackmail was accompanied by threats to beat the local Jews unless the demands were satisfied in so many hours. The Jews were compelled to fully furnish a club for Volksdeutsche in Dr. Kurzer's house. The Jewish police coerced this organized robbery, often in a violent and merciless way. The German setback on the Moscow front in the winter of 1941 brought some encouragement to most Jews.

Some even hoped they would be saved very soon by the war's quick end. Others quoted the Polish proverb, "Until the fat becomes thin, the thin ones die." People got used to beatings and humiliating insults, to "searches" serving as a pretext for looting or bad treatment. The fact that there were several informers and traitors ceased to be considered unusual. Jews learned to circumvent rules and to bribe the superiors, managers and commanders of every kind, a dubious and often risky undertaking.

During this period, many Jews occupied quite responsible professional positions, owing both to their skills and knowledge of German. Many were trusted to some degree by their German superiors and had certain influence. Through them important information could be obtained. They served as mediators in redemption of the arrested and so on. But in most cases, these people and, of course, the Germans profited from their privileged positions. The same goes for the Judenrat. Often the information released proved false, with the purpose of spreading confusion, mistrust and demoralization. Some of the professionals were honest or even naïve people, manipulated by the Germans. It should be noted that some of the "mediators" got megalomania and were convinced that nothing bad would happen to them or to their families. Obviously, such phenomena were characteristic not only to Bolechow. It seems, however, that especially in Bolechow their end, at the hands of "the trusted friends" was very cruel. In the interval between the first and second action, rampaging Germans killed several Jews. Some Jews were bitten to death by the trained dogs of the Gestapo. Some were sent to Stanislawow, a prison from which no one returned, not even their bodies. Others were sent to Kalusz prison or elsewhere. According to regulations, every Jew aged fourteen and over had to start working. In fact, the majority of young people were already working. Often their age was falsified in order to find a job. Soon all the employed received special cards (Ausweis) issued by the Security Police and S.D. in Drohobycz. Card numbers in Bolechow were mostly from 114,000 to 116,000. Along with this document, white armbands with the Star of David were distributed. Each armband contained the corresponding number with a letter A in the center of the Star of David. Both were embroidered in red. Until December 1, 1942, working Jews got wages although they were extremely low. In some places of work, like Hobag G.M.B.H., later Delta G.M.B.M., the former State Great Sawmill, poor meals were given to workers in a canteen. Because of such situations, Jews resorted to selling or bartering their various belongings very cheaply. Unfortunately, toward the fall of 1942, many had little or no belongings left. Of course, Jews had to do the most difficult or most degrading work as defined by the rules. On the other hand, a working day consisted of only eight hours, but later was increased to nine hours (and in Delta to twelve hours). Despite the hard work and bad treatment, including beatings, the great majority adapted.

In the early summer, news spread about new actions on a huge scale in the whole of ex-Poland, including the immediate vicinity. The new kind of action was called "wild action." The official name used by the authorities and mentioned in announcements was "Aussiedlungsaction," roughly meaning displacement or transfer action. In August, wall placards appeared signed by Major-General Katzmann, the police and SS commander in "Distrikt Galizien." Their subject was the transfer and, mainly, a warning, of the death penalty for infringement of instructions on the transfer day. Christians helping Jews to escape were threatened with death too.

Here it is suitable to briefly describe the character of this new sort of action. With the exception of particular methods and idiosyncrasies applied by various action commanders, the actions went on as follows: First, wall placards were posted specifying the exact time and place of reporting by the Jews. Sometimes classes were mentioned; the old, children, sick, unemployed or all. There were instructions about the amount of food and clothing to be taken, mostly twenty kilos. Usually only a few hours elapsed from the posting to the time of reporting. The head of the Judenrat was detained because he was thought to be personally responsible for the fulfillment of the orders regarding the "transfer." It was only in the first actions that some Jews reported as instructed. In no way could the Judenrat gather so many in such a short time. Therefore, actions were carried out by the Germans and their aides, while arresting the Judenrat head. The whole thing obviously was aimed at further terrorizing the Judenrat. In eastern Galicia in general, Jews were either mass murdered, mostly in Jewish cemeteries, or sent by cargo trains to the death camp at Belzec. The camp was active from roughly spring 1942 until early spring 1943 when it was destroyed and all traces of it carefully erased. During its activity, mass executions in the towns stopped, for the most part.

If, after the action, Jews still remained as planned beforehand, then Judenrat's head was freed. In August Bolechow was terrified by the action in Dolina where all its 3,000 Jews were murdered in one day. As already stated, many Bolechowers believed in the Dolina's Judenrat's head's ability to prevent catastrophe, in contrast with his counterpart in Bolechow, Dr. Schindler. An electrified atmosphere spread throughout the township. Feverishly, hiding places were being improved and rucksacks packed with food. Rumors often spread, soon to be denied. All had the feeling of forthcoming disaster. Many started to spend nights in hideouts or in Christian's homes and many did not report for work. The tension and fear reached a degree beyond description. In the first days of September, SS men arrived in Bolechow, not something unusual. But one of them told a Jewish woman on Szewska Street, "It will begin on Thursday." The news spread immediately. Somewhat later, so it was told, a telegram was received by the Judenrat coming from Stryj saying, "The parcels did arrive." This was the password agreed upon in case those in Stryj obtained reliable information about the action's start. On September 3rd, at dawn, three rifle shots were heard from the town center. Then shots became more frequent and some were mingled with the screaming of the wounded and the executed. The noise of the breaking down of doors and cupboards accompanied by sobbing, curses and yelling could be heard everywhere. This was the typical tumult of an action; a combination of horrifying voices, strong enough by itself to break people's spirit.

So the murderous gang of the "Flying Brigade," an expression in common use but quite unclear, entered into the action, aided by the Ukrainian police, Jewish police and other organizations.

On Wednesday night, Judenrat was approached by the action's command with an order; gather 2,000 Jews in the Rynek in the morning. Dr. Schindler and the members of the Judenrat were arrested since the order was rather formal and not feasible. This was in accordance with the common practice in actions, as explained. The action lasted for three days. This time most of the old, sick and children were killed on the spot. In some cases, old women were strangled. The skulls of the elderly men were crushed with rifle butts and infants' heads were smashed into walls or telephone poles. Many living on the outskirts of town, which meant relatively far from the concentration point in the Magistrate's courtyard, were shot in their homes or yards. On the Dolinska Street whole families were shot dead in the yard of Mr. Levi's house. They were the families Levi, Kuddish, Zauderer, Streifer and more.

Since most of the hideouts proved to be primitive and resembling each other, some were no match for the searchers. Often the crying of babies caused the hidden to be found. Some mothers strangled their babies with their own hands to prevent their crying. Elsewhere the hidden tried to kill the children while the parents protested. This was the background to horrible tragedies. In some cases children and adults disclosed the hiding places of their families, being promised life for their treason. Such promises were never fulfilled. The traitors died in even more cruel ways than others. Some Germans liked to appear as "justice makers" so the punishment was for both being Jews and traitors. But generally, on the verge of death, Jews behaved with courage and dignity, sometimes evoking amazement among the Germans. In particular many were the manifestations of family love and devotion. In these days, Bolechow seemed an incarnation of horror. Hundreds of dead and those in agony lay in the streets, yards, houses and ditches. Streets filled with mobs penetrating hiding places, beating, murdering, extraditing and, above all, robbing. Nearly all Jewish houses were subject to break-ins and pillaging. There were some 2,000 detainees in the courtyard of the Magistrate and the adjacent part of Rynek Square. Many perished there, the old and the weak in particular. For three days the victims suffered from thirst and hunger in the extreme heat. The honest among the Jewish policemen tried to do their best to supply some water and food. But their opportunities were very limited. Still, thanks to this and the efforts to obtain a little food at a high price, brought some relief to a part of the unfortunate in their last days. Jewish policemen and undertakers used carts to carry the killed to the Jewish cemetery. In Szewska Street the passing of blood dripping carts became an everyday event during that period. It was told that one person managed to feign as dead, during that action, and was transported in the death cart. He dared to stop feigning death only when already in the grave. The martyrs of the second action, some 400, were buried in several mass graves in the western part of the cemetery next to the majority of other victims of the Holocaust. Although heavily guarded, many succeeded in escaping from the concentration spot. Others, by various ruses, joined the groups of liberated employees. While releasing the specialized workers, no importance whatsoever was attached to the famous Ausweis cards. On Saturday, September 5th, in the afternoon, some 1,600 heavily escorted Jews, made their way to the railway station. Some religious elders were told to sing "My Shteteli Belz," a Jewish folk song (although Belzec is a different place). In the station, more of the employed were freed.

At the same time others were cruelly butchered. It happened as a result of the attempts made by many to escape. No one succeeded. All those who tried were killed. After packing some 120 people per freight wagon, the train started slowly moving in the direction of Lwow toward an unknown destination. The Germans claimed that all were being transported to a distant working place. To some extent it seemed plausible because of the systematical extermination of the children, the old, etc. On the other hand, the horrible conditions of transportation and some quite direct allusions did not leave much hope. So, some tried to escape the death train. A few succeeded. Upon returning to Bolechow, after several days, they gave full details about the hellish conditions in the locked wagons. The density was unsupportable (120 or more instead of 40 as per standard). People suffered to death of suffocation, thirst or hunger. Many died and some lost their sanity. Various vague rumors circulated as to the fate of the deported but this time only a few believed that anyone survived. After the liberation of Galicia, it only became clear the victims of the second action had been gassed at Belzec. Along with hundreds of thousands of Jews from the region they were buried in huge graves. Later their remains were exhumed and burned. The whole Belzec complex was totally eradicated in early 1943. This was in order to erase evidence of the crime in the wake of the deterioration of Hitler's army's situation on the eastern front.

The "Great Action," as the second action was called, differed from the first action in many ways: public executions (although not of hundreds or thousands), searches in Christian houses, apparently better and more methodical planning, participation of the Jewish police and groups of "Hitlerjugend (Hitler's youth organization) brought from outside. Paramilitary organs of "Railway Guards" (Bahnschutzpolizei) and "Forest Guards" also joined. Helmets were commonly worn, a kind of novelty at that time.

The worst murderers proved to be the Ukrainian policemen, Luhovyi, Demianyn and, above all, the depraved sadist Matowiecki. Another horrible assassin, equal only to Matowiecki was Strutynski, also a Ukrainian policeman. The German Piatke of Stryj Schupo (Schutzpolizei), chief of Bolechow's Ukrainian police, had dogs trained to literally tear their victims to pieces.

Some Jewish policemen showed extraordinary ability, enthusiasm and initiative when searching the hiding, often being praised by the Germans and Ukrainians.

When some 2,500 Jews returned from the woods, villages and hideouts they found a looted and deserted town. Dead bodies were still lying everywhere. Again, many noticed that their neighbors and other Gentiles were wearing their clothing or using their household goods or furniture. This was despite the execution by the Germans of several looting villagers. It seems the Germans decided to monopolize this "branch." They sent great amounts of commodities and furniture to Lwow by lorries. It appears, however, they only took interest in goods of higher quality.

The impact of the "Great Action," most probably carried out under the command of Captain (Hauptsturmfuhrer) Hans Block of Drohobycz, was enormous. But most people soon recovered. It seems that one of the main reasons for this was that the people now saw these events as inevitable and almost natural. Only a few days elapsed and life returned to "normal." Simultaneously, effort restarted to improve hiding places, finding Christian friends, obtaining "Aryan" papers, etc. At this time some survivors of the fully liquidated Jewish communities started coming to Bolechow, from Skole in particular. Most were young people.

Others continued on their way to Hungary. Some began to hide with the aid of Christians. They would remain hidden for a long time; until the liberation. Others took refuge in elaborate hiding places for the same purpose. After the action, the attitude of most Gentiles coming from the lower classes sharply deteriorated. This probably happened for the following reasons: new victories of Hitler's armies, further evidence showing that the Jews would be subject to total extermination, the fact that Jews knew a lot about the perpetrators of the robbings and murders. Most of the Polish intelligentsia behaved with hypocrisy at that time. Their aim was to gain the confidence of their Jewish acquaintances so as to obtain payment for the promises of future help. Scores succeeded in improving their financial condition or even enriching themselves at the Jew's expense. They got bolder because they succeeded in this manner. The formerly mentioned Podole barter business continued and flourished in this state of affairs.

B. The Second Action

The second action began on August 20, 1942. A few hours before, the news reached those destined to die about what was awaiting them. In addition, they knew that Jews had been killed in actions in other cities. They hurried to take refuge through the various means that they had prepared for themselves. That day at dawn, the Germans enlisted the militianists, the Ukrainian citizen volunteers, and the Jewish militia, and commanded them to find and take out all who were in hiding, arrest them, and bring them to the yard of the city hall. The searching and snatching lasted for 36 hours.

My parents, my sister of blessed memory, and I were among them.

Masses of people were brought along with us. Everyone was forced to lie face down. The wicked militianists were permitted to perpetrate any acts that their hearts and eyes desired. Very many people were murdered on the spot by their hands. Among the victims was Dr. Blumenthal of blessed memory, who loved his fellowman. He was a popular man, revered by the community.

The action in the yard of the city hall lasted for 60 hours! The Satanic executioners took their vengeance upon us for two and a half days!

A significant number of the afflicted people died from the torture, beatings, hunger and thirst. The extent of the cruelty went beyond anyone's imagination. Pregnant women were beaten mercilessly. The wicked people beat their bellies. They snatched infants from their mother's arms, tossed them, and broke their heads against the stone walls or the telegraph poles. I was an eyewitness to the atrocities that took place in the yard of the city hall. Therefore, I permit myself to describe them.

The nationalist Strotinski presided over the actions of the Ukrainians. The monster Strotinski, a trampling beast, a hater of humanity, overtook even the Nazi mass murderers with his evil. May he be cursed, may G-d curse him when he sleeps, when he arises, and when he goes along his way! May his name be blotted out forever! This despicable evildoer, this destructive demon, is responsible for the murder of thousands of martyrs.

After the slaughter in the yard of the city hall, those who remained alive were brought to the train station, where they were loaded upon train cars. Each car was designed for 20-30 people, but they packed 100-120 people into them. The small windows were covered with barbed wire. An armed German guard stood at each door. This "load" was transported to the crematoria of Belzec.

Aside from me, one woman by the name of B. Glass (with us today in Israel) saved herself by jumping from the moving car. One by one, including my unfortunate family, they were murdered at Belzec. Approximately 4,000 of our Jewish brethren were murdered in the second action.

C. The Third Action

On October 24, 1942, the Judenrat was ordered to extradite 400 Jews to the Gestapo. The task was carried out by the Jewish police. Only on the third, and last, day the Ukrainian police were approached to "give a hand." The victims were detained in Rand's house on Kosciuszko Street. Workers of various factories, unless they were highly specialized workers, counted among the arrested. The conditions under which the arrested were held was quite comfortable compared with the previous actions. For money one could easily acquire food and something to drink. During this action, whoever had the means to bribe the Judenrat, the Ukrainian and the Jewish police, was released. To replace the freed, poorer people were arrested. In fact, they only recently turned poor since the bulk of the original paupers had already disappeared in the spring. This base practice, in addition to being a means for extorting money, also represented the policy of the Judenrat to get rid of the poor. They were considered an element lacking the ability to survive. Finally the 400 were packed into a freight train and transported to an unknown destination (We later learned it was Belzec). A couple of weeks prior to the third action, all Jews were ordered to settle in a special quarter. It was restricted to Rynek and the streets Szewska and Kazimierzowaka, and their adjacent lanes.

Everybody moved on his own, without pressure, after finding a dwelling. Many occupied flats, now empty, as a result of the "great action." Still there was a great shortage of flats. Therefore, quantities of furniture and household goods had to be left behind or sold for next to nothing. There were no walls or fences around the quarter, nor guards. No restrictions on movement outside the compound were imposed. There were complaints by the mayor deposited in Stryj about this and other similar subjects. "Aryans" also lived in the quarter. It looked like the only reason for creating it was to gather the Jews in one place to make future actions easier.

D. The Fourth Action

Some weeks after the third action, from the 20th to 23rd of November, the fourth action took place. 300 Jews were caught by the Jewish police. This time it was without the help of the Ukrainian police. Again, they were put into a cargo train. In all aspects this action resembled the third action. But now, the employed were exempted. The equipment of he "policemen" consisted of axes, picks and so on used to break the "bunkers" (i.e.: kinds of hiding places). In order to prevent the arrested from escaping, they used various tricks such as taking away the men's trouser belts, thus making running impossible. They also tied the victims to the policemen with ropes They held them on leashes like dogs. All this was mainly because they had no real weapons.

Toward the end of November a new instruction was published by Major-General Katzmann. It announced that starting December 1, 1942, the Jews of Galicia would either stay in ghettos or be interned in labor camps. Up until this time ghettos only existed in larger and medium sized towns. People were free to choose between the labor camps and the ghetto in Stryj. In Bolechow only the camps would remain. As usual, those who would not comply (i.e.: remain in Bolechow but not in a camp) were threatened with the death penalty.

Consequent to those instructions a vivid debate developed among the Jews as to what was preferable: the ghetto or the camps. A great majority decided to remain in the Bolechow camps. Some claimed that the whole issue was nothing more than a stratagem and that all would be killed on December 1st. In fact, the four camps were already in existence before this official date. They were Delta, tanneries/leather factories, water management, "Wasserwirtschaft" dealing with river maintenance, and United Town Industries (together) and the barrel factory. It does not mean that camps were constructed. In fact, some blocks of Jewish houses, or separate houses, were adapted to this purpose. The houses were surrounded by a wooden fence about two meters high. The entrance was through gates watched by Jewish policemen. In some houses kitchens were installed along with three tiered bunks. The arrangements were far from uniform. In most cases people had their own beds, sleeping six or seven per room. Several hundred left for the Stryj ghetto, mostly those unfit to work. They were permitted to move individually with no restrictions as to quantity or kind of belongings to take with them. But, of course, again the transfer caused the added loss of property.

It was not by coincidence that the subject of households is being mentioned. The lack of possessions meant too often death by starvation. All the horrible events, coming rapidly in sequence after the second action, brought disastrous blows on the psyche of many. There were many suicides, sometimes by whole families. The poison business flourished. Often fakes were sold. Most suicides occurred during the actions so as to spare the torment. People did not want to die at the hand of the murderers. Many people kept poison with them at all times. In contrast with this phenomenon reflecting despair, numerous others spent unlimited energy on efforts to survive.

E. Bolechow After December 1, 1942

More than a thousand Jews remained in Bolechow. About 850-900 were in the camps. The others belonged to groups as follows:

A. Jewish police. Some 40 – 50 men, residing in a house on Kazimierzowska Street.

B. The employees of the "Litter Collecting Service," about 50 people, dwelling in private houses situated in the ex-Jewish quarter. In fact, most did not work.

C. Staff of the Jewish hospital serving the camps. The hospital, earlier funded by Judenrat, was situated in the quarter of Ruski Bolechow opposite Landes Leather Works. It counted a few dozen.

D. Physicians Dr. Landes and Dr. Rinnthal continued to live in their homes. They mainly treated the Christians.

In town and the surrounding area many Jews hid illegally but their numbers are unknown. Some lived in various "bunkers" on their own or were hidden by Gentiles. Others were hiding in the camps, among them a number of small children. Almost without interruption, small groups of Jews passed through Bolechow, survivors of annihilated communities or those who escaped from ghettos and camps. Here they sometimes succeeded in finding food or even time and a means to heal their diseases and wounds on their way to the forest or to Hungary. Unfortunately, many were caught and executed on the spot.

All the inmates were given a new insignia, in the form of a white cloth badge, a square of about 5 by 5 cm. In its center, embroidered in black were either the letter "R" or "W." Each letter was stamped by the seal of the "Police" and SS," over which everyone had to embroider his personal number (as per old "Ausweis"). One had to bear the badge on the left side of the chest (so as to "hit the heart straight" according to their joke).

The letters "R" and "W" were the initials of the Ruestungsindustrie (Munition Industry) or the Wehrmacht (Army). The "R" was considered better, perhaps because the majority got the letter "W," (Water Management, United Town Industries, leather factories and Delta Saw Mills).

The new era had begun with rather superficial changes to the lifestyle of the remaining Jews. Apart from living in concentration under slack supervision, (this provoked complaints from the Ukrainian local authority), basically there was little change. As already stated, many lived in camps beforehand. Most continued to work in the same place.

The food distributed was not sufficient to sustain life because of the interruptions of supplies. People had to buy provisions at Christian groceries or from the peasants. There was only tighter supervision with respect to hygiene and exterior order. Large boards were posted on the gates and walls of the camps on which was written: "Compulsory Labor Camp Bolechow – Jews" and other details. There were rare cases of illness in the camps. Most people seemed healthy. They were also reasonably well dressed. A state of partial hunger only existed in the last weeks. This was in spite of the hard work. Sometimes work continued for 48 hours or more with only brief interruptions. However, in general, work lasted 9 hours (also during the night shift) and in "Delta" it lasted 12 hours. Most people were already hardened and held on. Till the end, Jews kept responsible positions and sometimes many "Aryans" were under their charge. As already stated, this caused many an illusion of being important and thus not subject to harm. It seems these illusions had been nourished on purpose by the Germans who gave calming messages in profusion.

At the same time they enjoyed valuable "presents."

Apparently, important factors acted in favor of the Jews in labor camps: heavy bombardments of German industries, sending hordes of Poles and Ukrainians to forced labor in Germany, mobilization of young Ukrainians to form the SS division "Galizien" and the defeats of the Axis forces. This probably explained the existence of the camps of Bolechow until the end of August 1943. In Drohobycz and Boryslaw they existed until the Russians came. It seems that the penetration of Soviet partisans under Kolpak, indirectly brought the liquidation of the camps.

During the winter of 1942/3 the remainder of Bolechow Jewry felt relief. The illusion of safety was mainly fueled by the fact that the Stryj ghetto still existed. It was clear the "unproductive" element would be liquidated first. Some ascribed the calm to German defeats, mainly in Stalingrad. As it looked, the old unbiased optimism made a comeback. This was perhaps a reaction after a long period of despair. In any case, such attitudes always brought enormous damage. In the camps even a sort of folklore evolved, including songs, saying, jokes, etc. During that time an attempt was made by a group of young people from Lwow and Bolechow to cross the border into Hungary. News spread about their betrayal by the guides, who turned them over to the border guards.

According to a new regulation issued about then, Jews would be kept in prison for a maximum of 24 hours and either freed or executed. However, at the same time, the power of the Ukrainian police versus the camp inmates was restricted. This created a paradox: there was more freedom after being locked in the camps. In the last days of February, around one hundred young people were brought from the Stryj ghetto. The group consisted of ex-Bolechowers who now joined the workers in the barrel factory. They were lodged in its camps. At dawn of March 5th, these camps were surrounded by strong forces of the SS and Ukrainian police. All believed the hour of the final action had come. But after some time it became clear that the aim was only to capture the newcomers from Stryj. Jewish policemen arrived and took the unfortunates out, promising they would be sent to the Janowski camp in Lwow. This was an infamous labor camp in Lwow where thousands died. The group was escorted to the Magistrate. There they were held until the afternoon (pending the digging of the grave). Then they were led, until heavy guard, including the "Ordnungsdienst," to the Jewish cemetery. There they were ordered to completely undress and had to wait an additional two hours as the grave was still incomplete. Some tried unsuccessfully to escape. All the others were shot. The Jewish policemen intended to leave the cemetery but suddenly the

Germans and Ukrainians surrounded them. Prior to being executed, the Jewish policemen performed a kind of military parade with salutes, standing at attention, etc, literally to the verge of the grave. Finally they, too, had to undress. Apparently their commander, the lawyer Pressler, son-in-law of Dr. Schindler, had slapped the face of the Nazi superior officer. It should be mentioned that early in the morning several Jewish policemen fled, since they felt endangered. On the next day, Dr. Schindler committed suicide.

Equally, on March 5th, the Stryj ghetto was liquidated. Its thousands of residents were shot outside of the town in the village of Holobutowo.

These events depressed the remainder of the Bolechow Jews.

Already in the initial Katzmann's order related to the establishment of the camps, there was mention of March 31, 1943 as the final date of the camps "legal existence." The majority of inmates did not notice this detail, at least at the beginning, since they were used to living from one day to the next. A period of four months seemed fantastically long. Various "big shots" promised the camp's legality would be extended beyond March 31st. Then an instruction came to again register all the inmates. An anxious wait started toward the fateful date but the camp's people still had hope (provided there was any sense in logical thinking under the Nazis). The employees of the "Litter Collecting Service" already knew they were fated to die. One after another news came about the annihilation of this group in various places.

It seems worthy to briefly comment upon this "service." For reasons totally unclear unless one considers the German mania for recycling, they enjoyed a privileged status. In every action they were among the first to be freed. They were given a special great round tag made of tin, which had to be attached to their lapel. Several tens of Jews enrolled as employees of the "service." In fact, most never worked. And, they profited by their safety. They were among the few allowed to remain in their houses. But suddenly they fell into disgrace and, being aware of this, they made desperate efforts to escape. Most failed. The majority were arrested by the Ukrainian police and shot dead in the Jewish cemetery by the infamous Matowiecki.

This massacre took place on March 12, 1943. The number of victims was 28. The service's manager Joshua Freilich was released and kept at his duties as before.

Contrary to previous fears, nothing happened in the camps on March 31st or afterward. From March until June, a relative calm reigned. The life in the camp continued as before. The only difference was the complete lack of watchmen. As already mentioned, even when manned by Jewish policemen, the guard was quite inefficient.

During this period - and it seems such was the state of mind in the whole of Poland – many Jews developed a mentality of resistance. Unfortunately, this happened too late and without proper momentum. As an example of this new spirit, an event in summer can be recalled.

A group of about ten young Jewish men and women were hiding nearby the camp of the barrel factory. They consisted of survivors from nearby towns. People in the camp fed them. When the Ukrainian police discovered them, they did not beg for their lives. Neither did they try to bribe the policemen, or even try to escape. They attacked the policemen with knives and succeeded in wounding several of them. After quite a long struggle all were killed except one man who succeeded in escaping in spite of the great numbers of policemen and hooligans.

The Germans knew what happened and apparently there was an inner dispute between the economic circles and the political party circles (including the SS who were in charge of the camps and had the last word) as to whether to keep or abolish the camps. As already stated, there was a shortage of labor in Galicia then and many skilled professionals stayed in the camps. The cost of running the camps was next to nothing, so the German firms greatly profited and wanted the situation to continue.

It appears the protagonists of the "final solution" had the lower hand until the summer of 1943. The situation changed when news spread about the dangerous fermentation and uprisings in the ghettos of Warsaw, Bialystok and Cracow. The penetration of the brigade of Soviet partisans, under the renowned major-general Kolpak, into the Carpathian Mountains no doubt played a major role. In June the people of Water Management and the United Town Industries started feeling they were in danger. The economic importance of these enterprises was rather low, except for the leather industry. The inmates of Water Management used to pay their directorate for each day of work. In other camps no such thing existed. In June they were requested to pay increasingly higher amounts until it finally became absurd.

In the early morning of July 6th, the two camps were surrounded by many Ukrainian policemen brought from outside under German command. Some 100 people were brought to the Magistrate, "town hall" and put into two big cells. The magistrate was turned into a police station and prison. Again, several were killed when trying to escape but a number of inmates succeeded in avoiding capture and hiding. As told by survivors, the Ukrainians tried to convince the Jews they were only being taken to work in nearby Dolina. However, all of them knew the waiting in the Magistrate Building would end when the grave was ready.

In the morning, Ducio Schindler succeeded in snatching the rifle of a policeman and almost killed him, but was disarmed by many thugs. A German who appreciated his courage spared his life. He later approached the arrested and proposed a massive flight.

It was agreed that in Szewska Street, leading to the Jewish cemetery and the so-called "Horses Cemetery," when they heard a whistle, the people would disperse in all directions. In the afternoon they were led toward the cemetery. Schindler's whistles were heard but nobody moved. Ducio decided to give the example and broke into the chain of escorting policemen. Wounded by many bullets, he agonized for hours in a yard. The remaining people were brought to the vicinity of Dolzka, a place where dead horses used to be buried and the Jews were executed.

Ukrainian policemen prevented robbing the deserted camps. Several Christians trying to break in were arrested. Later, the Germans took some objects and the camps were abandoned to the pillagers. Gentile witnesses said this time, in particular, many jewels and watches were thrown into the Mlynowka stream, as well as torn dollars and local money banknotes. A new "pleasantry" in the camps was: "We work like horses and therefore we are being buried in a horse cemetery."

At other camps nothing changed on the surface. At this stage, thousands of soldiers of Vlassov's army (ex-Russian POWs under German command) arrived in Bolechow and its surrounding area. They were soon joined by units of other nationalities, mainly Azerbaijanis and Tatars who also collaborated with the Nazis. These were commonly nicknamed Kalmyks. The reason for their arrival was the penetration of the Soviet partisans in the mountains around Jaremcze after a near 1,000 mile march.

A strict night curfew was imposed on the whole population. Watchmen were placed every 50 meters on the roads and railways. An enormous tension reigned in the camps and almost everyone prepared to leave. On the days of July 25th and 26th, many did leave and nearly all the rest intended to do the same in the next hours. The authorities this time delayed their action.

On July 26th at around 4 P.M. an action started. Its aim, no doubt, was the total murder of the remaining Bolechow Jews. First shots were heard in the camp of the leather workers which caused flight from the other camps. Despite the participation of Vlassov's Russians, and many other police units, the action failed, lacking the surprise factor and poor planning. The Jews dispersed everywhere and most fled to the distant forests. Only one hundred were caught and about 80 were killed in various circumstances. After three days the arrested were freed and a kind of amnesty was published toward the others. And, since the massive fleeing was rather spontaneous, with only little planning, it could not hold up for long. Most had no choice but to return. The camps underwent a thorough pillaging; this time, it seems, mostly by Jews. Many people who came back discovered that fellow inmates sold their belongings unless they were already stolen by the Gentiles. In general, a minority with a dubious past did this. The returned greatly suffered. Some destroyed their banknotes and valuables when caught. The Germans started with an apparently new approach toward the remaining, seemingly out of fear that they would join the partisans or resist with arms. Indeed, during the last action, several Jews opened fire with pistols on the Germans in the camp of the leather industries.

Although there were no German casualties, as far as known, this left a strong impression. The coming days were marked by the arrival of SS Oberscharrfuhrer (sergeant-major) Grzymek and his aide, an Unterscharrfuhrer. They brought a suite of Jewish employees and servants and settled in Strassman's house on the end of Kolejowka Boulevard.

Soon Grzymek began his series of speeches to the camp people in German. As later proved, the aim was to calm the spirits and to lie. According to him, the policy toward Jews underwent a change due to the latest victories of the Allies. He said the American would kill Germans if the Germans killed the Jews. He claimed that a "great amnesty" was happening and encouraged Jews to pass on the news to all who were still hiding including the old and children. He promised that the construction of a central camp for all Bolechow Jews would start immediately. It would include, among other things, schools, kindergartens and a hospital. The speeches usually ended with strange declarations such as, "I am your father." The situation in the camps then abounded in paradoxes. So, for instance, the camps were watched by Ukrainians with pistols. But at the same time, Jews were allowed to freely move, not only in town but in the surrounding area as well. The guards' presence was explained by the need to protect the Jews. Simultaneously, the area of the camps was reduced to a minimum. The camp of the barrel factory that used to consist of seven houses now consisted of one. The meager food rations were abolished. Many suffered from hunger and some collapsed. They were taken to camp's hospital, which still functioned on a relatively high standard. The overcrowding in the camps became unbearable, Many slept in the yard or in the factories.

In the meantime, the "promised" camp's construction proceeded at a feverish pace on an open space between the refinery and Dolina Road. Its form was typical of concentration camps, strongly fenced by barbed wire, etc. Pending this, the "Father" (as ironically nicknamed in the camps) Grzymek was extorting money as he could, through the people in charge of various camps ("Lageraelteste"). As usual the collecting of money was accompanied by scandals and acts of violence.

August 22nd was determined as the day of transfer to the new camp. Everyone had to take a bath in the "Mikveh" (ritual bath) situated on Kazimierzowska Street, put in operation especially for this. Owing to the great bustle, many were able to escape, the conditions being favorable. Prior to moving into the new camp there was much arguing about whether to join the camp or to flee. Most agreed that the camp would exist for long. Hardly could one believe the miserly German would invest in something profitless. On the other hand, there was fear of heavy guards, etc., preventing the possibility of escape. Tens left their hiding places and entered the camp. So, after an interruption of many months, again Jewish children and the old could be seen – but not for long.

F. The Final Annihilation and "Judenrein" ("Free of Jews") Period

On August 25, 1943 the new camp was surrounded by strong forces consisting mainly of Vlassov soldiers. About 1,200 people were escorted to the Jewish cemetery and shot including hundreds from Skole who had, at the time, been brought to the camp. This time a new method of murder was used. The victims were shot upward into the neck from a very short range and simultaneously pushed by the murderer's leg into the grave. In former actions sometimes the victims were ordered to enter the grave and lay down over the killed, to be shot in their turn. Mostly, however, the victims were shot with rifles and machine guns from some distance while they were standing on the verge of the grave. As a result, quite a number were buried while slightly wounded or even unhurt. This resulted in many stories, widespread among Jews and Christians alike about sighs from the graves and earth moving on the surface. It seems, however, that the main purpose of the new method was saving bullets. As far as known, there were no successful escapes. The "Father," Josef Grzymek, originally from Silesia, nicknamed the "butcher of Lwow," ran wild and horribly tortured his victims before killing them.

In the camp, Vlassov's soldiers arranged a kind of auction for the commodities left. The graves were covered with a layer of lime and Bolechow became "Judenrein," free of Jews. To celebrate this joyful event the brass band of Salina Salt Works paraded through Bolechow. It seems plausible that some 300 Jews remained in forests, hidden by Christians or hiding on their own in various places. Probably a half of them were discovered and executed by the end of September. These people, mostly deprived of outside help (i.e.: the Gentiles), also used ramshackle and primitive hideouts, if any at all. Many fell into the hands of hostile Christians when searching for food and were handed over to the police. The Christians who brought the Jews to them in order to exploit them financially, of course, hastened the extraditing. The more prudent among such Christians gave preference to poisoning or simply slaughtering the hiding and burying them in secret. Indeed, the possibility of punishment then seemed a sure thing. Quite a number of Gentiles sincerely desired to save Jews by hiding them. In this period Fascist Italy collapsed and all believed Germany would soon surrender. Unfortunately, things evolved differently, putting both the hiding and their benefactors in a most difficult situation.

In the autumn of 1943 if Jews hidden by Christians were discovered, the latter could still expect only to be reprimanded – in most cases. This was despite the draconian regulations threatening death for helping Jews. On the face this could seem quite unlikely. But for certain the German and Ukrainian police had good reasons for such a policy. The main one was the relative weakness of their armed forces in the region. This was along with the background of the growing underground armed forces of Ukrainian nationalists, directed against both Germans and Russians. At this stage the Ukrainians became deeply disappointed in the Germans. Although hating Jews, the Christians considered it unacceptable to die because of giving shelter to Jews. They were taught by the Germans themselves that a Jew's life was not worth a penny, so why kill an Aryan because of a miserable Jew. In addition, almost everyone had some business with Jews, to profit from their distress. If one hid the Jews during an action, no one could know whether he really wanted to save them or extradite them. In cases of prolonged hiding, some Christians paid with their lives, such as the Pole Zdzislaw Szymanski and his sister.

In the autumn of 1943 a stricter approach began, perhaps because of fear that any Jews would survive. Ukrainians at this stage also felt a strong hatred for the Germans and were not ready to be punished by them because of the Jews.

Even before, when the camps still existed, a directive was issued by Katzmann promising 5,000 zlotys and twenty liters of vodka for each Jew denounced. It seems that until the Judenrein period, in fact, only a small fraction of this was given to informers. The lion's share was shared among various supervisors. Now, however, the income of many decreased. There were no more Jews to blackmail or rob. Many became interested in receiving the reward being now paid, if not fully, at least in its greater part. This probably was due to pressure by the interested. Germany's defeat then appeared as though it would soon come. May feared heavy punishment for their involvement in crimes. They were searching for the hiding Jews with almost endless energy. Some spent weeks combing the fields and woods to find a Jew. Others were eavesdropping in the night, putting their ears on the walls and windows to catch a suspected voice or noise.

In the winter of 1943/1944, Jewish houses were put up for sale for almost nothing. Some were dismantled in order to get various building materials and wood for heating. However, the main reason was trying to discover caches of valuables that indeed still existed in many Jewish houses. As a result, most of the ex-Jewish homes were severely damaged.

Despite the mild winter, the hiding Jews had to face some of the most complicated problems. Searches for Jews then attained a peak. Villages were combed by the army using dogs and aided by the peasants who were idle in this season. During the winter at least 100 Jews lost their lives. Some fell while fighting as members of the Babij's partisan group. Some 40 people, the Josefsberg family and others, were revealed in Huziejow village, hidden by the local miller. This happened because of criminal negligence by one of the hiding. He went to his former home to pick up valuables out of the cache on hearing that the house was being dismantled. The miller and his wife also paid with their lives. Sixteen people were found in a cave at Gerynia Forest. They had been smoked out and then shot and buried. The Ungar family was among them. Only nine of these people were certified as dead by 2004.

Smaller groups were revealed and shot. People hiding Jews were exposed to incessant intimidation and coaxing. So, for example, during a public meeting in the village of Gerynia, people were told that presently all over the world Jews were being annihilated. The Soviet army was doing the same and also killing those hiding Jews. After the meeting two Jews were turned over to the authorities.

The hope for the war's quick end vanished. At the same time it became clear that sheltering Jews was a difficult, death-threatening task. Thus, some decided to kill and secretly bury the Jews they were hiding. One can assume that in most cases they succeeded. But it also happened that such attempts became publicly disclosed. Eight members of the Wohl family hiding at Gerynia were poisoned. However, as the poison proved ineffective, they were butchered and buried in the fields. From time to time the bodies of Jews who died of cold and starvation were discovered in the woods. In the winter of 1944, four bodies were found hanging from the trees. These Jews apparently committed suicide.

During the autumn several Jews handed themselves over. It is worthwhile to mention the case of the ex-policeman Kopel, who appeared before his "friend" the deputy-commander of the Ukrainian police asking to be killed by him personally. The request was fulfilled.

In the spring and summer of 1944 several lonely Jews were found and executed. The last case occurred about a fortnight prior to liberation. During this period the general interest shifted to other subjects, such as the massive appearance of bands of Ukrainian nationalists, the activities of the Polish underground, mutual killings between Germans and Ukrainians.

Searching for Jews ceased to be lucrative or easy. However, the Jews were mercilessly tortured and killed if found. The Ukrainian nationalist bands policy was the murdering of Jews. So, for example, when Bandera's people got information about Rozia Adler hiding in the village of Hoszow, they requested that she be handed over. After robbing her, she was murdered. This happened in early summer of 1944. In the winter, Ukrainian nationalists had already started attacks on the Polish population, by killing a family of seven at Polanice village. They finally set fire to all Polish houses in the neighboring villages. Whole families were burned alive. Several families of Poles were murdered in Bolechow proper, although not in great numbers.

Many Bolechow Poles took refuge in Stanislawow. It should be noted that there was some anti-German activity by the Polish underground, most likely the Armja Krajowa (A.K.), reaching its peak with the setting on fire of the barrel factory. However, all their activity stopped after the arrests of some people and their execution in Stryj. Much more important seemed to be the operations led by groups of armed Jews during the winter of 1944. Among other things, they attempted to kill the butcher Matowiecki in Bolechow. He narrowly escaped. In another incident Ukrainian police were attacked by an armed group. In fierce exchanges two policemen were killed and the rest fled. These actions were ascribed to Babij's partisan group. He was a Ukranian communist from Dolina and served in the Ukrainian police after the German invasion. He later deserted and organized a partisan unit, manned almost exclusively by Jews and based in Dolina Forest. Until the autumn of 1943, they showed nearly no activity. Despite the incessant combing by German, Hungarian and Vlassow armies, most group members perished. Their deeds still greatly impressed the population. Many feared the armed Jews in the later period. As a result, whenever Jews were revealed, relatively great forces were deployed in order to apprehend them, taking minimal risks.

In one case, to illustrate, when rumors spread that a Jew armed with a pistol was hiding at a farm in Gerynia in the spring of 1944, the Ukrainian police merely promised they would soon come to deal with him.

Some sectors of the Ukrainian nationalists (U.P.A. of Bandera) fought the Germans for some time. A German unit of 22 soldiers riding in the narrow gauge mountain train (Kalejka) near Bubniszcze was attacked and annihilated.

During the spring of 1944 Stryj, Drohobycz, and Lwow underwent heavy air bombardments, mainly by hundreds of American planes based in the U.S.S.R. The blasts were distinctly heard in Bolechow. Leaflets were dropped. Heavy military traffic started on the roads. Jewish labor companies were attached to the Hungarian troops. But at the same time horrible news spread about the exterminations of Hungarian Jewry.

At the end of June the thunder of artillery could be heard from the east. Its stopping depressed the few Jewish survivors. In July army movements attained their peak. The Germans started entrenching themselves in Bolechow and its surroundings. Guns were placed in many locations.

Prior to this, much of the industrial equipment was dismantled and sent to Germany. Since spring, hundreds were employed enlarging and improving the roads. Many tombstones from the Jewish cemetery were used. Some were crushed into gravel and others were used whole to pave the sidewalks.

Finally, bands of hungry soldiers mercilessly robbed the peasants of their food, provoking general hate of the Germans. The same Ukrainians that welcomed them with enthusiasm were now expecting the coming of the Soviet liberators. But this was only a temporary mood. The echoes of heavy fighting was heard from the direction of Dolina. The Russians arrived there but were repulsed. A strong force of Soviet paratroopers had been, for quite some time, in the mountains. Now they barred the only road of retreat for the Germans at

Cisow. For three days there was an artillery duel. The Russians used, among other things, the Katyusha rockets and the German 220 mm. heavy guns and six-barrel mortars.

Thousands of projectiles hit the town causing heavy damages. Finally light weapon fire could be heard. Soviet infantry stormed Bolechow as the enemy retreated in panic, leaving their dead. Bolechow was liberated August 9, 1944 by forces of the 4th Ukrainian Front, under General Petrov. Notorious collaborators and German citizens as well as the Volksdeutsche fled weeks earlier. Most Ukrainian policemen joined the Bandera forces.

The surviving 45 Jews, including 2 children, started to leave their hideouts. The horrible Nazi rule was over.

Most of the survivors settled in an ex-Jewish house on Szewska Street for security reasons.

Indeed, the bands of Ukrainian nationalists still presented danger. It was 1954 before they were finally suppressed. Later, many started various occupations in enterprises restored by the Soviets with great energy. Most finally left for Poland in 1945, during population exchanges between the U.S.S.R. and Poland. Five to seven Jews remained. Later they were joined by several people who returned from Russia and by Soviet Jews. One of them fell in combat while in service within the "Extermination Battalions," a unit created by the Soviets to fight the Ukrainian nationalists.

The Russians converted the Great Synagogue into a military store. Nothing was done by the authorities to honor the memory of the victims. The mass graves remained deserted and neglected.

After some years the grave at Taniawa was properly arranged and a commemorative plaque was affixed – citing "Soviet citizens" – according to then Soviet policy. In 2003 the grave was in a bad state again and the plaque had vanished.

Jewish Bolechow completely disappeared.

[Hebrew page 145 & Yiddish page 340]

3. The Tragic Destruction of Bolechow Jews
by Benno Reisman
Translation from the Hebrew by Jerrold Landau

As an eyewitness to the final days of the Jews of Bolechow, I wish to describe them.

I was captured numerous times by the enemy, but I was saved from death by miracle or by coincidence. At first I wandered around in the forests, and then I found refuge with the farmers of Jaworow. My friend Munzio Turkel, a youth from Bolechow, was together with me. The aforementioned farmers demanded a specific sum of money from us in return for refuge. We were forced to give them our savings from home. The transfer of money was fraught with mortal danger. We succeeded in this difficult task, and in return, the farmers put a barn at our disposal. The only exit was from the attic. We spent 21 months in the small, dark barn. We breathed a restricted amount of air through a tiny window in the attic. An opening was made in the wall through which our food was served once a day. Our daily fare consisted of four potatoes and a half a loaf of bread. We lived in these dismal conditions until August 1944, when the Soviet regime conquered the town.

One day during that time, in the morning when I was still sleeping, they came to draft me to the Red Army. This step was taken thanks to the Ukrainians, because 15-16 Jews returned to Bolechow after its liberation from the Nazis. The Ukrainians feared that we would give testimony regarding their "good deeds" during the Nazi occupation, so of course they wanted to remove us from the city. Therefore, they approached the Soviet authorities to carry this out.

Almost all of us were drafted and sent to the front. I was wounded there. After I recovered, I was discharged from the army, and sent to Bolechow as a civilian. The local authorities recognized my military activities, and therefore employed me as a supervisor. To my dismay, I could not maintain myself in that job, since the Ukrainians stalked after me at every step and turn, and investigated my deeds.

When Poland was liberated, I decided to leave the city to search for my brother, the engineer Gustav, who served in an important role in De Gaulle's army in France. My other brother Max succeeded in making aliya to the Land.

A. The German Conquest

The Red Army was forced to retreat on July 2, 1941. The citizens and the military government left the city. A small group of sappers destroyed all strategic points, such as the bridges and storehouses. The residents of the city were in a state of confusion and perplexity because of the bombardment. Even though it

was a clear summer day, the streets were empty of people. The stores were shut. Ukrainian gangs took advantage of this propitious time to ransack and pillage Jewish stores as well as Soviet storehouses. A Ukrainian militia was then organized whose members organized themselves to patriotic duty. First of all, they arrested Jews who were suspected being Communists or Komsomolets (Communist Youth). In truth, this was personal revenge.

Leah Schindler, Ben-Zion's daughter, was among the first victims. She was murdered in a cruel and unusual fashion.

Battalions of the Hungarian-Slovakian army entered the city on July 6, 1941. The Ukrainians greeted them with joy and offered them flowers. All at once, shouts filled the air: Long live Germany! Death to Jews and Communists!

The Hungarian army took over the government of the Stanislawow region. The Ukrainians were not happy with this, for the Hungarians set limits to their freedom and "good deeds", and fined them. In this regard, the Ukrainians turned to the supreme German authority in Stryj with the request that the government be turned over to the Germans. They acceded to their request. The German regional minister and his official took up residence in Bolechow.

The minister ordered the establishment of a Judenrat. Its members included Dr. Schindler, Dr. Archie Reifeisen, Pressler, Buma Krauthammer, and others. The aforementioned committee was put under the direction of the official and his officers.

Dr. Harasimov was appointed as mayor of the city. His son-in-law, the former police chief Simkov, was appointed as head of civil defense.

The German city commissar took up residence in the home of Dr. Kleinberg. The cleanup and furnishing of this house to make it fitting for the residence of the commissar was the task of the Judenrat. Archie Reifeisen was made responsible for everything. The Judenrat turned to the residence of Bolechow to donate furniture, rugs, pictures, crystal, and valuables without delay, since the task had to be finished in seven days. Of course, a thorough cleanup had to be arranged from a technical perspective. A day or two was required for this. The day the task had to be finished was the Sabbath. The official summoned the members of the committee, lined them up, and shouted in a commanding voice, "Who is responsible for this task?" Dr. Reifeisen came forward from the line and said, "I!" The "refined" official got angry with him and slapped him on the cheek. He did the same to the rest of the committee.

After this embarrassment and degradation, Dr. Reifeisen turned to his friends and said, "The Germans will not be able to slap my cheeks again".

The next day, we were shaken up to the depth of our souls. The wonderful man, lover of his fellowman, Dr. Reifeisen, put an end to his life! He hanged himself in the garden next to his home! With is tragic but honorable death, we lost one of the fitting members, most reliable, who took responsibility and protected us.

At this point, the gloomy era began, full of suffering and tribulations. The Jews were forced to work in backbreaking labor: the building of bridges, the laying of railway tracks, etc. Every worker was given a quota that had to be filled, and he bent under his burden. It was particularly difficult for those people who were not fit for manual labor. The taskmasters punished and tortured in a cruel manner, without a scintilla of mercy.

The Jewish committee was established, and it had many tasks: the work office, the office of living arrangements, and the supply division. The headquarters of the committee was in the Jewish public school on Shuster Street. Dr. Schindler was the chairman, and his son-in-law Pressler was the director of Jewish civil defense (the "militia"). The task of the militia was to supervise that the citizens were following the orders of the Judenrat. These orders were effectively the orders of the Germans.

The commissar utilized his position for his own benefit and personal objectives. For example, he demanded that within a short time he be provided with butter, hides, textiles, foodstuffs, etc. These provisions were difficult to obtain even without this command. Not only the commissar, but also the Gestapo, jumped upon such items. The members of the committee were cruelly beaten if they were not able to provide the provisions.

After this time, the order was given that all Jews were to wear a blue band with a Star of David upon it. The hours that one could be on the street were restricted. Entrance to restaurants and places of entertainment, travel by rail, use of the post office, etc. were forbidden. Radios and other valuable items were confiscated. With the threat of death, all Jews were ordered to give over their furs, including their fur scarves.

The Ukrainian "militia" pillaged the houses during the daylight and the darkness of night. They conducted "searches" so to speak – and at such a fitting time, they would steal and take anything that they came across, despite the fact that this was against the law. Those who were robbed had to be quiet, without any recourse for complaint.

The committee rationed food. The portions were small and filthy. Since it was difficult to purchase additions to the scanty portions, a barter market was created. On account of the shortage of food, the elderly, weak and young swelled up and died of hunger.

In 1941, the regional minister, under the direction of the Gestapo of Stanislawow, commanded that a contribution be imposed upon the Jews of Bolechow. The value was 4.5 kilograms of gold, a vast sum of cash and valuables. This had to be collected within a number of days. If the property was not given over, lives would be taken (in an action). The committee asked the residents to give over money and jewelry without delay. The requested amount was given over quickly. The poor, unfortunate donors thought that the property would save their lives. The naivete! The action was carried out within a number of days.

B. How I was Saved

The director of the "Union of Civic Manufacturing" (Fareigente Stadt-Industrie) recommended me to the Gestapo director as a fitting worker. Thus I was removed against my will from the transport train. At this decisive and tragic moment, I refused to leave my family to their fate. However, the militianists did not pay attention to my refusal, and they forcibly dragged me from the train.

For a brief moment, I was able to see the receding trains, which carried all of my loved ones. I loathed my life. I could not shed tears. It seemed as if the earth was opening up beneath me, and I was sinking.

At that time, I lost my faith in the goodness of humanity. I saw it as a bloodthirsty beast. An evil beast, lacking a heart, not created in the Divine image. I only had one burning desire in my heart: Revenge! Revenge!

After the second action there was a brief lull, a respite from the diligent destruction of our Jews.

C. The Ghetto

Once again there was a decree. The Jews were ordered to leave their homes and go to the ghetto. It was located on Shuster Gasse, Ringplatz (the market square), Bahn Gasse, and the side alleys.

Jews of Perehinsko, Rozniatow, Weldzirz, and surrounding villages were brought to our ghetto.

It was forbidden to leave the ghetto. Violation of that decree was punishable by death.

D. The Jewish Work Camp

The Jews who were employed in the factories and workshops were housed in special premises on the Train Street. These were surrounded by barbed wire fences, and it was forbidden to leave them without a permit. Permission was only given to go to and return from work. The supervision of the camp was in the hands of our own militias and the Ukrainians. The latter, may their names be blotted out, degraded, cursed, and acted with cruelty to the workers, as was their way.

Pregnancy was forbidden for women. If perchance a woman gave birth, she had to turn over the infant to the hands of the Gestapo. On occasion, a mother succeeded in hiding her child. When the Nazis, may their names be blotted out, discovered this, woe to the poor mother and her child.

Our brethren worked in this abyss and hell until December 1942.

E. The Liquidation of the Camp

It was the beginning of December, 1942. After the paltry supper, tired and worn out from all the toil, the workers lay down to sleep without realizing that this was their last night. It was midnight. The Gestapo and the Ukrainians, may their names be blotted out, surrounded the camp, attacked the innocent workers, and shot many on the spot. The rest were dragged to the cemetery. They were shot and buried in a communal grave.

With the liquidation of the camp, our militias were superfluous. They were no longer needed, so their members were shot one at a time.

Very few Jews remained in the ghetto after this murder. The final victims were known as "fulverte" or "zamler Juden" (valuable ones, or trash collectors).

F. The Witnesses who Remained

Our brethren who hid left the city and joined the partisans, or hid once again with the gentiles of the villages. My friend Munzio Turkel was among those who survived. The Germans knew that there were Jews in hiding. Therefore, they threatened with death anyone who would give refuge to Jews or assist them. As a result, obviously only very few people jumped onto such rescue actions.

G. The Brave Ones who Perished

Not all of our brethren were taken out to be killed like sheep to the slaughter, without opposition and without revolt. Many fought and inflicted casualties upon our enemies. Let my soul perish with the Germans and Ukrainians!

There was not an equal situation. The man-eating enemy was armed a thousand times stronger than we were. Despite this, we fought.

I do not remember the names of all the mighty ones who took revenge before they died. However, I do remember two: Davidze Schindler of blessed memory (the son of Ben-Zion), and Yossi Nagal (the son of Shalom Nagal, the owner of the restaurant).

H. Conclusion

Thus were our brethren killed and slaughtered. Not only the elderly, the sickly, the weak – people whose time has come. No, no! Most were children, adults, and healthy people; thirsty for life, desiring of life, loving of life, embracing the arms of the world.

Members of all social classes, workers, craftsmen, teachers, maskilim, scholars, simple folk, officials, merchants, members of the free professions.

People who, thanks to their efforts, diligence, persistence, talents and culture, raised the level of the town, so that it served as a sign and example to other towns throughout Galicia.

May their souls be bound in the bonds of eternal life.

[Hebrew page 151 & Yiddish page 347]

4. My Gloomy Visit to my Hometown after World War II

by Esther Jakubowicz (Vitashka)
Translation from the Hebrew by Jerrold Landau

In October 1945, after the defeat of the Germans, I returned to Lwow from Russia. When I was in Lwow, I thought to myself: The last appropriate chance to see your hometown is now given to you. Despite the danger from the Ukrainians who fought against the Bolsheviks, I set out towards Bolechow. Woe to my eyes for what I have seen! A terrifying vision!

This town, the majority of whose inhabitants were Jewish, and in which a vibrant Jewish life pulsated, was now desolate and left without Jews.

The Ukrainians organized themselves into groups in the forests and fought against the Russians. The Poles moved to western Poland, and the Germans retreated with Hitler, may his name be blotted out, to Germany [1].

Shaken to my foundations, perturbed and dumbfounded, I began to wander through the streets of my town, seeing if I would meet anyone. I arrived at Salina. There was no change in it, except that its workers were Russian. From there, I arrived at the section of the street where Salka Schneid, Dr. Blumenthal, and Fishel Brokenstein had lived. I returned to the German Settlement and went until the "Large Bridge", but I did not come across a living soul.

The Civic Garden was as if it was in mourning over the destruction of its inhabitants. The Evangelical Church, Forestry School, and Sokol Hall were all destroyed.

The small bridge (The Lawka) was half destroyed. The waters of the Sukiel had dried up. The "Lazenes" were cut down. Among everything, there was no trace of our existence.

The Houses of Moshele Taffer, Shlomo Sheps, the teacher Hendel, and Rabbi Mendele Landau (a personality worthy of special mention) were standing in ruins. The pharmacy and the houses of Rabbi Yosef Horowitz and of Kurtzer had been bombed. Most of the houses had either been pillaged, destroyed, or occupied by the Russian Army.

The street of the synagogue and the "Kleine Kloiz", "Polishe Kloiz", "Sadigura Kloiz" "Groise Kloiz" Beis Midrashes – were in mourning. They stood in silence. Their holy arks were empty and gloomy. There were pieces of Torah scrolls rolling in the garbage heaps.

The "Shul" that had once been so full of splendor and glory, was used by the Russians as a warehouse for merchandise.

The cemetery, including the communal grave that had been dug by our pure brethren, may G-d avenge their souls, prior to their being shot by the murderers, was destroyed. Its gravestones were broken and cut down.

The lot of Bahn Gasse was the same as the lot of all of the streets. The chair factory and the mill of Yisrael Laufer, Alter Schneid, and Yaakov Kramer were still standing, as was the printing shop of Hirsch Mordechai Elendman, but they were boarded up. What about the house of the Russian rabbi, Rabbi Shlomo Perlow? In that house, weddings used to be conducted with great splendor, in which Hassidim from all over Galicia participated, with the dressed up relatives riding on horses, literally like Cossacks, as they were happy and rejoicing. Now, death and bereavement emanated from it. Fear! Terrors!

Furthermore, the butcher shop, the tannery of Jerzy Frei and Yudel Kimmel, the candle factory of Yoel Halperin, and the cheder of Wolf Diengott – in all, there was destruction and death.

At the sight of the extreme destruction and desolation I thought: To what shall I compare you, oh my dear town? To a bereaved mother, a mourner, a mother that had been cut down in her life. Gloomy, downtrodden, bereaved.

As my lips murmured, "remember, and do not forget", I left my destroyed childhood area, my hometown of Bolechow.

[Hebrew page 152 & Yiddish page 349]

5. Information from Yad Vashem
Translation from the Hebrew by Jerrold Landau

On May 3, 1946, testimony was presented in Munich by a resident of Stryj, Shmuel Zeliger (file number: Munich archives, testimonies, 191/76). He related: "On a frightfully cold night in January 1942, Ukrainian gendarmes and policemen invaded the homes of the poor people (in Stryj), and rounded up about 800 people. Several hundred were also brought from Zydaczow, Mikolajow, Zurawno, Chodorow, Bolechow, Dolina, Bobrka, and Skole. They were all loaded on village wagons and transported to the mountains. Many froze along the way. Almost all of the children froze. The rest were left in abandoned farmers' cottages. The strong ones fled and returned to Stryj. The rest of them, that is more than 80% of them, died of cold and hunger.

Memorial to the martyrs in the Bolekhov Martyrs Forest

Translator's Footnotes:

1. Obviously literary license, as Hitler was not personally involved in the war with Russia.

INDEX

F

Feder, 31, 160
Fierberg, 90
Frank, 17, 18, 200
Frankel, 47
Franz Josef II, 113
Franz Yosef, 178
Franz Yosef the First, 159
Frei, 72, 232
Freilich, 216
Freud, 83
Fridlender, 163
Fridman, 202
Friedlander, 58, 59
Friedman, 65, 67
Friedmann, 65
Frisch, 160
Frischman, 77
Frost, 97
Fruchter, 77

G

Galuchovski, 47
Gartenberg, 58
Gedzinksy, 8
Gedzinsky, 7, 8
Gelber, 27, 28, 36, 42, 61, 62, 65
Gelernter, 96
Gertner, 130, 177, 190
Glass, 112, 211
Goethe, 117, 120
Goldenberg, 38, 39, 40, 41, 45, 46, 50, 51, 53, 62, 65, 66
Goldman, 165
Goldschlag, 57, 72, 159
Gordin, 177
Gordon, 158
Gottesman, 139, 160
Graber, 62
Graubard, 89
Griffel, 179
Grifl, 163
Gripel, 142
Gruss, 97
Grzymek, 219, 220
Gurka, 69
Guzkav, 66

H

Ha-Levi, 57
Halevi, 114
Halperin, 59, 142, 232
Halpern, 165

Harasimov, 226
Harasimow, 196
Harkavy, 62, 63
Haszower, 131
Hauftman, 193
Hauptman, 159, 160
Hausman (Eshel), 147
Hausman-Eshel, 1
Hauzman, 177
Hendel, 1, 2, 3, 7, 29, 59, 76, 89, 90, 97, 98, 142, 177, 231
Herschaut, 185
Herzl, 102, 139, 174
Hildesheimer, 58
Hirsch, 37, 39, 48, 49, 100, 101, 104, 126
Hirsh, 27
Hirshhaut, 147
Hofman, 190
Homberg, 32, 36, 37, 53, 61
Horowitz, 18, 203, 204, 231
Hurvitz, 30, 61

I

I. B. M., 166
Ichel-Adler, 138
Israel of Zamosc, 30

J

Jabotinsky, 103, 104
Jacob, 128
Jakubowicz (Vitashka), 231
Jasz, 168
Josefsberg, 77, 221
Joseph II, 16, 17, 32, 64
Joseph the second, 27

K

Kahut, 130
Kaiser, 59
Karchin, 160
Karelman, 77
Katz, 2
Katzmann, 199, 207, 213, 216, 221
Kaufman, 76, 159
Kesler, 190
Kimmel, 159, 232
Klausner, 49, 55, 61, 62, 63
Kleinberg, 226
Kleinbort, 177
Klenbard, 77
Kohler, 199
Kohn, 37, 159
Kolpak, 215, 217

V

Valik, 190
Vaytsner, 165
Verber, 167
Vilgut, 58
Vinitzky (Altman), 132
Vishnitzer, 25
Vlassov, 218, 220
Vlassow, 223

W

Wachstein, 63
Weber, 3, 161, 170
Wechsler, 133
Weilgot, 143
Weisbard, 125, 143
Weitzner, 144, 185
Werber, 141
Weschler, 97
Wissel, 74, 75

Wohl, 125, 143, 222
Wolf, 143, 144

Y

Yaari, 27
Yeger, 190
Yost, 41, 62

Z

Zamoscer, 61
Zauderer, 208
Zeiman, 157
Zeliger, 233
Zeman, 32, 35
Zif,, 113
Zigel, 74
Zipper, 73, 103, 139
Zuckerman, 205
Zvi, 17, 19, 25, 27
Zweig, 77

www.ingramcontent.com/pod-product-compliance
Lightning Source LLC
Chambersburg PA
CBHW061835260326
41914CB00005B/1001